Children of Palestine

STUDIES IN FORCED MIGRATION

General Editors: Stephen Castles and Dawn Chatty

Children of Palestine

EXPERIENCING FORCED MIGRATION IN THE MIDDLE EAST

Edited by
Dawn Chatty and Gillian Lewando Hundt

Berghahn Books
New York • Oxford

First published in 2005 by

Berghahn Books
www.berghahnbooks.com

Library of Congress Cataloging-in-Publication Data

Children of Palestine: experiencing forced migration in the Middle East / edited by Dawn
    Chatty and Gillian Lewando Hundt
        p. cm. -- (Studies in forced migration ; v. 16)
    Includes bibliographical references and index.
    ISBN 1-84545-010-8
        1. Refugee children--Middle East. 2. Refugees, Palestinian Arab--Middle East. 3.
    Children, Palestinian Arab--Social conditions. 4. Children and war--Middle East. 5.
    Forced migration--Middle East. I. Chatty, Dawn. II. Lewando Hundt, Gillian. III. Series.

HV640.5.P36C45 2005
305.23'089'9274--dc22

                                                                            2004055058

British Library Cataloguing in Publication Data

A catalogue record for this book is available
from the British Library.

ISBN 978-1-84545-010-6 hardback
ISBN 978-1-84545-120-2 paperback

To Nick and Otto

Contents

List of Figures and Tables

Maps

Figures

Tables

Acknowledgements

This project has occupied more than half a decade of our lives, and we find it hard to identify all the people who helped to bring this book to fruition. We owe so much to so many. We are particularly grateful for the encouragement we received in the early stages of the development of this project from Carolyn Makinson, then at the Mellon Foundation, and Dr David Turton, then director of the Refugee Studies Centre. It was they who originally conceived of a small case study of Palestinian children in the Gaza Strip and it was they who encouraged us to think big and develop a wide holistic approach to Palestinian refugee children and young people in the wider Middle Eastern context.

In the course of setting up the fieldwork upon which this book is based we were grateful to Professor Riccardo Bocco, then director at CERMOC in Amman, who gave freely of his time to help us identify potential Palestinian researchers for this effort. We would like to thank him, and also Professor Huda Zureik and Rosemary Sayigh who helped similarly in Lebanon and Syria.

We are particularly grateful to Rualla Khadouri, Maha Damaj and Mezna Qato, who all served as research assistants to the project, providing administrative and editorial help to the project throughout its three-year life. To Maha, a further thanks for the wonderful job she did in producing the project newsletters which appear in Appendix III.

To Jason Stanley and Dr Gina Crivello we give a special thanks for so carefully reading through the various drafts of the manuscript, checking references and standardising transliteration.

Finally, we would like to thank all the Palestinian children and young people, their parents and caregivers, who took part in the study. All gave generously and freely of their time and the project would not have happened without their cooperation. We remain particularly grateful to all those families who so graciously accepted our constant questioning and recording of narratives.

List of Abbreviations

AAA	American Anthropological Association
ARCPA	Lebanese NGO working with Palestinian refugees
BFG	boys' focus group
CERMOC	Centre d'Etude et de Recherches du Moyen-Orient Contemporain
CRC	Community Rehabilitation Centre
EC	European Community
F	female
FAFO	Norwegian Institute for Applied Social Science
G	generation; G1 refers to the first-generation, G2 to the second-generation and G3 to the third-generation (see glossary for definitions)
GAPAR	General Association for Palestinian Arab Refugees
GDP	Gross Domestic Product
GFG	girls' focus group
GNP	Gross National Product
HH	household; HH20 refers to HH code no. 20
IGO	intergovernmental organisation
IPS	Institute of Palestine Studies
JD	Jordanian dinars
M	male
MAMAH	Information Network on Arab Maternal Health
MCC	Multifunctional Community Centre
MPI	Migration Policy Institute
NAJDEH	Lebanese NGO working with Palestinian refugees
NFE	nonformal education
NGO	nongovernmental organisation
ORT	oral rehydration fluid
PCBS	Palestinian Central Bureau of Statistics
PLO	Palestine Liberation Organisation
PMoE	Palestinian Ministry of Education

PMoH	Palestinian Ministry of Health
PNA	Palestinian National Authority
PRA	Participatory Rapid Appraisal
PRCS	Palestine Red Crescent Society
SCBS	Syrian Central Bureau of Statistics
SCF	Save the Children Fund
SIT	social identity theory
SLA	Lebanon Southern Army
UN	United Nations
UNESCO	United Nations Education, Scientific and Cultural Organisation
UNHCR	United Nations High Commissioner for Refugees
UNICEF	United Nations Children's Fund
UNRPR	United Nations Relief for Palestine Refugees
UNRWA	United Nations Relief and Works Agency for Palestine Refugees in the Near East
UNSCOP	United Nations Special Committee on Palestine
WPC	Women's Programme Centre

Map 1 Journeys of Migration of Study Households (1947-9)

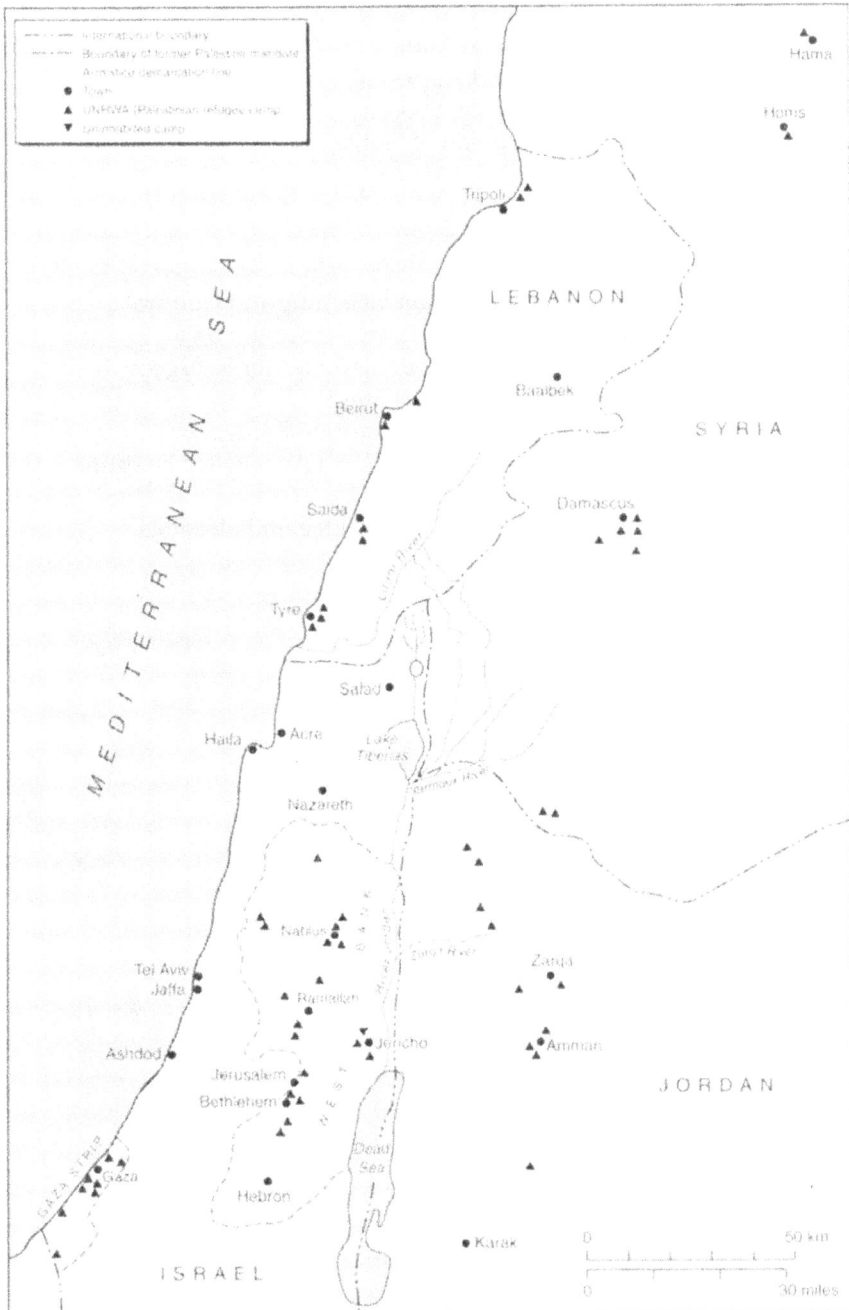

Map 2 Palestinian Refugee Camps

PMoH	Palestinian Ministry of Health
PNA	Palestinian National Authority
PRA	Participatory Rapid Appraisal
PRCS	Palestine Red Crescent Society
SCBS	Syrian Central Bureau of Statistics
SCF	Save the Children Fund
SIT	social identity theory
SLA	Lebanon Southern Army
UN	United Nations
UNESCO	United Nations Education, Scientific and Cultural Organisation
UNHCR	United Nations High Commissioner for Refugees
UNICEF	United Nations Children's Fund
UNRPR	United Nations Relief for Palestine Refugees
UNRWA	United Nations Relief and Works Agency for Palestine Refugees in the Near East
UNSCOP	United Nations Special Committee on Palestine
WPC	Women's Programme Centre

1

Introduction: Children of Palestine Narrate Forced Migration

Dawn Chatty and *Gillian Lewando Hundt*

Dawn Chatty
I am a social anthropologist with long experience in the Middle East as a university teacher, development practitioner, and advocate for indigenous rights. I have taught at the University of California, Santa Barbara, San Diego State University, the American University of Beirut, the University of Damascus, Sultan Qaboos University and the University of Oxford. I have worked with the regional offices of various international agencies including UNDP, UNICEF, FAO, IFAD, and USAID. My research interests include Middle Eastern ethnography, nomadic pastoralism and conservation, gender and development, health, illness and culture, and coping strategies of children and adolescents in prolonged conflict and forced migration. My most recent book is *Conservation and Mobile Peoples: Displacement, Forced Settlement and Sustainable Development* (ed. with Marcus Colchester), Berghahn Press, 2002. I am currently University Lecturer in Forced Migration and Deputy Director of the Refugee Studies Centre, Queen Elizabeth House, University of Oxford, U.K.

Gillian Lewando Hundt
I trained in social anthropology and sociology at the University of Edinburgh and my research and teaching is principally in the area of Sociology of Health, Medical Anthropology and Qualitative Research Methods. My research is largely in the area of gender, ethnicity and promoting equity in health. It ranges from the practical – setting up new service models e.g. mobile provision for Palestinian Bedouin in the Negev – to the theoretical – exploring ideas of risk, the social construction of statistics, and the social impact of innovative medical technologies. My current research programme has two foci – community perceptions of health, and the politics and practice of research and its impact on policy and provision. The themes underpinning my wide ranging interests are a concern with addressing social inequalities in health and health care, an imperative to elicit the local voices of marginal groups so that they impact on local policy and provision, and a strand of work on the politics of research. I am currently Professor of Social Sciences in Health at the University of Warwick, U.K.

Palestinian children and adolescents living both within and outside of refugee camps in the Middle East are the focus of this study. For more than half a century these children and their caregivers have lived a temporary existence in the dramatic and politically volatile landscape that is the Middle East. These children have been captive to various sorts of stereotyping, both academic and popular. They have been objectified, like their parents and grandparents, as passive victims without the benefit of international protection. And they have become the beneficiaries of numerous humanitarian aid packages, which presume the primacy of the Western model of child development as well as the psychosocial approach to intervention. The aim of this study is to move beyond the stereotypes and Western-based models to explore the impact, which forced migration and prolonged conflict have had, and continue to have, on the lives of these refugee children. Furthermore, the study seeks to elicit the voices of individual children, in the context of their households and their community. This approach, both participatory and ethnographic, challenges many of the assumptions concerning the *sui generis* nature of the Palestinian case and at the same time it supports the trend in much multidisciplinary research to bring cultural context closer to the heart of the discussion.

The 1980s was a decade of special interest in children. In 1987, an independent commission of the United Nations (UN) presented to the 42nd General Assembly a report entitled *Winning the Human Race*. The report included significant sections on the protection of children, on urban youth, street children and refugee children. Its contributors included Sadaka Ogato, Sadruddin Aga Khan and El Hassan bin Talal. At about the same time, the first Palestinian uprising, or *Intifada*, in the West Bank and Gaza was emerging and the eyes of the world focused on Palestinian children and youth, the stonethrowers who were challenging the Israeli military occupation of their land. During this tumultuous period, the UN commissioned a study of children and armed conflict, known as the Machel Report, which was released in 1996. In the West Bank and Gaza, a number of studies were conducted in the late 1980s and early 1990s on the impact of physical violence or the *Intifada* on children's psychological or physical development. These studies, mainly from the perspective of psychiatry or developmental psychology, focused on the child alone, while the community and the society remained in the background.

In 1993, the Oslo Agreement was signed, which signalled a period of hope and expectation for Palestinians in the West Bank and Gaza, but not elsewhere in the Middle East. As Oslo put aside the question of the 'right of return' of Palestinian refugees, the world seemed to refocus on the West Bank and Gaza, leaving Palestinian refugee children and their families in Syria, Jordan and Lebanon out in the cold. In 1998, the same year that the Convention on the Rights of the Child had been adopted by 191 parties, a renewed interest was emerging among researchers and donors alike for understanding how Palestinian children and young people were accommodating prolonged conflict and forced migration in their lives. An exploratory suggestion by the Andrew Mellon Foundation to the Refugee Studies Centre, University of Oxford, to conduct a case study of the impact of forced migration on Palestinian children in Gaza was rejected as too narrow, and thus probably lacking any potential for making a significant contribution to our knowledge. The Refugee Studies Centre countered with the suggestion of conducting a region-based study that would draw in Palestinian refugee children in Lebanon, Syria and Jordan along with those in the West Bank and Gaza. The positive response of the Andrew Mellon Foundation to the counter-suggestion resulted, in 1999, with the launch of this multidisciplinary, holistic study of the effect of forced migration on Palestinian children in refugee households in five field sites in the Middle East. Each team was made up of Palestinian researchers locally connected with institutions of education or health research. A general methodology and research strategy was outlined for each team which involved an initial rapid participatory phase of trust building and data sharing followed by a more intense phase of in-depth interviewing and life-history taking from children and their significant caregivers. Each team developed and modified its approach to fit the specific history and context of its field setting. The interviewers and local researchers were, by and large, residents of the refugee camps and communities where the fieldwork was conducted.

There are, in the literature, numerous case studies of Palestinian refugee children (Abu Hein et al. 1993; Baker 1990; Punamaki and Suleiman 1990; Qouta et al. 1995; Thabet et al. 2002). These are most often case studies set in a single Palestinian refugee camp or a cluster of such sites. They are generally based on psychological or psychiatric standards and measures derived from Western concepts of personhood and trauma. No multidisciplinary, regional study, however, has been undertaken to link, compare, or contrast the lives of these children over the five countries and territories where Palestinians were allowed to take refuge after their expulsion or flight from mandated Palestine in 1948 and from the West Bank in 1967. After decades of separated communities, this study seeks to explore Palestinian refugee children's perceptions of themselves and their futures in the context of a lifetime of forced migration in the specific cultural setting of the Middle East.

This study examines what happens in children's and young people's lives when they and the households they belong to are uprooted and forced to move. Unlike psychological and psychiatric-based studies, which focus on the individual in isolation, this study considers the lives of Palestinian children and young people in the context of the family group, the community and the wider social, economic and political arena.

It explores the ways in which children and young people within households are changed by past and current episodes of forced migration. This includes examining the ways in which individual rites of passage from childhood to adult status are affected by forced migration and the impoverishment which ensues. It also examines the transformations to family organisation and structure. It looks at the changes in informal and formal education and differential access to labour markets and its significance to children and young people. And it studies the transformations in Palestinian community cohesion in refugee camps and the way in which social institutions such as marriage, employment and care of the elderly are changed and adapted to suit new circumstances.

This book addresses the concerns of young lives affected by forced migration. It takes a holistic perspective and endeavours to see the child not just as an individual but also in the context of the family, the community and the larger society. As such it is influenced by anthropological writing which focuses on social suffering (Bauman 2001; Davis 1992; Hastrup 1993; Kleinman 1997). Through a contextual participative approach, which elicits Palestinian voices both as researchers and participants in the study, the way in which social, political and economic forces shape the lives of individuals and generations within families (Farmer 1997) is communicated to the reader. The narratives of coping with conflict and forced migration are individual and familial experiences and yet are shaped by structural violence – remote and near political and military decisions that have impacted on day-to-day living – displacement, curfew, unemployment, restricted access to travel or education, social discrimination and, in some sites, lack of civil rights and citizenship.

Background

The First World War had been hailed as the 'War to End All Wars'. Yet, in hindsight, it would appear that the international order which emerged from that rubble and was enshrined in the League of Nations did little to reduce the fighting that has marred most of the twentieth century. The last half of the twentieth century actually saw an increase in warfare throughout the world (Kaldor 1999; Walter and Snyder 1999). It has resulted in much disruption of the social, economic and political infrastructure of civilian life everywhere. It has fragmented households and communities and contributed to massive increases in the number of forced migrants worldwide. By the end of the twentieth century, the United Nations High Commissioner for Refugees (UNHCR) estimated 14 million refugees worldwide and the United Nations Relief and Works Agency for Palestine Refugees in the Near East (UNRWA), the special UN agency set up to provide basic services to Palestinian refugees, estimated 4 million registered and unregistered refugees in the Middle East.[1] Whereas in previous conflicts between national armies, the casualties were mainly soldiers (e.g., First World War), the Second World War and subsequent conflicts in Vietnam and Cambodia involved heavy bombing of civilians. Between 1947 and 1948, approximately 750,000 Palestinians fled from their homes and farms in British-mandated Palestine as a direct result of their being targeted by Jewish armed militias, mainly the Haganah, but also the Irgun and Stern Gang. In recent political conflicts in the 1980s and 1990s, for example in the former Yugoslavia and Rwanda, women and children have become targets, survivors and forced migrants (Ressler et al. 1988, 1992).

Much of the research undertaken on the effects of forced migration on men, women and children has been in the domain of psychology and psychiatry and explores the trauma and coping strategies of these victims and survivors (Ahern and Athey 1991; Ahmad 1992; El-Bedour et al. 1993; Mollica 1990; Rousseau et al. 1998, 2001; Young 1992). This body of work raises two fundamental concerns regarding the concepts and methods that are applied to the work.

Nearly all psychiatric and psychological research amongst forced migrants employs concepts that are based on Western ideas of pathology. These concepts often do not correspond to local illness taxonomies and classifications, as many field studies and critiques have shown (Ennis-McMillan 2001; Kleinman 1980, 1990; Young 1982, 1992). In Guatemala, for example, ethnographic studies have identified eight possible causes and types of diarrhoea, of which only one would be considered suitable for treatment by oral rehydration fluid (ORT) – the treatment recommended by the World Health Organization (Scrimshaw and Hurtado 1988). In Pakistan, studies have shown that widespread rejection of ORT is based on indigenous beliefs that diarrhoea is either a normal part of teething and growing, is caused by malevolent spirits or is a 'hot' illness which requires a 'cold' form of treatment. They classify most Western medicines as 'hot' and therefore inappropriate for a diarrhoeal child (Mull and Mull 1988). Work by Kleinman and his colleagues in the field of mental health has identified clear differences between lay and professional taxonomies (Kleinman 1986). Somatisation, the cultural patterning of psychological and social disorders into a language of distress of mainly physical symptoms and signs, is a serious problem encountered by mental health professionals in making psychiatric diagnoses across cultures and in different societies (Helman 2001: 182). Even between England and France, differences in psychiatric diagnosis are significant enough to suggest that there are cultural and conceptual variations between both countries' practitioners (Van Os et al. 1993). The use of Western diagnostic criteria and scales developed using professional disease classification may, therefore, be conceptually at variance with local and indigenous classifications. Scales for measurement, family well-being and stress management indexes are also liable to the same criticism (Goldberg 1978; Langner 1962; McCubbin and Thompson 1991).

The methods used in much research in the domain of psychology and psychiatry also present some difficulties, since they limit the extent to which mental health can be conceptualised in the surrounding culture and society. For example, our early exploratory discussions with Western researchers in Gaza revealed some confusion among the fieldworkers regarding their findings. The results of their questionnaires with children and young people, trying to establish a hierarchy of fears among this cohort, showed a strong community-centric focus to their worries rather than the anticipated egocentric focus one would expect in Europe or North America. Such findings could only be understood within the wider cultural context of Palestinian family and community cohesion, the study of which benefits from qualitative research approaches. Recent research in the psychosocial field, particularly amongst practitioners, is beginning to incorporate qualitative methods in its design (Ager 2002; Dawes 1992; MacMullin and Odeh 1999; Wessles 1998). Still more needs to be done, and, in the case of Palestinian refugee children, where the development psychological approach holds sway, further effort is required in order to effectively contextualise and thus validate research findings.

Research on children and young people, in general, is based on Western models of childhood and child development (Boyden 1994, 2002; James 1998; Scheper-Hughes 1989; Scheper-Hughes and Sargent 1998). Perhaps the most fundamental principle which grounds these models is the belief that all children throughout the world have the same basic needs, pass through the same developmental stages, react in like manner to armed conflict and forced migration and employ similar coping strategies. These models are rooted in Jean Piaget's four stages of child development and may have even earlier associations with the Romantic and Reform movements of Europe (Cunningham 1991, 1995). Cross-cultural studies of children and childhood, however, increasingly show that there are wide variations in how childhood is defined and experienced around the world. When childhood begins and ends and the behaviour considered appropriate for young people tends to vary quite widely between different societies. Like childhood, the category of 'adolescent' is socially constructed and in many cultures is not even recognised as a meaningful category (James 1998). In some communities, individuals of the age of 12 or 13 are expected to take on the roles and responsibilities of (what is Western-defined) adults: marrying, raising families, seeking gainful employment and caring for younger siblings and the elderly in the household. How individuals in such cultures react to and cope with forced migration is bound to be different from individuals in cultures where adolescence is recognised as a transitional category from childhood to adult responsibility.

Discussions with international organisations' programme officers in the Middle East have revealed that the underlying issues that inform their programmes – such as child labour, early marriage and early school-leaving – are set from headquarters in New York or Geneva and are based upon Western assumptions of appropriate child development rather than an understanding of the cultural, social, political and economic context in which these phenomena occur. This has created serious disjunctures between policy making, programme development and successful implementation on the ground. Research is only now beginning to show that our Western-based assumptions of child development are not universal and that children do not automatically progress through the same sequence of development stages (Dawes and Tredoux 1989).

This study, grounded in the conceptual debates mentioned above, has developed a multidisciplinary approach to research on children and adolescents affected by prolonged conflict and forced migration. It takes into account the social and cultural variations found throughout the world and draws upon the concepts and techniques of anthropology, sociology, psychology, economics and educational studies (Allen 1989; Eisenbruch 1991). The child is not considered in isolation, but within the context of his or her extended family, household and community. Innovative work in this vein is just beginning to emerge among local and national nongovernmental organisations (NGOs) and intergovernmental organisations (IGOs) in the Middle East, which needs to be supported, improved and documented. In the Gaza Strip, the Community Mental Health Programme currently visits everyone released from detention at home and is moving firmly in the direction of developing a more household- and community-oriented approach. In Lebanon, Save the Children Fund (SCF) experimented with creative partnerships with children – as exemplified by the photographic workshop which it initiated among Palestinian adolescents in an after-school club in Lebanon in 1998–9. This SCF study sought to work with youths, to understand and communicate young people's perspectives through their self-generated representations of home and community. It was able to move away from the image of children and adolescents as victims and political activists and instead viewed them as human beings with perceptions, thoughts and concerns that needed to be documented and shared. Their photographs linked individual concerns and aspirations with broader histories of community and displacement. Other local NGOs such as NAJDEH and ARCPA have undertaken creative oral history projects that integrate children and young people in both the design and the running of the projects.

Rather than looking at the pathology that develops in situations of conflict and forced migration, this study examines the coping strategies and resilience among children and their significant caregivers. The experiences of children and young people of different ages and genders have been explored and the following issues have emerged as significant to all the five research sites: how the experiences of girls differ from those of boys in terms of exposure, opportunities, constraints and responsibilities within the household and the community; how past experiences of forced migration amongst the older generations impact on children and young people; and how active involvement in a political cause is mediated by children and young people, and what coping mechanisms are involved.

The justification for a regional rather than a single-country approach was built on the assumption that the different political and economic experiences of each field site would impact significantly upon the way in which the experience of forced migration was felt by individual communities. This proved to be very much the case, as the experiences of conflict and of forced migration differed markedly from field site to field site. The Gaza Strip and the West Bank field sites have faced extensive periods of active conflict with the Israeli army and settlers as well as some minor confrontations with the Palestinian National Authority (PNA). A number of psychological and psychiatric studies of children in this area have been carried out (Abu Hein et al. 1993; Baker 1990, 1991; Punamaki and Suleiman 1990; Punamaki et al. 1997; Qouta et al. 1995) and some participatory and less extractive work is just beginning to emerge (MacMullin and Oudeh 1999). In Jordan, there have been three successive waves of Palestinian forced migration in 1948, 1967 and 1991, while active conflict with the Jordanian army has also been intermittent. In Lebanon, armed conflict has occurred between militias and the subsequent Syrian and Israeli occupations. This means that the experience of the 1948 and 1967 forced migrations, as well as internal displacements resulting from continuing instability, need to be addressed. There is some published research on the Lebanese situation concerning children (Bryce and Armenian 1986; Farhood et al. 1993; Ryhida et al. 1986), and IGO and NGO projects are also beginning to explore more participatory approaches to project development.

Palestinians in Lebanon, Syria and Jordan experience varying degrees of social discrimination, political disempowerment and economic disadvantage. Many of these Palestinians are stateless and have been so since 1948. It is this group of Palestinian refugees that feels particularly isolated and removed from the central core of current activity and negotiation. It is their 'right of return' which was left as an afterthought to the Oslo negotiations and which the more recent Geneva Accords proposes to do away with, giving compensation and third-country resettlement priority in finding a final negotiated peace for all Palestinians and Israelis. Therefore they share a collective memory and experience of surviving conflict and forced migration which we can study from the perspectives of yesterday's and today's children.

The specific design of this regional case study is not meant to obscure the many broad characteristics concerning forced migration, childhood and adolescence that are comparable to other settings outside of the Middle East. A broader view of the issues can contribute to improving knowledge, policy and practice among Palestinians and other refugees around the world (Agerbak 1992).

Aims and Objectives

The aims and the objectives of this study are to investigate the direct and the indirect effects of forced migration on children and young people in the region. Particular emphasis is placed on the social context of the effects of conflict, the attitudes to and incidence of violence within and outside the households and the coping strategies of families with children and young people living with the effects of forced migration. Our aim is to move away from the medical or psychological meaning of 'coping' and to allow an organic sense of what it means to live one's life under such conditions to emerge from the interviews and oral narratives of Palestinian young people and their caregivers. In some cases, it is clear from the context of the narration that 'coping' is perceived as 'managing or surviving'. In other cases, it is given a broader, more holistic interpretation closer to the sense of managing or getting by. In part this is a reflection of the impact of the Arabic terms that the teams decided to use to convey the sense of the project, but also it reflects the very palpable feeling of community recognition of political realities and the sense of making the best out of very difficult circumstances.

The study also seeks to develop a multidisciplinary approach in research on children and households affected by forced migration which can be used in both applied as well as theoretical contexts. In addition it aims at developing, in cooperation with local practitioners, programme managers and policy makers, participatory methods relevant to situations of forced migration which focus on children, young people and caregivers. One anticipated outcome of this study is the generation of concepts regarding children and households affected by forced migration that are culturally and socially sensitive to local contexts and that could be successfully applied to policy, practice and programme development. And finally, it is hoped that the study will identify coping structures, strategies and mechanisms from which lessons might be learned and disseminated to researchers, practitioners and policy makers concerned with children and young people in the Middle East and elsewhere.

Multidisciplinarity

The study team brought together researchers from a number of disciplines within the social sciences – anthropology, sociology, political science, education and psychiatry. The Jordanian team was led by Dr Randa Farah. She had just completed her doctorate in anthropology on Narrative and Identity amongst Palestinians in Jordan, was based with CERMOC (Centre d'Etude et de Recherches du Moyen-Orient Contemporain) and had particular expertise in narrative collection and analysis.

The Syrian team was led by Dr Adnan Abdul-Rahim. He had a background in political science and education and was based with the General Union of Palestinian Women and worked with UNWRA and UNICEF (United Nations Children's Fund) in developing and implementing programmes for youth and also UNRWA kindergartens.

The Lebanese team was led by the sociologist Dr Bassem Serhan, who had many years of experience teaching in universities in Lebanon and Kuwait and was based at the time with the Welfare Association, and Ms Samia Tabari, who had recently completed an MA in International Communications and Development from City University, London.

The West Bank team was led by Dr Salah Alzaroo, who received his doctorate in Continuing Education from the University of Warwick on the role of formal and nonformal education in Palestine.

The Gaza team was led by Dr Abdel Aziz Thabet, a psychiatrist with a record of published research on the mental health of children in Gaza based within the Gaza Health Services Research Centre.

Dr Chatty had worked extensively amongst Bedouin on issues of migration, conservation and development in Lebanon, Syria, Jordan and Oman. Professor Hundt had carried out EC-funded research amongst Palestinians in the Negev and Gaza in the area of health and health care (1995–9) and, with Dr Oona Campbell, coordinated an EC network on Arab Maternal Health (MAMAH), which had a regional newsletter and meetings supported by Dr Alzaroo (1996–8). This spread of disciplinary expertise meant both that there was considerable learning within and between teams and that within the project framework each team developed its own emphasis.

Field Setting

The social and political conditions of Palestinians in the countries in the region differ in relation to rights to citizenship, their proportion within the entire population of the country and their access to employment and housing. They form a politically, socially and economically disadvantaged group within the region and within the countries they live in, and many of them survive in conditions of poverty and have an age structure to their population in which the young predominate numerically. With the exception of those living in Jordan, none of them had rights to citizenship until 1995, when the Palestinians living in Gaza and the West Bank had the right to Palestinian passports issued by the Palestinian Authority.

Please refer to Map 1 and Map 2 in the preliminary pages for details of migration routes and whereabouts of refugee camps.

Lebanon

In 1949, there were 110,000 Palestinian refugees in Lebanon and, in 2001, that number rose to some 370,000 (UN 2001) refugees registered with UNRWA. It is estimated that there are a further 10,000 Palestinian refugees who are unregistered. Overall, 53 percent live in camps and about 20 percent live in 'unofficial' camps. Lebanon denies all Palestinian refugees civil rights. They need work permits for employment and these are issued only when there are no Lebanese available to take on the work. Unemployment is high at 40 percent. Health and educational services are in decline, especially those provided by UNRWA, because of budget limitations.

Syria

The number of Palestinian refugees in Syria is estimated to be more than 400,000 by GAPAR (General Association for Palestinian Arab Refugees), the Syrian administrative department responsible for Palestinian refugees (GAPAR 2000). Of these, 370,304 are registered refugees of 1948 and their descendants, for whom UNRWA has records, as well as those who came from Lebanon and Gaza during the last two decades. They make up less than 2.6 percent of the Syrian population. Of these, 45 percent are less than 19 years old and the average family size is six members. There are ten camps in Syria near Damascus and Homs (see Map 1) and three additional sites. The largest camp is Yarmouk camp with 90,000 inhabitants. Many of the Palestinians are socioeconomically disadvantaged – 26 percent of families live below the poverty line, 22 percent on the poverty line and UNRWA had 24,000 hardship cases registered in 1999 (UNRWA 1999). They do not have Syrian nationality.

Jordan

Jordan has the largest number of refugees in the diaspora – 1.6 million refugees are registered with UNRWA. These registered refugees constitute 32 percent of the total population. Jordan is the only Arab country that has provided citizenship rights to most refugees. There have been repeated armed conflicts in the region (1948, 1967, 1990–1) resulting in waves of Palestinian forced migration into Jordan, and internal armed conflicts (1968, 1970–1). These refugees face a variety of discretionary barriers to full integration as citizens. Refugees from 1948 have full citizenship entitlements, while refugees from 1967 and later waves of forced migration do not.

The Gaza Strip

The Gaza Strip is 50 kilometres long, 5–12 kilometres wide and in total comprises 362 square kilometres. There are four towns, eight refugee camps, fourteen villages and in total a population of more than 1 million. The population is predominantly young: 47 percent are under 15 years of age and 5.2 percent are 60 years and over. In 1998 there were 798,444 registered refugees, of whom 54.8 percent were living in camps, comprising approximately 75 percent of the population of the Gaza Strip. UNRWA provides education, health and relief services to refugees living in and outside camps. The Palestinian Authority provides services to residents (non-refugees).

West Bank

Palestinian refugees constitute 37 percent of the population of the West Bank. In 1997 542,642 refugees were living in the West Bank, of whom 26 percent were living in the nineteen camps and 74 percent were living outside the camps (PCBS 1999). Nearly half the population (45 percent) is under 15 years of age – 17.5 percent are between nought and 4 years of age and 27.5 percent are between 5 and 14 years of age.

Shared History

Two bitter struggles came to a climax in 1948 in the former British-mandated Palestine: one was the birth of the state of Israel; and the other was *al-Nakba*, or the Catastrophe, a term used to describe the 1947–8 War in Palestine, when armed Jewish militias occupied most of Palestine and forced the indigenous people to flee. More than 750,000 Palestinian people left their homes and places of work and took refuge in camps hastily set up by the Red Cross and other humanitarian agencies in the West Bank, the Gaza Strip, Lebanon, Syria, Jordan and Egypt.

A special agency was set up in December 1949 by the United Nations (UNRWA) to manage Palestinian refugee camps and provide health, education and humanitarian aid. Today, Palestinians rank as the largest refugee population after the Afghanis. Globally, one in three refugees is a Palestinian. Despite its dramatic scale and longevity, the Palestinian refugee problem remains poorly comprehended. In order to understand why their case has remained marginalised and unresolved for more than half a century requires coming to terms with the way their recent history is intertwined with the aspirations of the European Jewish Diaspora.

Between the sixteenth century and the end of the First World War, Palestine was an integral part of the Ottoman Empire. As this began to crumble prior to the end of the First World War, European powers began to vie for control of the Arab Ottoman provinces. Between July 1915 and March 1916, Sir Henry McMahon began to correspond with the Sharif of Mecca, al-Amir Hussein. Their exchanges resulted in the McMahon-Hussein treaty whereby Great Britain agreed to recognise and support the independence of the Arabs, should they revolt against the Ottomans. A few months later in May, Sir Mark Sykes (Secretary to the British War Cabinet) revealed a contradictory agreement with France and Russia, which would have the lands of the Arab Ottoman Empire divided up so that France would take the territories that would emerge as Syria and Lebanon, Britain would take control of what would become Iraq and Transjordan, while Palestine was to be placed under international admin-istration with Russia agreeing to the management of Jerusalem (Tannous 1988: 62–3). The Bolshevik Revolution in 1917, however, undermined that agreement, when Russia withdrew and divulged the, until then secret, Sykes-Picot agreements to the rest of the world.

In 1917 – less than a year after the Sykes-Picot agreement had been signed – the Balfour Declaration was revealed. On 2 November 1917, Lord James Balfour, the British Foreign Secretary, sent Lord Rothschild, a British leader of the Zionist movement in London, a letter pledging sup-port for the establishment in Palestine of a 'national home for the Jewish people':

Foreign Office
November 2nd, 1917

Dear Lord Rothschild,

I have much pleasure in conveying to you, on behalf of His majesty's govern-ment, the following declaration of sympathy with Jewish Zionist aspirations which have been submitted to, and approved by, the Cabinet. 'His Majesty's Government view with favour the establishment in Palestine of a national home for the Jewish people, and will use their best endeavours to facilitate the achievement of this object, it being clearly understood that nothing shall be done which may prejudice the civil and religious rights of existing non-Jewish communities in Palestine, or the rights and political status enjoyed by Jews in any other country.' I should be grateful if you would bring this declaration to the knowledge of the Zionist Federation.

Yours sincerely,
Arthur James Balfour

With the close of the First World War, the League of Nations was established and in its Covenant, signed in 1919, the Palestinian people were recognised as an independent nation placed 'provisionally' under British mandate. Other Arab peoples, who were under the rule of the defeated Ottoman Empire, were also placed under mandate, some British and others French. In 1922, the League of Nations issued the British Mandate and incorporated the Balfour Declaration in its articles, perhaps not recognising that a fundamental inconsistency now existed in its articles of incorporation. On the one hand the British Mandate required Great Britain to act as 'custodian' (in Article 22 of the Covenant) to the Palestinian people who were 'not yet able to stand by themselves' as an independent state. At the same time, the incorporation of the Balfour Declaration into the League of Nations Mandate for Palestine (Articles 2, 4, 6 and 7) clearly contradicted significant parts of the original Covenant. These articles allowed Great Britain to consult with the Jewish Agency on matters pertaining to land, Jewish immigration to Palestine and settlement, without referring to or consulting with the indigenous Palestinian people.

Over the next three decades, the Jewish percentage of the population of Mandated Palestine was to alter dramatically. In 1918, the Arab population of Palestine was estimated at 700,000 people, of whom 574,000 were Muslim, 70,000 Christian and 56,000 Jews. By 1944, the number of Jews in Palestine was as much as 135,000 out of a total population of 1,739,624. Between 1946 and 1948, the number of Jews in Palestine increased to 700,000 or about a third of the total population of about 2,115,000 (Farsoun and Zacharia 1997: 79).

In 1947, the United Nations dispatched a Commission of Inquiry, the United Nations Special Committee on Palestine (UNSCOP), to Palestine. The Commission returned and proposed the partition of Palestine, and, on 29 November 1947, the United Nations General Assembly Resolution 181, known also as the Partition Plan, was passed. According to the Plan, the Jewish state was to comprise 56.4 percent of the territory while the area allocated to the Palestinian Arab state was 42.8 percent. Jerusalem was to become an international zone. At the time the resolution was passed, Jews owned 7 percent of the total land area in Palestine, Palestinian Arabs owned the rest. By this time, Palestinians constituted nearly 66 percent of the population of Palestine (Farsoun and Zacharia 1997: 77–80).

The day following the UN Partition Plan, armed conflict spread throughout Palestine. Zionist paramilitary organisations – especially the Haganah and the international volunteers who came to assist them – engaged in a system of what David Ben-Gurion called 'aggressive defence': every Arab attack must be met with decisive counteraction, destruction of the site, expulsion of its residents, and seizure of the location. After the Irgun and Stern Gang massacre at Deir Yassin village in

1948, the Arab states assembled in an Arab League, to consider intervention in Palestine with their regular armies (Farsoun and Zacharia 1997: 114). By the time the Arab armies decided to intervene, most of the major cities and towns in Palestine had already fallen to the Haganah and other Jewish militias. Among the Jewish fighting force, there were 52,000 men in the Haganah, 14,000 in the Jewish Settlement Police (which had been trained and armed by the British) and 27,000 Second World War veterans as well as numerous paramilitary groups. The Haganah – later renamed the Israeli Defence Force – and other Jewish militias were superior to the local Palestinian forces and the Arab armies combined. Most of these Arab states had only just snatched their independence from French or British mandate and were not prepared for international campaigns. Egypt was still in a semi-colonial relationship with Great Britain. Lebanon and Syria had only just been granted independence from France in 1946 and 1943 respectively. And Jordan's King Abdullah was alleged to have given orders to his British-commanded Arab legion to secure only the part of Palestine – the West Bank – allotted to him in secret talks with the Zionist leadership.

The Palestinians were defeated and on Friday, 15 May 1948, Ben-Gurion declared the establishment of the state of Israel. Henceforth, 1948 marked two contrasting historical experiences: for the Zionists, it was the culmination of the dream of creating a state for world Jewry, as a means to put an end to European anti-Semitism; for Palestinians it was the time of expulsion and destruction of their land and society. The dramatic and abrupt dispossession and displacement of Palestinians in 1948 attracted significant international attention. In June 1948, Joseph Weitz, Director of the Jewish National Fund, and Ben-Gurion met and put forward a plan for preventing the return of refugees to their home. This plan was formalised and adopted by the Israeli Cabinet on 16 June 1948. Arab governments, at the same time, refused to formally integrate Palestinian refugees, believing that this would threaten their right of return to their homes in Palestine.

Upon their expulsion, Palestinian refugees sought shelter in neighbouring countries, primarily in the West Bank and Gaza (which had fallen under the control of Jordan and Egypt respectively), Lebanon and Syria. The majority of Palestinians believed their expulsion would end in a matter of days – at most a few weeks. Most had not carried their belongings with them and many had left their doors open, while others took their keys. Today many hold on to the keys to their homes as a symbol of hope and resistance to exile.

After their initial expulsion during and consequent to the 1947–8 War, Palestinians were subjected to further displacement. During the Arab-Israeli war in 1967, Israel occupied the remaining 22 percent of Palestine, namely the West Bank and the Gaza Strip, as well as other Arab territory. As a result of the 1967 War, approximately 350,000 Palestinians were uprooted from the West Bank and the Gaza Strip – over half of them for the second time. The Israeli invasion of Lebanon in 1982 resulted in the death and displacement of thousands of Palestinians in refugee camps in that country. The Gulf War in 1990–1 caused another mass forced migration of Palestinians from Arab countries, estimated at 350,000 – mainly from Kuwait. In the middle of the 1990s, Libya evicted its Palestinian community of some 30,000, many of them straddled the Libyan-Egyptian border for months and some remained for over a year, unable to return to Palestine or find a country that would allow them in.

Local History, Demography and Histories

Each location in this study has experienced a unique set of historical and demographic realities which have shaped the way in which Palestinian identity is formed and maintained. For Palestinian refugees in Syria, for example, their presence and political experience in the country is perhaps the most stable and least affected by the continuous crises and armed conflicts in the region. This is partially a reflection of the tight control the government has maintained on Palestinian groups as well as its own citizens, never allowing unauthorised action on any of its borders. Most Palestinian refugees were settled into particular sites in the 1950s and remained there to this day, with more refugees arriving in Syria as conflicts involving Palestinians in neighbouring countries came and went. In Lebanon, on the contrary, continuous armed conflict throughout the 1960s, 1970s, 1980s and 1990s has intimately shaped the unending displacement and forced migration imposed on Palestinian refugees in that country. In the West Bank and also in the Gaza Strip, governance has changed dramatically over the past half century. The West Bank was governed by Jordan between 1948 and 1967, by Israel between 1976 and 1994 and by the Palestinian National Authority after 1994. The Gaza Strip moved from governance by Egypt, then to Israel and finally became, after 1994, the Palestinian National Authority. These changes in central authority dramatically affected the lives of the Palestinians and Palestinian refugees in these territories.

Lebanon[2]

Approximately 100,000 Palestinians fled to Lebanon in 1948 during *al-Nakba*, or the Catastrophe, from the Galilee region and northern Palestine (including the districts of Acre, Bisan, Safad, Tiberias and the vicinity of Haifa) when the state of Israel was established. Palestinian refugees were initially well received by Lebanese authorities and had great support and sympathy from the public. However, once it became evident that there would be no early return, the Lebanese authorities imposed strict measures on Palestinian refugees, especially those resident in refugee camps. Perhaps they feared that Palestinians might cause trouble by fighting the Israelis on the Lebanon-Israel border or by clashing with local militias. Whatever the reasons, the Lebanese government considered Palestinians a threat to the security of the state and thus entrusted Palestinian affairs to security agencies, especially to the army's intelligence department, known as the 'Second Bureau'.

During 1948 and 1949, the International Red Cross offered Palestinian refugees relief services, especially food rations. In 1950, the United Nations established UNRWA as a special body responsible for the well-being of Palestinian refugees in Arab host countries. The Lebanese state was relieved of any social or economic responsibility towards Palestinian refugees on its territory. UNRWA was held responsible for providing shelter, food rations, education and health care. UNRWA contracted the Lebanese authorities to settle Palestinian refugees in designated areas, which became fifteen camps that were officially recognised, administered and serviced by UNRWA.

During this early period Palestinians were considered temporary guests awaiting the international community's settlement of their problem. A special department within the Ministry of Interior was established to handle aspects of their affairs, such as issuing them identity cards and travel documents, registering their marriages, divorces and new-borns. Palestinian refugees were considered a special category with the right to residence in Lebanon, but no other social, legal or economic rights.

The Lebanese economy was developing rapidly; hence it welcomed cheap skilled Palestinian labour in agriculture and unskilled labour in construction and in manufacturing. Palestinian refugees did not need work permits to be employed in those sectors. A small number of Palestinians were employed directly by UNRWA, mostly teachers, nurses and clerks. They established themselves within the Lebanese economy, and formed a substantial proportion of Lebanon's unskilled and semi-skilled labour force. Many refugee families found it necessary to send their women into factories, agricultural fields, and domestic work. Palestinian refugee women often worked as servants in middle- and upper-class Lebanese homes.

During the early years of the Palestinian displacement, the Lebanese government absorbed most of the Christian Palestinian refugees through naturalisation. The remaining majority, who were Sunni Muslims, were not trusted by Lebanese authorities. Even before the civil war broke out in the 1970s, the relationship between Palestinian refugees and Lebanese authorities was coloured with tension. The same applied to their relationship with UNRWA. Because of its limited services, Palestinian refugees frequently held general strikes against UNRWA in the camps.

Palestinian refugees in Lebanon focused on educating their children to achieve transferable skills that could be used anywhere. Possessing higher education and technical skill enabled the second-generation Palestinian refugees to find work in Arab Gulf countries. The new income enabled the families concerned to improve their standard of living and to provide better opportunities for their children (the third generation). In 1970, a small percentage of Palestinian refugees in Lebanon settled in the Gulf States and Libya; some moved out of the camps and rented or bought apartments in Lebanese cities (e.g., Beirut, Sidon and Tripoli), while the remaining majority stayed in the camps.

When Palestinian fighters were expelled from Jordan after the Black September conflict with the Jordanian army in 1970–1, they moved their bases into South Lebanon, an area that came to be known as 'Fatah Land'. The official headquarters of the Palestine Liberation Organisation (PLO) were based in Beirut. Large numbers of nationalist and pan-Arab Lebanese youth joined the various PLO factions between 1970 and 1974. During the same period, the camps' populations witnessed a period of freedom, independence and relative prosperity. The PLO and its factions established a variety of social institutions and economic corporations that employed large numbers of Palestinian youth and adults, in addition to those recruited in the military sector or the militia. The PLO established a vast network of allies and supporters among Lebanese political parties and prominent politicians. However, Lebanese groups who rejected the presence of the PLO in Lebanon and who believed that 'weak Lebanon' could not be a major front from which Arabs could fight Israel, prepared for a showdown with the PLO. They believed that they had to defend the existing Lebanese political system (dominated by Maronites) by expelling the PLO forces from Lebanon.

In April 1975, Lebanese forces started their open battle against Palestinians, a battle that became absorbed as part of the Lebanese civil war (1975–90), into which regional players like Syria, Israel, Iraq and Egypt were drawn. The first two brutal years of the war were 1975 and 1976. The Phalange militias besieged and destroyed three camps that were in their area of control, namely Tal el-Za'tar, Jisr el-Basha and Dbayeh camps. Thousands of Palestinian families were displaced in all directions within Lebanon. In 1976 the Syrian army entered Lebanon in order to put an end to the civil war. The Syrians defeated the PLO and deployed their forces in many parts of Lebanon, including the capital. At that time the Lebanese army spilt on a sectarian basis. The Lebanese state became the weakest of all contending parties.

In June 1982, Israel invaded Lebanon, besieged Beirut, occupied half the country, and drove the PLO forces out of Lebanon and destroyed its infrastructure. During the Israeli invasion around 20,000 Palestinians and Lebanese (mostly civilians) were killed. Israel established a concentration camp in South Lebanon (Ansar), destroyed several Palestinian camps (e.g., Borj el-Shemali and Ein el-Hilweh) and forced internal migration and displacement among the population. Two of the major tragedies of the Israeli invasion were the massacre of Palestinian refugees residing in Sabra and Shatila camps, committed by Phalange Maronite Lebanese forces under the control of the Israeli forces; and the beginning of emigration from Lebanon by Palestinian families – mainly to Germany, Sweden and Denmark.

Between 1982 and 1985 the Lebanese Resistance Movement (mostly Islamist Shiites) replaced the PLO in fighting Israel. After Israel withdrew, the Palestinians attempted to rebuild their power in the camps and in Beirut. The Shiite AMAL Movement objected and began a siege of Palestinian camps in the South and in Beirut. Thus began the brutal Camps Wars that lasted from 1985 to 1987. The experience was one of the most difficult for Palestinian refugees in the camps, as described in their narratives. This period witnessed the largest waves of Palestinian emigration from Lebanon.

The civil war came to an end in 1990 and a Lebanese central government was reinstated. A process of rebuilding the Lebanese state, its political system, its bureaucracy and the divided cities, towns and villages resumed. Palestinians in the camps were left out of the effort and were socially and politically isolated. The camps were placed under Lebanese or Syrian control. The flow of emigration continued. Unemployment among Palestinians skyrocketed, especially as Arab labour markets became closed to them after the Gulf War. All Lebanese political parties and politicians agreed that Palestinians could not settle in Lebanon. Some Lebanese called for redistributing Palestinian refugees to other Arab and foreign countries. The fate of Palestinian refugees in Lebanon was discussed at the international level. A large number of reports and proposed plans about their fate were published in daily newspapers. Feelings of insecurity intensified and appear clearly in the narratives of Palestinians.

According to the 2001 figures of UNRWA, the registered Palestinian refugee population in Lebanon stands at 382,973 persons.[3] Palestinians in Lebanon have the highest ratio of camp residence, at 56 percent, followed by the Gaza Strip at 54 percent, whereas in Jordan, Syria, and the West Bank, it is 17.6 percent, 28 percent, and 27 percent respectively (UNRWA 2001). The Lebanese government severely limits camp expansion and reconstruction. Most camps in Lebanon have suffered massive destruction during the conflicts and the Lebanese government has prohibited their reconstruction or replacement.

Many Palestinians are forced to live in 'unofficial' camps and gatherings for the displaced. UNRWA does not administer these camps. The fourteen 'unofficial' camps, resulting from both natural population growth and internal displacement, are generally located at the peripheries of the twelve UNRWA administered camps. The choice of location was sought for social and practical purposes, allowing their inhabitants a shelter near their community and access to UNRWA services.

Syria[4]

The majority of Palestinians who fled Palestine and came to Syria were poor, illiterate peasants. They left their villages and towns in the northern part of Palestine and due to the geography of the region came to the southern parts of Lebanon where they were received as temporary refugees by the International Red Cross. Within a very short period of time they were transferred to Syria and were re-distributed around all the major Syrian urban centres. The refugees were first given shelter in mosques, schools and tents; later they were offered parcels of land by the Syrian government, which constituted the beginning of the establishment of the UNRWA Palestinian refugee camps in Syria. These UNRWA operations set up in the 1950s provided the refugees with food supplements, shelter, health and educational services. Nevertheless, the Syrian government was, and still is, one of the main service providers for Palestinian refugees in Syria. (Brand 1988)

The Palestinian refugees in Syria enjoy similar civil rights to the Syrian citizens, including equal access to employment in the public and private sectors, health and educational services (Brand 1988). In July 1956, the Syrian government issued Law number 260 to integrate Palestinian refugees into Syrian civil life. Palestinians residing in Syria have the same rights as Syrians in all things covered by the law and connected with the right to employment, commerce and national services, while preserving their original nationality (Brand 1988: 623; UNRWA 1992: 139). However, despite the Syrian Law of Integration, most Palestinians are not permitted to vote in Syrian elections, and they are not eligible for Syrian citizenship 'passports' (Brand 1988).

The traditional Palestinian social system based on Arab values of family and community is strong among these refugees. Thus the individuals' social identification and affiliations depend on their family or tribe, and especially their village of origin in Palestine. Social values were conservative with regard to education, freedom of movement and employment of females. Many felt that by keeping to traditional attitudes and values they sustain their social identity. Interestingly, traditional culture seems to be defended by both elderly and young generations.

From the beginning of the 1960s many Palestinians, especially refugees, participated actively in the Palestinian resistance movements. Thousands of Palestinians were killed in the *Fedayeen* (freedom fighters) activities against Israel, in the Black September campaigns in 1970 against the Jordanian army and in the Lebanese civil war during the 1980s. Moreover, the unstable political conditions in the Middle East, the emergence of the Palestinian revolution in the 1970s, the Israeli invasion of Lebanon in 1982 and the continual Israeli bombardments on Lebanon until recently had dramatically affected the demographic distribution of the Palestinian refugees in Syria and Lebanon, causing particular overcrowding in some camps.

The Palestinian refugee community in Syria is a young population with a large proportion of children compared to the elderly and middle-aged (Cattan 1988; Dickerson 1974; Friedlander 1980). UNRWA (2000c) statistics showed that, among refugees, the children and young people within the age group of 1–15 years represent nearly half of the population (46 percent) and more than 20 percent of this age group is below 6 years of age. The average number of children per family is between five and eight. A decrease in fertility has been noted, which could be due to the increase in marriage age for both males and females, as well as the family planning services offered by the UNRWA clinics and the Syrian Ministry of Health. There is also a significant decline in child mortality as a result of recent general campaigns of vaccination of children under 5 years of age. Child mortality decreased from 200 per 1,000 in 1960 to 32 per 1,000 in 1999. Nevertheless, UNRWA health reports indicate that 26 percent of the children below the age of five suffer from malnutrition, iodine deficiency and anaemia (UNRWA 1999; UNRWA 2000b).

Although the quality of housing and living conditions among Palestinian refugees has improved over the years, many Palestinian camps and neighbourhoods in Syria still suffer from overcrowding and lack of basic services, such as water, sewage systems, solid waste collection and disposal mechanisms (PRCS and PCH 1994). A Canadian report (Canadian Mission 1999) on the Palestinian refugees in Syria shows that only 80 percent have access to a water system. More than 400 families in Nairab camp near Aleppo still live in old French Army barracks lacking privacy or ventilation. Khan Eshih camp near Damascus still lacks a sewage system and solid waste management. Furthermore, a UNICEF report (1999) indicates that 48 percent of Palestinian families in Syria live below or on the poverty line; 15 percent of the families live in unacceptable housing conditions; only 9 percent of the children and young people have access to places of entertainment such as public parks and recreational clubs; and 24 percent of the children play in unsafe conditions. Moreover, an UNRWA report (2000a) declares that there are 27,529 hardship cases among Palestinian refugees including the ill, imprisoned, unemployed, divorced and widowed.

UNRWA runs twenty-three primary health care clinics with twelve laboratories in the Palestinian refugee camps. The Palestinian Red Crescent Society runs three hospitals and more than twelve primary health care clinics; other NGO clinics also present limited services to the Palestinian refugees (UNRWA 1999).

There are thirty-three Palestinian kindergartens scattered around the Palestinian refugee camps in Syria; less than 8 percent of Palestinian children within the age group of 3–6 years attend. There were 85,000 school pupils between the ages of 6 and 15 in UNRWA schools in the year 2000. School drop-out rates are low in the first years of schooling, but increase up to 14 percent in the preparatory stage and reach 50 percent at the secondary stage of schooling. The illiteracy rate is relatively high (20 percent) among people between the ages of 13 and 45. Vocational training for young people is limited (UNRWA 1999).

Recent UNRWA reports showed that 68 percent of the Palestinian refugees in Syria were originally from Galilee and 22 percent from Haifa and other coastal areas in British-Mandated Palestine (UNRWA 2001). The lack of accurate statistics and the high percentage of nonregistered refugees with UNRWA make it difficult to define the exact number of the Palestinian refugees in Syria. Nevertheless, current available statistics indicate that the number of the UNRWA-registered refugees in Syria is 389,877, in addition to an estimated 20,000 unregistered refugees.

Currently, Palestinian refugees in Syria live in ten refugee camps and three residential settings. This represents about 60 percent of Palestinian refugees in Syria. The aforementioned Canadian study (Canadian Mission 1999) shows that the majority of the refugee camps are situated around Damascus, where more than 302,363 Palestinian refugees live, while only 23,561 are in the south near Dara' and 34,369 in Homs and Hama; 28,582 live in the north around Aleppo, and about 5,000 are in the coastal area – mainly in Lattakyia. Interestingly, the largest Palestinian settlement, known as Yarmouk camp, which is located near Damascus and hosts a huge number of Palestinian refugees, is not recognised as a refugee camp by UNRWA (Brand 1988).

Jordan[5]

Between 700,000 and 900,000 Palestinians found themselves abruptly acquiring refugee status following *al-Nakba* in 1948. Two years following the 1948 war, the West Bank was annexed to Transjordan, which was renamed the Hashemite Kingdom of Jordan in March 1950. The annexation of the West Bank dramatically expanded the constituency and territorial base of Jordan, a factor that played a crucial role in the reshaping and development of the Jordanian nation-state.

Following its annexation of the West Bank, Jordan extended full citizenship rights to the majority of Palestinians living on the West and East banks of the Jordan River, including refugees who had been uprooted from their homes and lands during the 1948 war. Today, Palestinians with Jordanian passports represent the majority of the population. The demographic factor in favour of the Palestinians is a politically sensitive issue to the extent that statistics revealing the number of Jordanian citizens with Palestinian origins are unavailable to the public; government officials rationalise the inaccessibility of such data on the basis that such a revelation might incite ethnic conflict (Zureik 1996: 33).

There were three major armed conflicts that led to the influx of refugees into Jordan. The 1948 war or *al-Nakba* resulted in the displacement of an estimated 100,000 people who fled into Transjordan.[6] Four camps were established following the 1948 war, while the further six camps were erected as 'emergency camps' consequent to the 1967 war, when an estimated 400,000 people flooded into Jordan. For over half the population fleeing the 1967 Arab-Israeli war, this was their second displacement. Many of the 'second time' refugees had fled from camps in the West Bank and the Gaza Strip, such as *Aqbat Jaber* and *Ain al-Sultan* in Jericho, *Fare'a* and *Balata* in the West Bank and *Maghazi* and *Rafah* in the Gaza Strip.

A third exodus occurred during the Gulf War in the early 1990s, when approximately 400,000 expatriates were forced out of Gulf countries, mainly from Kuwait. Most of those expelled were Palestinians, many of them carrying Jordanian passports, who were classified as the 'Returnees.' It is important to note that a significant number of the Returnees had never lived in Jordan, having been born and spent most of their lives in Gulf countries. While working in the Gulf, the expatriates were an important source of remittances to Palestinian refugee families, as well as to Jordanians. Some 10 percent of the Returnees moved into refugee camps and/or needed UNRWA services. In addition, higher rates of unemployment were registered as the result of the large influx of Returnees into Jordan (Mrayyan 1994: 234).

The various categories granted to the uprooted Palestinians are accompanied by different rights and obligations, privileges and prohibitions. For example, those classified as 'refugees' refer to Palestinians who originate in the areas occupied during the 1948 war, while the 'displaced' refer to Palestinians uprooted during the 1967 war who originate in the West Bank. There are other such classifications, which make it even more difficult for the refugee population to rally around collective demands. The 'displaced' from 1967 are not eligible for all UNRWA services – in fact their descendents do not even appear in the Agency's statistical records. Similarly, those who fled the 1967 war from the Gaza Strip, many of them also 1948 refugees, acquired a different legal status; for example, the 'ex-Gaza refugees' are not eligible for Jordanian citizenship.

In addition to the three major wars, there were other conflicts that resulted in forced migration and internal displacement, such as the 1968 *al-Karameh* battle,[7] and the armed clashes around Black September in 1970–1, which led to the ousting of the Palestine Resistance Movement by the Jordanian government – along with a significant number of cadres – mainly to Lebanon. Consequently, the frequent relocation and uprooting resulting from armed conflict and the concomitant need to find shelter and livelihood, characterises the trajectories of Palestinians, particularly refugees.

Although the sense of Palestinian belonging to Jordan varies by factors, such as class, generation and legal status, and is influenced by the political context, Palestinians have maintained a sense of 'people-hood' and separate national identity. Moreover, Jordanian policies, mainly those that provide for preferential recruitment of Transjordanians in the public sector, aggravate the schism between the two communities (Brand 1995: 50–5).

Furthermore, the Oslo Agreement in 1993 and its collapse aggravated the issue of identity in Jordan in relation to citizenship and national belonging. Questions pertaining to the future of the Palestinians invoked popular resentment among Jordanians and Palestinians alike. The 'Transjordanians' feared that Jordan would turn into the Palestinian 'alternative Homeland', an idea propagated by the Israeli state, while the Palestinians in Jordan were concerned that the Oslo negotiations would abrogate their right of return and force them to resettle permanently in Jordan.

Of the approximately 3.7 million Palestinian refugees registered with UNRWA in Jordan, Syria, Lebanon, the West Bank and Gaza,[8] approximately 1.6 million registered refugees reside in Jordan and constitute 32 percent of its total population. This figure represents 42 percent of the total registered Palestinian refugee population in the region. UNRWA statistics also indicate that over half the Palestinian refugee population (56 percent) in Jordan is under the age of 25 (UNRWA 2000d). Around 18 percent of refugees in Jordan live in ten UNRWA camps established on lands leased from the government. These have become increasingly permeable, as inhabitants, pressed by overcrowding, have spilled over, forming new neighbourhoods in the vicinity. However, the socioeconomic status between those who live inside camps and those in close proximity are not very different, though the perceptions of 'inside' and 'outside' have political and cultural ramifications. According to UNRWA sources, the percentage of refugees living in 'camps' rises to 65 percent, if one includes those who have moved into the immediate vicinity of the designated legal boundaries of camps.[9]

West Bank[10]

The Arab–Israeli conflict of 1948 and the subsequent establishment of the State of Israel resulted in the dispossession and displacement of two-thirds of the Palestinian people, some of whom ended up as refugees in the West Bank. The Israeli army prevented the return of the internally displaced Palestinians to their homes for alleged security reasons (Morris 1987).[11] Following the war of June 1967, the Israeli military occupied the

West Bank and the Gaza Strip. Neighbouring countries faced another massive influx of refugees when thousands of Palestinians fled from the West Bank and the Gaza Strip.

The West Bank covers an area of 5,500 square kilometres. The area was part of the Hashemite Kingdom of Jordan during the period 1948–67. Subsequently, from 1967 to 1994, the West Bank was under Israeli occupation. In 1995, a total of 517,412 refugees were living in the West Bank. This number comprised 17 percent of the total Palestinian refugee population in the region and 37 percent of the total population of the West Bank. In 1997, the total number of inhabitants in the West Bank was 1,873,476, of which 951,693 were male and 921,783 were female. Of these, 18 percent were between nought and 4 years of age and 28 percent were between 5 and 14 years of age (PCBS 1998).

The West Bank camps are overcrowded but many of the original UNRWA concrete shelters have been replaced by multi-floor private homes. The refugees who live outside the camps form 74 percent of the total refugees in the West Bank while the remaining 26 percent live in the twenty-two refugee camps in the West Bank. Following the Oslo Definitions of Accords, refugee camps are located in areas A, B, and C, as well as in occupied East Jerusalem. This means that while some refugee camps are located in areas fully controlled by the Palestinian Authority, other camps are still directly exposed to Israeli military rule. Both of the study site camps – al-Aroub and al-Fawwar – are placed in area C according to the Oslo Accords and thus the Israel Civil Administration still controls all their civil and security affairs. Israeli soldiers guard the adjacent roads, patrol the camp and continue to chase after stone-throwing children.

Al-Fawwar camp has a total of approximately 3,000 inhabitants. The camp is located about 8 kilometres south of Hebron in a valley that is surrounded by mountains. Al-Fawwar is the name of a spring located near the camp. There are two basic UNRWA schools in the camp, one for boys and one for girls. The girls' school is divided into two sessions, the morning session and the afternoon session. The camp has three mosques, three kindergartens and one nursery. In addition, there are some organisations, such as the Women's Centre that was established in 1993, which organises several courses for women and runs a kindergarten and a nursery; the Youth Centre was established in 1957; the Disabled Rehabilitation Centre was established in 1990 and it runs a kindergarten. Moreover, there are four local centres, namely the al-Sabbar Cultural Centre, the Refugee Cultural Centre, the Palestinian Children's Cultural Centre and the Multifunctional Community Centre (MCC). Moreover, there is one UNRWA primary health care clinic in the camp, which provides free health services for refugees. The camp has nine cleaners and one UNRWA rubbish collection truck to collect the solid waste from both the al-Aroub and al-Fawwar camps. The latter camp has many public health problems, such as the open sewage system, the control of flies/mosquitoes and the contamination of drinking water.

Al-Aroub camp has about 4,000 inhabitants and is located some 17 kilometres north of Hebron, in a valley surrounded by mountains. Beit-Fajjar village surrounds it from the east, the Israeli settlement, Ifrat, from the north, Sheikh Alaroub village from the south and Beit-Omer village from the west. The name al-Aroub originates from the name of the neighbouring village Shyoukh al-Aroub. There are two basic UNRWA schools in the camp, one for boys and one for girls. The Women's Centre was established in 1976, and it holds several courses for women and also runs a kindergarten and a nursery. The camp has had a Youth Centre since 1968. The camp has nine cleaners.

Refugee children and young people in the West Bank are deeply affected by the waves of forced migration and prolonged conflict of the past half-century. The consequences of these events are ever present and include the expropriation of lands, loss of water resources, home demolitions, construction of Israeli settlements and bypass roads, violence, imprisonment, emigration, deportation and the imposed closures of the West Bank towns and villages. Many of these features of life have been revived and reinstated, especially during the first *Intifada* (1987–94) and the current *Intifada*. These conditions have profoundly affected the physical, economic, psychological and social aspects of Palestinian life.

The Gaza Strip[12]

Prior to 1948 the Gaza Strip was part of the southern district of British Mandatory Palestine. From *al-Nakba* in 1948 up to 1967 the Egyptian government administered Gaza Strip. During this period, Jordan incorporated the West Bank under its constitutional rules, broadening its charter to its residents and establishing common civil services for both Jordanians and Palestinians. Egypt, by comparison, set the Gaza Strip aside as an administrative territory and people from Gaza did not have Egyptian citizenship; on the contrary, they kept their nationality as Palestinians (Tamari 1992). After the 1967 *al-Naksa* (The Disaster), Israel occupied the whole West Bank and Gaza Strip.

During the years of the Israeli occupation, the Palestinian economy was very dependent on that of Israel. In December 1987 four residents of Gaza were killed in a traffic accident involving an Israeli military vehicle. Civilian protests over the deaths quickly escalated into mass demonstrations; thousands of people from Gaza City marched into the streets to erect barricades and started their civilian protest campaign. Within a week, the protests had spread to the entire areas of the Gaza Strip and the West Bank, and were being referred to as the *Intifada* (Uprising). The *Intifada* lasted for seven years. It ended with the signing of the peace treaty, partial withdrawal of the Israeli military occupation forces from areas of the West Bank and Gaza Strip and the handing over of the administration to the Palestinian Authority in 1994.

Following the signing of the peace agreement between the Palestinian Authority and Israel in the early 1990s, the Palestinian Authority started to rebuild the infrastructure of the Palestinian economy. The steady deterioration of the economic situation in Gaza has largely been due to the Israeli closure policies, which disrupted the established labour and commodity market relationships between Israel and the West Bank and the Gaza Strip. In 1998 Israel eased the siege on labour from the West Bank and Gaza Strip; this lasted nearly three years, and this period witnessed an economic recovery in the West Bank and Gaza Strip. This recovery ceased in the last quarter of 2000 with the outbreak of the Palestinian *al-Aqsa Intifada* in September and the tight Israeli military closures of Palestinian self-ruled areas. The internal chaos within Palestine, accompanied by the Israeli military strikes against Palestinian areas, resulted in a complete destruction of the Palestinian economy and the administrative structure, widespread closures of business, a high level of unemployment and a sharp drop in GDP. Another major loss has been the decline in income earned by Palestinian workers in Israel.[13]

Today the Gaza Strip comprises a narrow zone of land, located in the south of Palestine, constituting the coastal zone of the Palestinian territory along the Mediterranean Sea between Israel and Egypt. It is 50 kilometres long and 5–12 kilometres wide with an area of 362 square kilometres, and has five districts including four towns, eight refugee camps and fourteen villages.[14]

Within a very short time of the creation of the state of Israel, 250,000 Palestinian refugees fled their homes to the Gaza Strip. Its population tripled almost overnight, and the internal dynamics of the territory were transformed forever. There are now more than 800,000 registered refugees in the Gaza Strip out of a total population of nearly 1.5 million (UNRWA 1999). More than half of the refugee population (55 percent) lives in overcrowded refugee camps and the remaining 45 percent lives in villages and towns. The age distribution of the refugee population is as follows: 50 percent of the population is below 15 years of age, 19 percent are under 5 years of age and only 5 percent are over 60 years of age. Up to the age of 50, the ratio of men to women is weighted in favour of men. After 50, there are a greater proportion of women to men (PCBS 1997). UNRWA is the main provider of education, health and relief services for refugees living in and outside the refugee camps (UNRWA 1999).[15]

Unemployment is high because job opportunities are limited and access to work in Israel is restricted. However, a minority of people are still working in Israel; some work in local shops or workshops, others are farmers and fishermen, while the rest are employed by the Palestinian Authority, UNRWA, local or international NGOs and the private sector.

Some workers have to go through Israeli military checkpoints at the entrances of the Gaza Strip to reach their workplaces either in Israel or on their farms. As a result of the difficult economic conditions, many refugee families are currently receiving hardship assistance.

In the refugee camps, respiratory infections and gastrointestinal diseases are still significant causes of child mortality and morbidity, and are the result of the poor sanitary and environmental conditions. In many camps, sewage runs in open drains and accumulates in the sea and/or Wadi Gaza. According to the Palestinian Ministry of Health (PMoH) in 1997, the infant mortality rate was 3.2 percent, the crude birth rate was 3.75 percent and the annual population growth rate 3.4 percent. The life expectancy rate at birth is 69 years for males and 71 years for females (PMoH 1997). Despite poor living conditions, malnutrition was not a major public health problem (Ard Al Insaan 1997) at the time of this study but anaemia and parasitic infestations are two major problems (Abed 1992). Most children are fully immunised against the known vaccine-preventable diseases (PMoH 1997). UNRWA is the main health provider for refugees inside and outside the refugee camps.

Education in the Gaza Strip is provided by three principal sectors: the government, UNRWA and the private sector. UNRWA provides free education to the registered refugees.[16] Six years of schooling is often considered the minimum for literacy. Under this definition almost 84 percent of the Palestinian population of the Gaza Strip is literate (PCBS 1997). UNRWA provides free education for refugees up to the ninth grade. Each camp has schools that run two shifts and the classrooms are overcrowded. Many teachers complain about class sizes, students' behaviour and their limited ability to control them. Moreover, because schooling was severely disrupted during the *Intifada,* many children suffer from functional illiteracy (UNICEF 1997).

Until 1995, the educational curriculum in Gaza Strip was based on the Egyptian system of education. A Palestinian curriculum was introduced with the establishment of the Palestinian Authority. In the mid-1990s the Palestinian Ministry of Education (PMoE) unified the educational system between the West Bank and Gaza Strip, establishing a uniform twelve years of basic education. At the end of twelve years of schooling, students take the General Secondary Education Certificate Examination (*Tawjihi*). Admission into institutions of higher education is determined largely by the results of this examination.

The Gaza Strip has two universities of its own (Al Azhar and the Islamic) and branches of two other universities (Al-Quds and the Open University). In addition, there is a College of Science and Technology in Khan Younis and Vocational Training Centres located in Dair El Balah, Gaza and North Gaza.

In the early 1980s there were several projects run by the Israeli government in cooperation with UNRWA for rehousing refugees in Gaza. These housing projects provided refugees with financial compensation to enable them to buy a small piece of land and build their own house outside the borders of the refugee camps. Refugees who accepted such offers had to abandon their UNRWA refugee identity (ID) cards, meaning that refugees automatically lost their right to return to what had been their property in 1948. A small minority of the refugees accepted the offer, while others refused and stayed in the refugee camps. Since the signing of the peace agreement between the Palestinian Authority and Israel in the early 1990s, the refugees' right to return remains a central and unresolved issue.

In the Gaza Strip, young people live within three to four-generation extended families. In such families, gender, age and adult authority often dominate the relationships between family members. However, Palestinian society has witnessed some significant changes, including challenges to adults' authority. During the first and current Palestinian Uprisings, many adult men were either arrested or killed; their absence provided children with the conditions to develop independence and self-confidence. Furthermore, young people had the opportunity for active involvement in the daily confrontations with the Israeli troops.

For the last fifty-four years, Palestinians living in the Gaza Strip were exposed to a variety of stressful situations, including displacement, imprisonment, beatings, house demolition, killings, and constant social and economic pressure. A local epidemiological study of Palestinian children reported that out of 1,564 children, 96 percent had experienced night raids, 49.8 percent had been subjected to physical beatings which resulted in 8.7 percent having their bones broken, and 29 percent had been shot or wounded (Abu Hein et al. 1993). Other studies have explored the psychological and emotional problems that children have related to exposure to, or witnessing of violence (Abu Hein et al. 1993; Qouta et al. 1997; Thabet and El Sarraj 1992; Thabet and Vostanis 1998, 1999, 2000). Psychiatric and psychological research indicates that individual coping styles mitigate or exacerbate the effect of a stressor on psychosocial functioning.

Notes

1 These figures are derived from UNHCR and UNRWA sources: www.unhcr.ch/cgi-bin/texis/vtx/basics and www.un.org/unrwa.

2 This section is adapted from a longer piece prepared by Bassem Serhan.

3 UNRWA's registration figures include refugees residing outside of Lebanon, either temporarily for work or study or for emigration purposes. This category is estimated at 60,000–100,000 refugees. However, it is to be noted that there are also refugees who are not registered (NR) with UNRWA. UNRWA has surveyed some 14,000 NR, but the nonregistered are estimated to be around 30,000 refugees.

4 This section is adapted from a longer article prepared by Adnan Abdul-Rahim.

5 This section adapted from a text prepared by Randa Farah.

6 This figure excludes those who sought refuge in the West Bank and Gaza.

7 Al-Karameh was the first time that an organised Palestinian resistance movement, with some help from the Jordanian army, clashed with the Israeli army. Although the Palestinians were defeated, their ability to fight and inflict losses on the enemy boosted morale among Palestinians and in the Arab world, especially since it followed closely the Arab defeat in 1967.

8 This figure excludes Palestinians who are not registered with the Agency. According to official Jordanian figures cited in Zureik's book (1996), the number of Displaced Persons in 1994, who are not registered with UNRWA, totalled 500,417 persons and Displaced Persons carrying Israeli permits, another category referred to as 'Latecomers', totalled 88,211, while deportees were estimated at 12,500. Again this figure excludes Palestinians who did not register with the Agency and are not regarded as displaced (Zureik 1996: 23).

9 Jordan Refugee Camp Profiles, UNRWA, http://www.un.org/unrwa/refugees/jordan.html

10 This section was adapted from a piece written by Salah Alzaroo.

11 The United Nations Relief and Works Agency for Palestine Refugees in the Near East (UNRWAPRNE or UNRWA) was founded by the United Nation (UN) General Assembly Resolution 302 (IV) of 1949 to replace the earlier emergency aid provided by voluntary agencies and coordinated by the United Nations Relief for Palestine Refugees (UNRPR).

12 This section was adapted from text provided by Abdul-Aziz Thabet.

13 See: http://www.odci.gov/cia/publications/factbook/geos/gz.html#Intro

14 See: http://www.nationalgeographic.com/gaza/b024.html

15 See: http://www.arts.mcgill.ca/MEPP/PRRN/prfront.html

16 For more information see: http://www.palestine-net.com/education/it.html

References

Abed, Y. 1992. *'Risk Factors Associated with Prevalence of Anaemia Among Arab Children in Gaza Strip'*. Doctor of Public Health Dissertation, Johns Hopkins University, Baltimore, U.S.A.

Abu Hein, F., Qouta, S., Thabet, A. and El Sarraj, E. 1993. 'Trauma and Mental Health of Children in Gaza'. *British Medical Journal*, 306: 1129–30.

Ager, A. 2002. 'Psychosocial needs in complex emergencies'. *Lancet*, 360, Supplement 1, 21 December: s43–s44.

Agerbak, L. 1992. 'Breaking the Cycle of Violence: Doing Development in Situations of Conflict'. *Development in Practice*, 1(3): 151–8.

Ahearn, F. and Athey, J. 1991. *Refugee Children: Theory, Research and Services.* Baltimore and London: Johns Hopkins University Press.

Ahmad, A. 1992. 'Symptoms of Post-traumatic Stress Disorder among Displaced Kurdish Children in Iraq: Victims of Man-made Disaster after the Gulf War'. *Nordic Journal of Psychiatry*, 46: 315–19.

Allen, T. 1989. 'Violence and Moral Knowledge: Observing Social Trauma in Sudan and Uganda'. *Cambridge Anthropology*, 13(2): 45–66.

Ard Al Insaan (Terre des Hommes). 1997. *Nutritional Status of Palestinian Children.* Report.

Baker, A.M. 1990. 'Psychological Response of Palestinian Children in the Occupied West Bank and Gaza: An Exploratory Study'. *American Journal of Orthopsychiatry*, 60: 495–505.

———— 1991. 'Psychological Response of Palestinian Children to Environmental Stress Associated with Military Occupation'. *Journal of Refugee Studies*, 4(3): 237–47.

Bauman, Z. 2001. *Modernity and the Holocaust*. Ithaca, NY: Cornell University Press.

Boyden, J. 1994. 'Children's Experience of Conflict Related Emergencies: Some Implications for Relief Policy and Practice'. *Disasters: Journal of Disaster Studies and Management*, 18(3): 254–67.

———— 2002. *Social Healing in War-Affected and Displaced Children*. Working Paper, Oxford: Refugee Studies Centre.

Brand, L. 1988. 'Palestinians in Syria: The Politics of Integration'. *Middle East Journal*, 4: 621–35.

———— 1995. 'Palestinians and Jordanians: A Crisis of Identity'. *Journal of Palestine Studies* 24(4): 46–72.

Bryce, J. and Armenian, H. (eds) 1986. *Wartime: The State of Children in Lebanon*. Beirut: American University of Beirut Press.

Canadian Mission. 1999. *'Canadian Report on Palestinian Refugees in Syria'*. Unpublished manuscript, Damascus.

Cattan, H. 1988. *The Palestinian Question*. London: Croom Helm.

Cunningham, H. 1991. *Children of the Poor*. Oxford: Blackwells.

———— 1995. *Children and Childhood in Western Society Since 1500*. London and New York: Longman.

Davis, J. 1992. 'The Anthropology of Suffering'. *Journal of Refugee Studies*, 5(2): 149–61.

Dawes, A. 1992. *Psychological Discourse about Political Violence and its Effect on Children*. Paper prepared for the meeting on the Mental Health of Refugee Children exposed to Violent Environments, Refugee Studies Centre, University of Oxford, January.

Dawes, A. and Tredoux, C. 1989. *The Impact of Violence of Children: A Study from South Africa*. Paper presented at the Fourth Ethnography of Childhood Workshop, Victoria Falls, Zimbabwe.

Dickerson, G. 1974. 'Education for the Palestine Refugees: The UNRWA/UNESCO Programme'. *Journal of Palestinian Studies*, 3(3): 122–30.

Friedlander, D. 1980. 'Modernization Patterns and Fertility Change: The Arab Population of Israel and the Israeli-administered Territories'. *Population Studies*, 33:2.

Eisenbruch, M. 1991. 'From Post-traumatic Stress to Cultural Bereavement: Diagnosis of Southeast Asian Refugees'. *Social Science and Medicine*, 33(6): 673–80.

El-Bedour, S., Bensel, R. and Maruyama, G.M. 1993. 'Children at Risk: Psychological Coping with War and Conflict'. *International Journal of Mental Health*. 22: 33–52.

Ennis-McMillan, M. 2001. 'Suffering from Water: Social Origins of Bodily Distress in a Mexican Community'. *Medical Anthropological Quarterly*, 15(3): 368–90.

Farhood, L., Zurayk, H., Chaya, M., Saadeh, F., Meshededjian, G. and Sidani, T. 1993. 'The Impact of War on the Physical and Mental Health of the Family: The Lebanese Experience'. *Social Science and Medicine*, 36: 1555–67.

Farmer, P. 1997. 'On Suffering and Structural Violence: A View from Below'. In A. Kleinman, V. Das and M. Lock (eds), *Social Suffering*. pp. 261–83. Berkeley: University of California Press.

Farsoun, S. and Zacharia, C. 1997. *Palestine and the Palestinians*, Oxford: Westview Press.
GAPAR (General Association for Palestinian Arab Refugees). 2000. *Annual Census and Survey Report*. Damascus, Syria.
Goldberg, D. 1978. *Manual of the General Health Questionnaire*. London: NFER-Nelson Publishing Company.
Hastrup, K. 1993. 'Hunger and Hardness of Facts'. *Man*, 28(4): 727–39.
Helman, C. G. 2001. *Culture Health and Illness*. 4th edition. London: Arnold.
James, A. 1998. 'From the Child's Point of View: Issues in the Social Construction of Childhood'. In C. Painter-Black (ed.), *Biosocial Perspectives on Children*. Cambridge: Cambridge University Press.
Kaldor, M. 1999. *New and Old Wars: Organized Violence in a Global Era*. Cambridge: Polity Press.
Kleinman, A. 1980. *Patients and Healers in the Context of Culture*. Berkeley: University of California Press.
———— 1986. *Distress and Disease in Chinese Society*. New Haven and London: Yale University Press.
———— 1990. *Patients and Healers in the Context of Culture: An Exploration of the Borderland between Anthropology, Medicine and Psychiatry*. Los Angeles: University of California Press.
———— 1997. 'The Appeal of Experience; the Dismay of Images: Cultural Appropriations of Suffering in our Times'. In A. Kleinman, V. Das and M. Lock (eds), *Social Suffering*. Berkeley: University of California Press.
Kleinman, A., Das, V. and Lock, M. (eds) 1997. *Social Suffering*. Berkeley: University of California Press.
Langner, T.S. 1962. 'A Twenty-two Item Screening Score of Psychiatric Symptoms Indicating Impairment'. *Journal of Health and Social Behaviour*, 3: 29.
MacMullin, C. and Odeh, J. 1999. 'What is Worrying Children in the Gaza Strip?'. *Child Psychiatry and Human Development*, 30(1): 55–72.
McCubbin, H. and Thompson, A. 1991. *Family Assessment Inventories for Research and Practice*. Madison: University of Wisconsin Press.
Mollica, R. 1990. 'Communities of Confinement: An International Plan for Relieving the Mental Health Crisis in the Thai-Khmer Border Camps'. *Southeast Asian Journal of Social Science*, 18: 132–52.
Morris, B. 1987. *The Birth of the Palestinian Refugee Problem*. Cambridge: Cambridge University Press.
Mrayyan, N. 1994. 'The Economic Impact of the Gulf Crisis in Jordan'. In S. Shami (ed.), *Population Displacement and Resettlement: Development and Conflict in the Middle East*, pp. 234–5. New York: Centre for Migration Studies.
Mull, J. and Mull, D. S. 1988. 'Mothers' Concept of Childhood Diarrhoea in Rural Pakistan: What ORT Program Planners Should Know'. *Social Science and Medicine*, 27: 53–67.
Painter-Black, C. (ed.) 1998. *Biosocial Perspectives on Children*. Cambridge: Cambridge University Press.
PCBS (Palestinian Central Bureau of Statistics). 1997. *Population in Palestinian Territory*. Gaza: PNA.
———— 1998. *Palestinian Children: Issues and Statistics*. Ramallah: PCBS.
———— (1999) *Population, Housing and Establishment Census, 1997*, Statistical Brief (Summary of Census Results), Ramallah.
PMoH (Palestinian Ministry of Health). 1997. *The Status of Health in Palestine*. Annual Report, Gaza: PNA.

PRCS and PCH (Palestinian Red Crescent Society and Palestinian Council of Health). 1994. *An Overview on the Situation of the Palestinian Refugees in Diaspora: Demographic, Socio-economic Characteristics and Health Status.* Paper presented by the Palestinian delegation in Rome, 25–27 January.

Punamaki, R. L., Qouta, S. and El Sarraj, E. 1997. 'Relations between Traumatic Events, Children's Gender, Political Activity and Perceptions of Parenting Style'. *International Journal of Behavioural Development*, 21: 91–109.

Punamaki, R.L. and Suleiman, R. 1990. 'Predictors and Effectiveness of Coping with Political Violence among Palestinian Children'. *British Journal of Social Psychology*, 29: 67–77.

Qouta, S., Punamaki, R.L. and El Sarraj, E. 1995. 'The Relations between Traumatic Experiences, Activity and Cognitive Emotional Responses among Palestinian Children', *International Journal of Psychology*, 30: 289–304.

—————— 1997. 'House Demolition and Mental Health: Victims and Witnesses'. *Journal of Social Distress and the Homeless*, 3: 203–11.

Ressler, E., Boothby, N. and Steinbock, D. 1988. *Unaccompanied Children: Care and Protection in Wars, Natural Disasters and Refugee Movements.* Oxford: Oxford University Press.

Ressler, E., Tortorici, J.M. and Marcelino, A. 1992. *Children in Situations of Armed Conflict: A Guide to the Provisions of Services.* New York: UNICEF.

Rousseau, C., Drapeau, A. and Corin, E. 1998. 'Risk Factors and Protective Factors in Central American and Southeast Asian Refugee Children'. *Journal of Refugee Studies*, 11(1): 20–37.

Rousseau, C., Mekki-Berrada, A. and Moreau, S. 2001. 'Trauma and Extended Separation from Family among Latin American and African Refugees in Montreal'. *Psychiatry*, 64(1): 40–59.

Ryhida, J., Shaya, M. and Armenian, H. 1986. 'Child Health in a City at War'. In J. Bryce and H. Armenian (eds), *Wartime: The State of Children in Lebanon.* Beirut: American University of Beirut Press.

Scheper-Hughes, N. 1989. *Child Survival: Anthropological Perspectives on Treatment and Maltreatment of Children.* Dordrecht: Reidel.

Scheper-Hughes, N. and Sargent, C. (eds) 1998. *Small Wars: The Cultural Politics of Childhood.* Berkeley: University of California Press.

Scrimshaw S. and Hurtado, E. 1988. 'Anthropological Involvement in the Central American Diarrheal Disease Control Project'. *Social Science and Medicine*, 27(1): 97–105.

Tamari, S. 1992. 'The Transformation of Palestinian Society: Fragmentation and Occupation'. In M. Heiber and G. Overnsen (eds), *Palestinian Society in Gaza, the West Bank and East Jerusalem: A Survey of Living Conditions.* FAFO Report No. 151.

Tannous, I. 1988. *The Palestinians: Eyewitness History of Palestine under the British Mandate.* New York: I.G.T. Company.

Thabet, A.A. and El Sarraj, E. 1992. 'Cultural Influences on Post Traumatic Stress Reactions in Palestinians'. Unpublished paper.

Thabet, A.A. and Vostanis, P. 1998. 'Social Adversities and Anxiety Disorders in the Gaza Strip'. *Archives of Childhood Diseases*, 78: 439–42.

—————— 1999. 'Post-traumatic Stress Reactions in Children of War'. *Journal of Child Psychology and Psychiatry*, 40: 385–91.

—————— 2000. 'Post-traumatic Stress Disorder Reactions in Children of War: A Longitudinal Study'. *Child Abuse and Neglect*, 24: 291–8.

Thabet, A., Abed, Y. and Vostanis, P. 2002. 'Emotional Problems in Palestinian Children Living in a War Zone: A Cross-sectional Study'. *The Lancet*, 359: 1801–4.

UN (United Nations) 2001. *Report of the Commissioner-General of the United Nations Relief and Works Agency for Palestine Refugees in the Near East, 01 July 2000 – 30 June 2001*. General Assembly, official records.

UNICEF 1997. *The Situation of Palestinian Children and Women in the West Bank and Gaza Strip*. Jerusalem: UNICEF.

——— 1999. *A Report on the Situation of the Palestinian Children in Syria*. August, Damascus.

UNRWA 1992. *Basic Data on Palestinian Refugees and UNRWA*, October. Vienna: UNRWA.

——— 1999. *UNRWA and Palestinian Refugees – 50 years*. Gaza: UNRWA.

——— 2000a. *The Relief and Social Services Program*. Amman, Jordan.

——— 2000b. *The Report of the General Commissioner of the UNRWA Refugee Camps*. June.

——— 2000c. *The Situation of the Palestinian Children in the West Bank and Gaza Strip, Syria and Lebanon*. Amman, Jordan: UNICEF.

——— 2000d. *Report of the Commissioner-General of the United Nations Relief and Works Agency for Palestine Refugees in the Near East, 1 July 1999 – 30 June 2000*. General Assembly, Official Records, Fifty-fifth session, Supplement No. 13 (A/55/13).

——— 2001. *UNRWA Registration Statistical Bulletin*. Amman, Jordan.

Van Os, J., Galdos, P., Lewis, G., Bourgeois, M. and Mann, A. 1993. 'Schizophrenia sans frontiers: Concepts of Schizophrenia among French and British Psychiatrists'. *British Medical Journal*, 307: 489–92.

Walter, B. and Snyder J. (eds) 1999. *Civil Wars, Insecurity, and Intervention*. New York: Columbia University Press.

Wessles, M. 1998. 'Children, Armed Conflict and Peace'. *Journal of Peace Research*, 35(5): 635–53.

Young, A. 1982. 'The Anthropologies of Illness and Sickness'. *Annual Review of Anthropology*, 11: 257–85.

——— 1992. '(Mis)applying Medical Anthropology in Multicultural Settings'. *Santé, Culture, Health*, 7: 197–208.

Zureik, E. 1996. *Palestinian Refugees and the Peace Process*. Washington, D.C.: Institute for Palestine Studies.

2

Palestinian Refugee Children and Caregivers in Lebanon

Bassem Serhan and Samia Tabari

Bassem Serhan

I am a sociologist by training and an activist by inclination. I was born in the village of Kabri in the Acre province of Palestine in 1946. The head of the Serhan family was a Palestinian political leader and member of the Arab Higher Commission for Palestine. In 1948 Zionist militias demolished our family's house. After this incident the family, along with all the other residents of Kabri, fled to Lebanon leaving everything behind. The village was later razed to the ground.

I received my BA degree in sociology from the American University of Beirut in 1966. I was then granted a scholarship and grants from the University of Alberta (Canada), where I received a Master's degree in Sociology (1969). I returned to Lebanon in June 1969 in order to participate in the Palestinian struggle for liberation and freedom, giving up my Canadian-landed immigrant status. I joined the PLO Research and Planning Center. I was head of the Social and Educational Planning Department of the PLO Planning Center.

A scholarship from the Arab Institute for Social and Economic Planning and UNDP in 1977 enabled me to pursue a Ph.D. in sociology of development at the American University in Washington D.C. I received my Ph.D. in December 1980. I taught at several universities in the Arab world, including American University of Beirut (AUB), Lebanese American University (LAU), Kuwait University, Arab Planning Institute, and Western Mountain University (Libya). Currently, I am associate professor of sociology at Bahrain University. Furthermore, I established and coordinated a development programme for Palestinian refugees living in camps in Lebanon from 1996 to 2002. Welfare Association, the largest Palestinian non-governmental organisation, sponsored the programme.

Over the past 30 years, I have conducted numerous studies on various aspects of Palestinian society in exile including political socialisation, family relations, values, manpower and education, and the status of Palestinian women.

Samia Tabari

I am a Palestinian refugee from Lebanon. I inherited my own exile from my parents' hometowns of Tiberias and Jerusalem. I grew up in Beirut throughout the war years and studied at the American University of Beirut from where I was awarded a BA in sociology. I took an MA in International Communications and Development from the City University, London. I also completed the International Diploma in Humanitarian Assistance at the Centre of International Health and Cooperation at Fordham University, NY. At Oxford, U.K., I attended the International Summer School of the Refugee Studies Centre.

I am currently Projects Officer at a U.K.-based British charity overseeing implementation of projects primarily in the fields of education, disability and health throughout the Middle East. From 1990 to 2002 I was involved with a number of research projects and several NGOs active with the Palestinian refugee community of Lebanon. After participating in surveys by UNICEF and Save the Children Federation, I joined Association Najdeh as the External Relations Officer and then as Head of the Program Consultative Board, where I was engaged in planning, monitoring, and evaluating development projects targeting refugee women and children. As an independent consultant to the Arab Resource Centre for Popular Arts, I was involved in managing cultural projects such as film festivals and a resource library.

During this same period I consulted with international and UN agencies on evaluations and publications. I consulted with UNHCR on *'United Nations assistance to Palestinian refugees'* in The State of the World's Refugees: Fifty Years of Humanitarian Action, UNHCR, Geneva, 2000. I recently consulted with a Dutch NGO (NOVIB) on evaluating the programmes of a partner organisation in Egypt.

My publications include: 'Les Palestiniens: la troisième génération' (Palestinians: the third generation) an article published in Defis Sud (issue # 32, April-June 1998, Brussels) and "Health, Work Opportunities and Attitudes: A Review of Palestinian Women's Situation in Lebanon," a research paper prepared in collaboration with Leila Zakharia, which was published by the Journal of Refugee Studies, Oxford, in September 1997. I also contributed to drafting the Second Supplementary Report on the Rights of the Palestinian Child in Lebanon (for the UN Special Session on Children's Rights, 2001 and 2002). I was a senior researcher on a television documentary series about the 1982 Sabra and Shatila massacre, collecting and documenting the survivors' testimonies and reconstructing the massacre time-line through these testimonies, available data and expert opinions.

This chapter focuses on the impact of prolonged conflict and forced migration on young Palestinian refugees in Lebanon. The sample of this research includes nineteen households in three refugee camps and one urban area in Lebanon.[1] The specific variations to the overall team research methodology are discussed in Appendix I. In this chapter, the voices of Palestinian children and their caregivers are prioritised and, as much as possible, allow the findings of the study in Lebanon to emerge from the narratives.

Coping with Inherited Exile

We fled first to Nirba, then to Halta [South Lebanon]. It was winter and we slept out in the rain. Then we went to Kfarshuba where we stayed for two years. Then we moved to Abu Zibla Bridge where we stayed for three years. We lived there in straw houses. Then the Lebanese government moved us to the sand [Tyre]. We were not accustomed to living on sand. We stayed there for two months, then we came to this camp, which was all filled with thorns. They housed us in tents. We received rations since the time we were in Marjioun. Then men went to work using pitchforks and shovels and until today we still work as manual [agricultural] labourers. (HH7, G1, F: see list of Abbreviations for explanation)

Fifty-four years since the 1948 exodus, the Palestinian refugee community has borne many generations in exile. Children and adolescents now constitute the third and fourth generations of refugees. Palestinians who fled to Lebanon endured not only the hardships of refugee life, but also witnessed the many wars that struck Lebanon. A similar fate was likewise shared by the following generations.

UNRWA supports Palestinian refugees; yet UNRWA's mandate, unlike that of UNHCR (United Nations High Commissioner for Refugees) does not provide protection. Consequently, Palestinians are denied international protection, whether legal or physical, and remain dependent on the host country's policy. Left unprotected, Palestinian refugees witnessed a history of wars, massacres and violations of basic human rights. Host governments have issued their own policies towards their refugee community; the most austere were imposed on those in Lebanon. The Lebanese government still denies Palestinians their civil rights, severe restrictions on their employment being one of many. The authorities justify these limitations since they view them as a measure to avoid permanent refugee settlement in Lebanon, which would endanger the country's confessional social political system.

The life of Palestinians in Lebanon is saturated with stinging realities, past, present, and future. It is a life burdened by wars, internal displacement, lack of civil rights and insufficient services, compounded by meagre living conditions, poverty and an uncertain future. The effects of all these factors are detrimental to the community's physical and psychological well-being. Refugees endure high levels of anxiety and frustration. This chapter focuses on how Palestinian refugee children and adolescents cope with the realities outlined above. Coping mechanisms will also be examined in relationship to age and gender.

Caregivers: Adult Generation

I wish to have a house, freedom, and a big yard in front of the house, because my children are pressured [by the lack of space]. We are pressured too. My husband comes home, wanting to rest, but there is no rest. The children are bound to make noise, even if they are studying, if they ask a question related to their homework. This causes psychological pressures for both my children and husband. (HH12, G2, F)

The adult interviewees, including parents, teachers, and NGO staff,[2] spoke at length about the difficult living conditions and were gravely concerned by the growing frustration and anger in the camp. They listed problems such as lack of work and higher educational opportunities, congested space, social deviance, demoralisation and poverty. They especially noted the insufficient educational and recreational services available to children and youth and the effect this has on children's behaviour and attitudes.

Although basic education is UNRWA's biggest programme, constituting around 55 percent of its budget, the Agency's austerity measures have included restrictions on hiring teachers, building or renting new schools, as well as on expanding existing premises. Consequently, the class occupancy rate has risen sharply, averaging forty-three students per classroom. UNRWA school premises, lacking essential equipment and facilities, remain of poor quality. Moreover, UNRWA's secondary-level schools cannot absorb half of the applicants. On another level, despite the fact that there are numerous NGOs providing a variety of services for children and youth, most lack much needed space, equipment and educational material. Open play space is limited to narrow alleys, streets and damaged areas in the camp. Many of those living in the Gaza Building play in the corridors. Television is a main pastime for children and youth.

Parents mentioned the repercussions that the war had on the family unit and the whole community. They endured frequent internal displacement, loss of livelihood, houses and lives. Many men were detained and tortured. Mothers spoke of fear and the war's detrimental impact on the people's physical and psychological well-being, which is carried forward to this day. Parents emphasised their children's high level of anxiety and fear during the war. Women were separated from their husbands for long periods during the war; men were either busy earning a living or fighting, while women cared for the children and sought their safety. They experienced more frequent forced migration than their husbands, for they had to be on the move in order to protect their children. In general, mothers gave more detailed accounts of the traumas they experienced. Huda from Borj El-Barajneh camp, Beirut, said:

During the Israeli invasion, we fled from corner to corner, from shelter to shelter. I was dead scared... During the 1982 invasion we lived in a shelter. The cluster bombs rained on us. My son Bassel was shot in the arm. His friend Hamed was killed. My son carried him and came back with his clothes full of blood. My son was 17... My son got killed during the invasion. It was the last days of the fighting... My son had a hand grenade and his friend had a pistol. The joke turned into a quarrel... My son died on the way to Gaza hospital... My husband worked in Gaza hospital until the 1985 war broke out [camps war, 1985–7]... They [AMAL militia] shot him [dead] with 30 bullets... My children and I were in Rashidiyeh [camp in the South] at that time... Then came the six-month war [camp siege, 1985]. I stayed in the camp [Borj El-Barajneh] and managed to feed my children from the ration I had saved for a period of three months. However, we suffered during the remaining three months. I had to go around begging for food... My son brought home some mule meat. Then he brought a tray of cats' meat. We were unable to eat it. I told him to give it to people who would be willing to eat it. For 12 days we only had water and one rotten loaf... When the siege was over, we went out to buy things we needed. One day as we returned from the town, they [AMAL] began sniping at us. Many women were killed, including the daughter of our neighbours. My young children began working here and there to support ourselves... (HH3, G1, F)

The caregivers noted different ways in which children and youth react to or deal with existing realities; the most dominant were violent and deviant behaviour, quitting school or lowering ambitions, engagement in economic productivity, and emigration. Fatima, a mother living in the Gaza Building, summed it all up while describing her family's living situation:

Children became chaotic. They no longer respect us like before, because of the environment we are living in, we are fighting most of the time, in front of our children... At times, my daughter would be in a hurry to go to school, but there would be someone in the [communal] bathroom. We would knock and knock, but he/she would refuse to come out. We have no independence; we have nothing. I feel tied up, as if someone is suffocating me, little by little everyday. We are fed up; sometimes we curse and yell; we cannot help it. My neighbour takes my laundry off the line and throws it to the street. She says that it is her balcony although they [Popular Committee] told her otherwise. I feel humiliated. This forces me to raise my voice. My children are affected by this situation... My son befriended bad people once. They misled him and made him go on the wrong path. They wanted him to slaughter some sheep for them. They told him that they would give him 100,000 LL [US$ 66] for this. He used to work in a slaughterhouse. He went with his friends. He didn't know what they were up to. They stole sheep. My son left them... My son knows right from wrong... I wish that my children had studied, for education is beneficial. A diploma is a weapon in the hand, but as Palestinians, they cannot do anything with it. Work is becoming better [than education]. My daughter left school and learnt sewing. She is working now. She tells me, 'Mother, sewing is better. With a diploma, nobody will employ me. I am a Palestinian'... The children are 100 percent for emigration, but the father, my husband, refuses. Even my son, now engaged, wondered about life abroad, thinking that it would be as difficult as our life here. However, after he got engaged, he sees no future here. He tells me, 'if they can take us back to Palestine, then let them, but if not do you want to remain here without hope?'... The war was tragic. It was a miserable life – a miserable life in every sense of the word. It is just like the life of Palestinians in Lebanon now... in general, the socioeconomic conditions are equally difficult for everybody [refugees in and outside the camps]... (HH3, G2, F)

Teachers and NGO staff said that violence is increasingly prominent, especially amongst young boys. They blamed this mostly on the media for glorifying violence, on life frustrations, and on repressed energies and potentials. Smoking and drinking are also noticeable, while drug usage is present, but to a lesser extent. Violence is frequently manifested in fist-fights. Teachers added that the past wars and presence of political parties are other factors contributing to aggressive behaviour. Some mothers complained about their children's chaotic behaviour. One mother said that her son is very aggressive, always beating up his siblings and other children. Another said that her son started carrying a knife after his friends were killed in a recent fight[3] near Borj El-Barajneh camp. A third mother mentioned that her daughter is violent and frequently gets into fights. A father, living in the Gaza Building, stressed his fear for his son who had once pulled out a knife on someone.

Children and young people were observed to have a negative outlook towards the future and are suffering from declining ambitions. This is due to the constraints imposed on the refugee community in terms of lack of civil rights, as well as political instability; that is, not knowing where and what their future will be. An NGO member noted children's preoccupation with the 'idea' of war – during art sessions, many children, aged 14 and younger, frequently draw warplanes and prisons. She added that this affects their ambitions, for they feel that war will destroy their achievements.

The school drop-out rate is increasing, for children are aware of the restrictions imposed on Palestinian employment and thus are discouraged from pursuing further education. Overcrowded classrooms and housing do not offer a proper studying environment, and affect students' scholastic performance. Only one mother mentioned that her daughter had left school, for she constantly feared that the school would be air-bombed. Quitting school is not only linked to demoralisation – many children leave school in order to work and thus cope with financial difficulties.

Some children also engage in economic productivity while still at school. Mothers from Gaza gathering said that most of their children work during the summer break. One mother said that her son, now 11 years old, has been working since the age of 8, after his father was imprisoned. He works in a grocery store after school hours, earning less than US$ 2 per day. Another mother explained that children grow up before their time.

With limited opportunities available for refugees, caregivers confirmed that young people, mostly boys, are increasingly interested in emigration, to the extent of obsession. The desire to emigrate is seen as a method by which children protect themselves against their reality and as a possible way out.

Parents worry about their children on several levels. They feel helpless, as they cannot secure their children's basic needs, especially education. They fear a deadlocked future for their children, a sentiment that is shared by the other caregivers. They all had a number of propositions to combat demoralisation amongst the youth. Mothers insisted that UNRWA should provide a better education. Teachers said that schools ought to have more sports activities, field trips, spacious and better-equipped playgrounds, and equipment for practical exercises should be made available. They stressed the urgent need to have social and psychological counselling units at school for both parents and students.

Similarly, NGO staff recommended social counselling for children/youth. They also saw the need for increased awareness-raising activities with children on different issues, such as puberty, emotional problems and sex education. Teachers suggested a joint programme, between schools and youth organisations, for easing the prevalent violence amongst the youth. Lack of funds remains the main obstacle for implementing the forwarded recommendations.

Views of Children and Young People

> My grandparents were in Palestine. They said they were peasants and the Israelis came and told them to leave, and that they would let them come back a week later. My grandparents took nothing with them when they fled. The Israelis did not give them back their land. *Al-Nakba* is Palestine's sad day, when they [Palestinians] left our country. (HH2, G4, F)

We interviewed 138 children, aged 9–18.[4] This age category constitutes around 20 percent of the registered Palestinian refugee population in Lebanon (UNRWA 2001: 22). Discussions revolved around several topics, including war experience, education, living conditions, identity and personal worries. Children and young people represent the third and fourth generations of Palestinian refugees.

A recent UNICEF and PCBS (1999) study of 2,000 Palestinian boys and girls between the ages 13 and 18, in Lebanon reveals that most youth have no hope for the future. Around half of them endure anxiety on either a constant or irregular basis. This applies equally to boys and girls. Leisure and cultural activities for the youth are limited. Camps and gatherings lack libraries, clubs and proper public spaces. Youth further 'suffer from seclusion and deteriorated environmental conditions in the camps'. (UNICEF and PCBS 1999: 7–8)

This confirms what the caregivers said earlier. However, our interviews with children and young people portray a more positive image of children. Although they live in unfortunate circumstances, many resort to constructive coping mechanisms and are resolute to cope with their harsh realities by hoping for a better future. Hala, from the Gaza Building, is one of many who shared such sentiments as:

> I want education and work. I am studying to work, even if for one day, then marry afterwards. The important thing is to work. Work hard but find something [reward]. I want to prove to myself that I am capable of doing something, and in front of people [prove herself], and also to make our people [Palestinians] look better, that they worked and did something. (HH12, G4, F)

The next two sections highlight the incidence of violence in their lives. An investigation of how children and youth cope with their living situation will follow.

The Legacy of War

> ...we wish for better times for our children, and that they forget the war. The war is unforgettable. It is embedded in our memory. Until now, we react and yell without knowing why. We cannot help it. This is from the war. Many of today's illnesses are caused by the war. (HH3, G2, F)

All of the children were born in Lebanon, and most were born after the Israeli invasion of 1982. Some were too young during the Camps' Wars (1985–7), while those below the age of 15 were not even born at that time. Younger children do not remember anything about the wars that took place in Lebanon, while most of the older youth, 17 to 18 years old, have only a vague recollection of the war events. However, almost all of them have first-hand information about the wars that took place in Lebanon.

They heard detailed war stories, mostly from their parents, especially from their mothers. They know about major massacres and battles, and the atrocities that accompanied them. For instance, they heard of cases where pregnant women, during the Sabra and Shatila massacres, were cut up and their unborn babies removed. The children of Borj El-Barajneh camp also heard that people ate mule, cat and mouse meat, during the Camps' sieges. In a sense, the children inherited the psychological effects suffered by the earlier generations. Mahmud from Borj El-Barajneh camp said:

My grandmother told me that there was a war and that AMAL Movement fired at us and killed my grandfather at Gaza hospital near Shatila. They came to take the keys to the hospital's generator and to kill the patients. He refused to give them the keys, so they shot him and took the keys. They shut off the generator and killed the patients... I have Palestinian and Lebanese friends. Some Lebanese are really good...I confide my secrets only to Palestinian friends, because I am afraid that the Lebanese would tell their friends who might be AMAL members, AMAL would come to the camp and there will be war... (HH3, G4, M)

Some children have watched videotapes of the war. More recently, they all saw, on television, the aftermath of a massacre of Lebanese villagers committed by the Israeli army in May 1996. Many of those who did not have direct exposure to previous wars spoke of personal losses, such as the death and injuries of family members and relatives. Youth who experienced armed conflict recounted specific incidents they remember and stressed the damaging effects internal displacement had on their education and life in general. Ali from Borj El-Shemali said:

...all I remember is the war of AMAL Movement. I remember when I was a little boy, the fighters used to tell me to go and see if there were any AMAL members on the road. I used to go and prepare safe passage for them. I also remember how they [AMAL] came into our house and broke things while asking me 'where is your father', because they wanted to take him. They said to me 'where is your father or else we will explode the house'... In Majdeleon [Sidon suburb], we stayed in a building that was half-built and had underground garages. We lived in a garage, and our relatives lived next to us... Displacement affected us to a great extent. We lost our education. (HH7, G3, M)

In Beirut, Reem from the Gaza Building explained:

...all my uncles are dead...the shelter [was bombed] fell on them. My aunts too, the shelter fell on them [1982 Israeli invasion]... We had to leave five places. I was born in the south. We stayed there [Borj El-Shemali camp]... We went to Al-Damour [south but closer to Beirut]. We used to sleep in the car, we had no place and my mother had recently given birth. After Al-Damour, we went to Tripoli [north] and after Tripoli we went to Baalbeck [central-north], and after Baalbeck we came down to Shatila, and after Shatila we came here. I was very upset by this. (HH14, G3, F)

It is noteworthy to mention that children living in the city never heard stories from their parents about the war. Only one boy, age 17, had some knowledge, as his father was a political activist; however his younger sister, age 11, only knows that there once was a war. Although the city dwellers sample was small (six children), this somehow reflects differences between children living in the city and those confined in camps and gatherings.

In general, most children are worried about the resumption of war. Israeli warplanes still fly over Beirut and break the sound barrier, evoking fear, and embodying an ominous reminder of war. Hala from the Gaza Building said:

> I heard about many wars, but thank God, I did not live through them...I am very afraid of the war...When I hear a warplane, my heart starts beating. I get startled. Will people die, or live and become displaced? Will another war take place; some go this way and some that way? (HH12, G4, F)

Violence at School

> There are two or three teachers who are not good. They are bad with students, they are always hitting and yelling... No one can talk with them, they are always yelling, and they immediately hit... [It upsets me] that teachers beat us without understanding the cause, for example, we would be talking about something and the teachers immediately hit without knowing what's happening, or they solve everything with yelling and insults. (HH14, G4, M)

UNRWA prohibits corporal punishment at its schools; however, the overwhelming majority of children and youth expressed strong complaints about UNRWA schools, especially the brutal and violent behaviour of both male and female teachers.[5] Other research, such as that of UNICEF, corroborates such occurrences: "verbal abuse and harsh treatment by teaching staff are reported frequently and appear to be practised on a wide scale" (UNICEF 2000: 47).

Children reported that at times teachers hit them so hard that this resulted in nosebleeds. One group said that once a teacher broke a student's arm. Methods of beating involve hard slaps and the use of sticks, broomsticks and plastic water hoses. Reasons given include students' mischievous behaviour, not doing their homework, asking the teacher to re-explain the lesson, as well as the teacher's mood (no reason at all).

Almost all of the children suffer from teachers' verbal abuse. Teachers frequently insult them, call them names, discourage and yell at them. A group of girls said that teachers often insult their intelligence and tell them that they will become housemaids in the future. One girl reasserted that teachers should stop degrading students. Others, like Doha from the Gaza Building, elaborated:

> I would like to have understanding teachers. Teachers who don't yell at girls; and if we ask them to explain they would explain instead of immediately yelling. I once asked the teacher a question and she said, 'those who understood, understood, and those who didn't, didn't.' She refused to repeat the explanation. (HH13, G4, F)

Cruel treatment does not discriminate between age and gender; however, boys tend to endure more intense physical punishment. Most children disapproved of teachers' abuse. Still, the majority admitted that their parents also hit them, less frequently when they are above 14 years of age. In general, they supported corporal punishment induced by their parents, and saw it to be 'for their own good.' Only one girl, 17 years old, bitterly complained that her brother often hits and yells at her, although he is her junior. She elaborated that he once hit her with a plate, resulting in seven stitches on her face. At another level, some children were concerned about the frequent disputes between people in their community. They also noted fights amongst youth.

Trapped Potentials

At our house, all the walls leak [seepage]. The staircase [of the building] is broken. There aren't any places for fun, no playgrounds, and no clubs. There isn't even a club in the vicinity... There is always garbage on the stairs; we always have mosquitoes, roaches, and many insects... It is always dark, no light or electricity. Water is scarce... I don't like the overcrowding. The houses are facing each other and there are 12 houses on each floor... When we enter the building, we smell the garbage and sewers are overflowing. I would like to live in a good environment, to see roses when entering the building, not garbage. But no one hears me; no one hears what is in my heart. (HH14, G4, M)

All children described their physical environment with utter dismay. Poor housing conditions, inadequate infrastructure, insufficient recreational centres, lack of open space and playgrounds were at the top of their list. Girls further complained about the absence of sports and cultural clubs exclusively for girls. Girls felt especially confined in their living environment. They live in a traditional community and, because of the congested space, they feel that people are constantly watching them. Some children said that they do not have any privacy at home, while others noted segregation from the host community. Doha, from the Gaza Building, said:

The house is small. This balcony is communal. If you go out to sit by yourself, people come and it becomes noisy; and at home people keep on coming and going. The bathrooms are also communal... Living here is not nice. There's no independence. I would like each house to have more rooms, a balcony, and a bathroom. (HH13, G4, F)

Additional complaints about schools, aside from the reported violence, included overpopulated classrooms, unavailability of computers, and the absence of cultural and sports activities. The school's double-shift system imposes difficulties, as class hours and subject material are condensed, thus negatively affecting their apprehension. Many children also said that they were struggling with the newly introduced school curriculum.

Moreover, most of them admitted that their overcrowded and noisy homes limit their studying capabilities.

Discharging Pressure: Coping Strategies amongst Young Palestinian Refugees

> Resilience is the human capacity to face, overcome and be strengthened by or even transformed by the adversities in life. Everyone faces adversity; no one is exempt. With resilience, children can triumph over trauma; without it trauma (adversity) triumphs. (Grotberg 1995: 10)

The manner in which children depicted their living conditions is similar to that of the caregivers. However, conversations with the children also reveal how they interact with their surroundings and extract the available resources that enable them to better cope with current realities. Many children and young people described aspects of their physical and social spaces in positive terms. Almost all value the security they derive from their families and friends. They appreciate the cohesiveness of their community and being around people they identify with. Many have dreams and aspirations. Some choose to defy reality, while others choose to take it as a matter of fact. All of them have a strong sense of identity.

Grotberg (1995) mentions three sources of resilience that assist children in overcoming adversity: I Have, I Am and I Can. The first (I have) is availability of external support, that is, people who love, guide and help them. The second source stems from their internal sense of self, to know who and what they are, as well as a willingness to be responsible for their actions (I am). Children's capability in problem solving and taking action is the third source (I can). As noted above, these sources are indeed available to many of the children we spoke with. The children's narratives reflect various coping strategies to which they resort. The most prominent include: (1) family and communal solidarity; (2) preservation of identity; (3) emigration; (4) lowering expectations; (5) quitting school; and (6) defiance of reality (see Figure 2.1). [7]

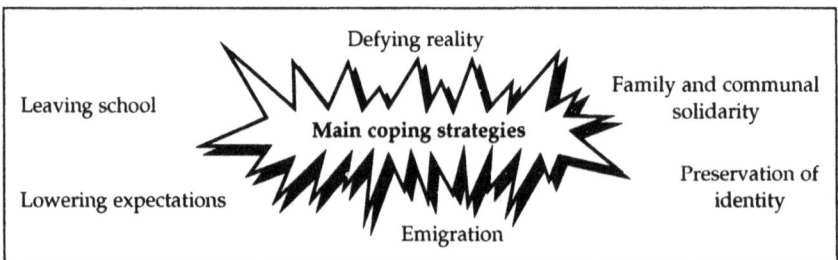

Figure 2.1 Coping Strategies among Young Palestinians in Lebanon

Family and Communal Solidarity

Our findings show that Palestinian refugees have strong family ties. Children and adolescents feel that they can depend on their families, both nuclear and extended. They are highly protected by their families. Their relationship with their parents exhibits little tension, generally related to parental strictness, more specifically towards girls. They are especially confident of their parents' love and care, and appreciate what they do for them even when they cannot afford most of their children's demands. On the contrary, some children even feel that they do not do enough to help their parents. Many of them confide their secrets to family members, while others seek peer support. Hassan from Borj El-Shemali camp stated:

> My parents do not interfere with my [choice of] friends unless I am behaving in a bad way. I do not get upset if they are right. I ask my parents' opinion, especially my mother, on all matters. I feel that my mother can understand me better, and she finds a way to tell my father... My parents meet whatever they can of my demands. I do not demand things I know they cannot realise. For instance, I want to travel [emigrate] or to buy a car. I know they cannot realise that, so I try to do it myself. I am saving money from my work. My father pays me for helping him at the bakery. On personal matters, I talk to my mother most, and also to one friend. If I am in big trouble, I tell my father, or my cousin who can help me. (HH7, G3, M)

Aida, also from Borj El-Shemali, relayed a different situation than that of Hassan, showing differences in how males and females are treated:

> My parents interfere in the choice of my female friends. They force me [not to see them] if it is in my best interest. My parents have an old mentality... When they upset me I keep silent because it is useless to argue with them. I ask their opinion when I go out, but I do not consult with them on love matters because they tell me not to have a relationship. My parents satisfy all my wishes. Sometimes, they cannot afford my demands, but that does not make me mad. I do not tell my mother about my personal affairs because she would tell my father or elder sister. That's why I keep my personal life to myself. I do tell my aunt, who is also my friend... If I am in trouble, I seek my aunt's help. (HH10, G3, F)

In their narratives, most children go beyond the camp's physical representation. Living in a Palestinian community gives them a sense of security and community protection, especially as most feel that the Lebanese are hostile towards them. It also signifies their belonging to a collective social sphere. One girl noted that the camp keeps Palestinian people together. A 15-year-old boy added that if there is a dispute between two persons or families, the community intervenes and settles the differences.

They counterbalance the negative and positive aspects of camp life, and rationalise their existence in camps. Rasmiyeh, from Borj El-Barajneh, reasoned:

> Living in the camp is not that bad. You feel that you live among Palestinians like yourself. We are accustomed to camp life. Also your economic condition is similar to those around you. The way of life is the same... Now, as long as we are not living in our country, we need a replacement. We have the camp as a setting to live in temporarily instead of our country, till our cause is resolved... (HH2, G3, F)

Latifeh, also from Borj El-Barajneh, said:

> I like living in the camp. I was born and raised here. I do not like to live outside because I feel that my heart is in the camp... you feel that they all care about each other... Outside [of camp], people quarrel... if one dies, his neighbour would not know that. We are so close to each other that if one does not see his neighbour for one hour, he would go check if there is anything wrong... Also, staying in the camp is economical... (HH4, G3, F)

It is to be noted that children living in the Gaza gathering for displaced refugees do not see many redeeming aspects in their physical environment. Their living situation is much harsher than that of the camp. They all want to change residence. They listed some advantages of being in Gaza gathering, which included having a close market-place, free electricity and water (when available), no rent, and some good neighbours. A 16-year-old boy added that Sabra area is the 'mother of the poor'.

Youth clubs and centres, where available, constitute a support network to some children and adolescents, who participate in youth activities. Many of those who don't participate stated that appropriate youth centres are lacking. Females further endure traditional constraints, and therefore many spend their free time at home. Most children resort to a combination of entertainment methods: hang around with friends, play on the streets (boys only), visit relatives, listen to the radio and frequent recreational clubs where possible. Several boys and girls were thankful for having friends and relatives living close by as this helps them to endure boredom and have a nice time.

Preservation of Identity

Although most children have scant knowledge of the 1948 Exodus of Palestinian people, all have a definite sense of their identity, at an individual and collective level. They know that most Palestinians were forced to flee their country, that Israelis/Jews occupied their country, and as a result they are refugees. They are Palestinians and are members of their refugee community, which is dispersed in many countries. Most children and young people know their village or town of origin in Palestine. Many speak about Palestine with nostalgia, which is generally transmitted through their grandparents or through their parents who have also inherited nostalgic sentiments from their forefathers. Nada, from Borj El-Shemali camp, explained:

> I am from Palestine, from Na'imeh. I am here because there was a war in our country and we were displaced and we had to leave our country... My grandmother tells me about the Palestine war. She tells me how they left when the war broke out inside Palestine and people were being killed... She said they kept moving from one town to another and that they lived in tents along the beach... She also told me that she wishes we could go back to Palestine and live in dignity instead of being displaced from one country to another. (HH9, G4, F)

Youth clubs/centres and, to a lesser extent, UNRWA schools also play a role in their formation of identity.[9] Both mediums disseminate information on Palestine's history and geography. Clubs and centres further expose children to Palestinian traditions and customs, including music and dance. This serves as a rich representation of culture and allows the communication of its values. Lubna, from Borj El-Shemali, said:

> I am from Loubyeh. I am here because the Israelis forced us to leave Palestine... My grandparents kept telling me about Palestine and how beautiful our country is. My parents tell me that the Jews [Israelis] told them to leave for 10 days and then they could return... My grandmother used to tell me how they filled water from the spring. She told me about their dress. I acted in a play [at a youth club] and wore a traditional Palestinian dress... (HH8, G4, F)

Children's living situation and surrounding environment further accentuate their identity awareness. An 11-year-old girl said that her accent made her realise that she is a Palestinian. Others elaborated:

> I am a Palestinian from El-Houleh. I am here because we were displaced from Palestine long ago. We were born in Lebanon and we are still here. Since my birth [early childhood] I knew I was Palestinian, my mother told me and I knew [of my identity] when I went to UNRWA school. (HH8, G4, F)

> On our way to school, we pass by an institute [vocational centre]. They [male students] keep harassing us and cursing the Palestinians. One day we were ready to fight back... We beat them up with sticks... (HH5, G4, M)

The surrounding environment especially affects city dwellers, as they live amongst Lebanese. A couple of children are hesitant to express their identity, while others defend their identity. Ramzi, a city dweller, stated:

...for a while, I felt that saying the word Palestinian was something shameful. I became ashamed of saying Palestinian... Slowly, slowly, I felt that there is nothing wrong in being Palestinian... I started to show them that the Palestinian is not what they imagine. (HH15, G3, M)

In general, children and young people take personal pride in their identity. It gives them a clear point of reference. Two siblings noted that having a Lebanese nationality does not erase their Palestinian identity. Most of them have a strong desire to return to Palestine. Although they are well aware that it will not happen in the near future, their wish for liberation and stability remains. Mahmud, from Borj El-Shemali camp, elaborated:

I am from Al-Zouk. I am here as a result of the [Palestinian] exodus. I knew I was a Palestinian when I was born [early childhood]. My parents are Palestinians and used to tell us about Palestine. I have the Lebanese nationality, but I am Palestinian. I have Palestinian blood...however, if they are going to send us back to Palestine, I will tear up my Lebanese identity card... My parents say Palestine is like heaven. My grandmother tells me about Palestine. They say Palestine is a good country. My parents also talk about return. (HH10, G3, M)

His sister, Aida, explained in her interview:

My parents say there is hope, by God's will, to return to Palestine. I heard that they [political news] want to take us to Canada. I do not like that. I would prefer to go to Palestine. I have obtained the Lebanese nationality, but I will not give up my original nationality. If I were asked to choose between settling in Lebanon or going back to Palestine, I would choose Palestine. (HH10, G3, F)

Al-Aqsa Intifada against Israeli occupation had a visible impact on the refugee community in Lebanon. The death of two Palestinian young men by Israeli bullets at the Lebanon-Israel border further intensified the community's reactions. The two men were gunned down while Palestinian refugees from Lebanon were demonstrating in protest of the Israeli aggression, less than a month after the start of the *Intifada*. Posters of the two martyrs and of *al-Aqsa*, maps of Palestine, slogans on the right of return, graffiti, banners, and more flooded the camps in Lebanon. Murals of Mohammed Al-Durra, the 12 year-old Palestinian boy who was shot and killed on September 30th, 2000, at the Netzarini junction as his father shielded him from Israeli bullets, also appeared in the camps.

The Palestinian *Intifada* also had a perceptible effect on children. Several NGOs noted that most of the children's drawings reflected identification with the current *Intifada*, showing recurring images of stone throwers, Israeli tanks, Al-Aqsa Mosque, and the Palestinian flag. The *Intifada* was also a main subject of dialogue. The caregivers further detected signs of trauma among some children, who were constantly agitated and frequently speaking of the disturbing images they saw on television. The caregivers spoke to the parents about sheltering their children from frequent exposure to such images.

Some of the children and youth were re-interviewed shortly after the resurgence of the Palestinian Uprising, in order to detect any changes in attitude. Many of them reported that they had been active in demonstrations in support of the Palestinian people, denouncing Israeli aggression. They could not comprehend why children were being killed. They frequently cited Mohammed Al-Durra as an example. It was evident that the *Intifada* has empowered their sense of identity and elevated their hope for return to Palestine. Ramez, from Borj El-Barajneh camp, said:

> I cried when I saw Mohammed Al-Durra die. He was not fighting and they killed him... We should stay here [in Lebanon and not emigrate] so that we can fight to liberate Palestine. There is hope. The Arabs are more motivated than before... (HH6, G4, M)

Emigration

Like the caregivers' testimonies, emigration, as a coping strategy, frequently surfaced in the children's narratives. Boys and girls expressed a desire to emigrate; they listed a number of destinations: Sweden, Denmark, U.S.A. and others. Young people, especially boys, were more eager to emigrate. This can be attributed to the fact that young people in general are more aware of their living situation. They are also at a stage where they start planning for the future, while recognising the realities unfolding around them. On another level, boys, in Palestinian society, are given more freedom than girls, including the choice to emigrate.

Children and young people often hear about members of their community emigrating. Some already have relatives abroad. The thought of emigration helps them think of a better future, which is in contrast to their current living conditions and the grim future they face in Lebanon. Hassan, from Borj El-Shemali camp, confirmed:

> Of course I thought of emigrating. I am Labeled a refugee, wherever I go I will remain a refugee. Nothing changes, so it makes no difference to which country I go... If we get the chance now, we would leave... I would like to go to Canada. What harm would it do me since I am doing nothing here? I will try Canada, maybe my situation will improve... (HH7, G3, M)

Raef, from Borj El-Barajneh camp, argued:

I definitely thought of emigrating. I thought of that last year and this year. I wanted to go to any European country. The reason is life here – one feels suffocated. We live in a graveyard here in the camp. I am not happy at all... I want to emigrate because first of all I will live a free life, the way I want, without much exhaustion. The second thing is that you feel settled, you are respected at work. Abroad people respect you, you have a future, you could get married there... (HH6, G3, M)

The desire for emigration does not eliminate their wish for return to Palestine – however, it is seen as more realistic. Others confirmed that they would not lose their identity by living abroad. Rajeh, a city dweller, said:

...I also need to be a citizen of some country... There are Palestinian-Americans who did not lose their national identity and are still very proud to be Palestinian... (HH16, G3, M)

Lowering Expectations

The caregivers have spoken of declining ambition, mostly related to children's attitude towards pursuing education. This was also reflected in the children's narratives; however, for some 'lowering expectations' was a way of cushioning themselves from facing life's harsh realities. They feel that they are unable to change the course of their life and accept it as their destiny, a collective destiny.

Some resort to faith in dealing with their adversity, for they see that whatever God bestows upon them is approved. Others hope that, with "God's will" things may improve. Latifeh explained:

My mother told me to continue my education. I said all my friends dropped out, why should I stay in school, am I going to be a doctor or something like that?... I am quite satisfied the way I am now. I do not need anything and I am happy. Whatever comes from God is welcomed and acceptable. (HH4, G3, F)

Samira reasoned:

I want to be a physician because I feel that it is a nice and humanitarian occupation. I am not sure I can realise my ambition, unless our financial situation allows it. Maybe by the time I go to college everything will change, if God wills. (HH2, G4, F)

Quitting School

In line with the caregivers' testimonies, dropping out of school was connected to general demotivation and to economic reasons. The children's narratives further revealed that many leave school because of school-connected reasons. These include the school's physical condition and the lack of computers, a dearth in sports and recreational activities, teaching methods, and especially teachers' harsh treatment of the children. Aida elaborated:

> I quit school four years ago ... However, when I was at the school in Sidon, I was satisfied. That school had discipline. The teachers explained any lesson I did not understand. They did not differentiate between boys and girls. In the Borj El-Shemali school, when I asked the teachers to explain they used to say dirty words and ask me 'why don't you understand?'... I was a good student and I wanted to continue my education. Also, there was a teacher who always hit me on my back ... (HH10, G3, F)

Leaving school for economic reasons was more evident in the boys' narratives. Some boys felt the need to help their fathers, who were not earning enough to support their families. On another level, only girls mentioned that they quit school in order to help their mothers in household chores and in taking care of ill members in the family. For some children, work was seen as a solution for dealing with financial difficulties and a more productive option than completing education, especially as they are deprived of their civil rights. Jamal, from the Gaza Building, noted:

> Life was difficult so I thought it was better to work... but even if I had gotten the diploma, what can I do with it? A Palestinian can do nothing here...You cannot work, or in regards to the future, there are no stable jobs or a stable life. (HH13, G3, M)

And Mohammed, from Borj El-Barajneh, elaborated:

> First, I worked in freezers and washing machines maintenance. Then I worked at a butcher's shop. I worked there two days then left that job because I wanted to be with my friends on the streets. I worked in a bakery... Then I worked a whole year in repairing heaters and boilers and I was good at it. Now I am working, in tiling, with my uncle. Now I am settled. I used to regret leaving school because we had two days vacation and my parents used to buy me everything, and there was no hard labour. However, I do not regret leaving school because I am doing well at work. (HH5, G4, M)

Defying Reality

Children and young people continue to hold on to their aspirations and dreams. Some even think of alternatives for overcoming foreseen obstacles. Others focus on the school's positive aspects, and try to make the best out of their schooling situation. Children value education and see it as a means for achieving their aspirations. School is also a place where they can spend time with their friends and meet new people. As noted earlier, the caregivers did not observe this resilient attribute.

Most of their aspirations revolve around their future professions; for instance, many children aspire to become doctors, engineers, musicians or lawyers, and are determined to realise their dreams. For others, notably girls, having their own family is also a part of their future plan. Raef clarified:

> My father sent me to work for a car electrician, and he registered me in a vocational institute... I do not regret leaving school... For the future, if God wills, I will open a [car mechanic] workshop and be a master of my vocation, get married, and be independent. I have every chance to realise my ambition. In four years, I would know the market well and I would have my own customers. (HH6, G3, M)

And Nawal, from Borj El-Shemali camp, affirmed:

> ...I believe education is important for girls and boys in their future. I would like to be a doctor or a teacher. If my parents have no money to pay for my education, I would work every summer and save up for my university fees. I will work in agriculture or in houses [cleaning]... (HH11, G4, F)

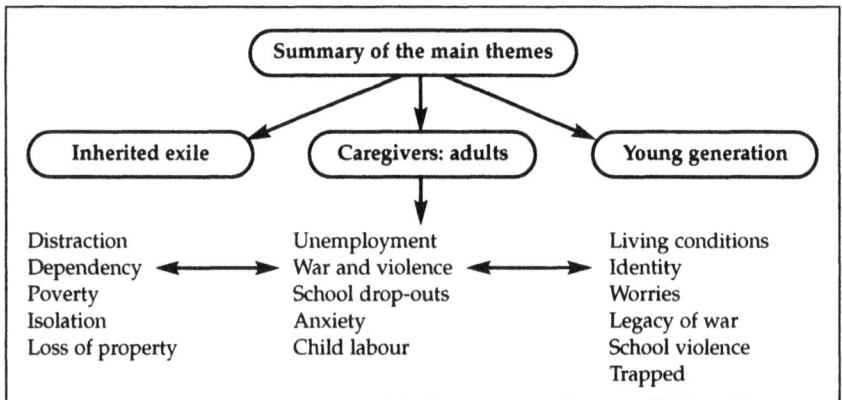

Figure 2.2 Lebanon: Summary of the Main Themes

To a lesser extent, some children linked their aspirations with national-istic sentiments. A 10-year-old girl, from Borj El-Barajneh camp, said that she would like to become a journalist in order to write about the Palestinian cause and the situation of the camps' poor neighbourhoods. Her other option, as she explained, is to become a lawyer in order to defend the innocent and punish the oppressors.

Conclusion

Palestinians in Lebanon endure high levels of frustration and anxiety due to the realities enmeshed in the past, present and future lives of all gener-ations (Figure 2.2). Images of war are continuously reproduced, while their current situation is deteriorating, and their future remains uncertain.

Caregivers listed different strategies through which children and young people cope with their living situation. They noted that children are generally demotivated, which affects their desire for education; they resort to violence and deviance, contemplate emigration, while some become responsible at an early age (work). Caregivers see children as helpless, which is often the case in many cultures, especially in a tradi-tional one.

Although some of the coping mechanisms mentioned by caregivers surfaced in the children's narratives, it remains evident that most children and young people are not passive. Many are resolute about improving their lives. They derive strength from support networks available in their social and communal environments. They have strong nationalistic senti-ments, which gives them a clear sense of self, a sense of belonging, exis-tence and continuity. They have learnt to adapt and shelter themselves from unpleasant realities. They react and opt for alternatives. Many of the children resort to a combination of these coping strategies.

Other coping methods may be further explored. Backing up what the caregivers said, some of the children also spoke of youth in their commu-nity who indulge in drinking, smoking, taking tranquillisers and sniffing glue. On another level, NGO staff noted that some young girls elope in order to escape pressures faced at home. Pressures include traditional constraints and congested housing conditions. These dimensions need further exploration.

The interviewers reported that most participants, especially the 15–18 age group, appreciated the opportunity allowed in this research to express themselves. It was clear that they needed an outlet to express their feelings, thoughts and concerns. In general, venues that provide coun-selling services for Palestinians in Lebanon are very limited. Beit Atfal Al-Sumoud is the only NGO that has a family-counselling programme, targeting around 470 children and young people. The related centre is based in Beirut and takes in cases from other regions. There are no other similar services. This stems from the fact that such programmes are highly costly and are not priority programmes for many donor agencies. Moreover, service providers put more emphasis on other educational and develop-ment programmes, which are seen as a more urgent need for the survival of the community. In general, psychological health care is de-emphasised and on some levels is seen as taboo.

Educational, recreational and psychological programmes need to be enhanced and made readily available to Palestinian children and young people. The related programmes must address and pay special attention to the several problems noted in the children's narratives. They should aim to empower the youth in order to strengthen their current ability to cope with the challenges of life as refugees and stateless people.

Notes

1 The authors would like to thank the team of field interviewers for their con-tribution and hard work: Sana Hussein, Fayza Khalaf, Su'ad Hammad, Samia Jammal, Mahmud Jum'a, Hiba Izhamasd and Mohammed Hamzeh. The authors further express their gratitude to all interviewees and people of the camps for their time and their warm welcome.

2 These included seven group interviews with parents (forty-one mothers and fathers) in addition to parents present in the nineteen households (in-depth inter-views), six interviews with teachers (twenty-five to thirty teachers of elementary, intermediate and secondary levels), and interviews with nine NGOs. All inter-views were conducted in the year 2000.

3 On 24 February 2000, two Palestinian boys, ages 14 and 16, were stabbed to death and a third was seriously injured. The incident took place near Borj El-Barajneh refugee camp. A Lebanese gang attacked them, for they were friends with a group that the gang disliked. There was no fight. The three boys were attacked quickly and brutally. The murderer, an ex-convict, turned himself in. The whole incident was hushed down for fear of a Palestinian-Lebanese clash.

4 These included group interviews with 100 children and in-depth interviews with thirty-eight. Both genders were represented almost equally in the inter-viewed sample. All interviews were conducted in the year 2000.

5 Excludes four children, city dwellers, who do not attend UNRWA schools. They attend private schools and had no complaints about the treatment of teach-ers.

6 With the exception of children living in the city.

7 Most of these coping strategies, except for identity and emigration, do not apply to children living in the city. Reminder: the sample of city dwellers includ-ed only six children, and thus we cannot generalise their situation.

8 Youth clubs and centres, as well as nearly all kindergartens, are mostly run by NGOs, while some are run by Islamic groups.

9 This applies less to city dwellers, as most of them do not frequent clubs in the camp. Two of the six children have never been to any of the camps, while four of them are in private schools. The remaining two who attend UNRWA schools benefit from basic lessons on Palestine.

10 UNRWA provides assistance for mental patients. The Agency has limited its beds at mental institutions to forty-three. The age range of current patients, as of May 2001, is 18-62 (only one 18-year-old, a male). The average age is 41. Gender distribution: 65 percent male and 35 percent female.

References

Grotberg, E.A. 1995. *Guide to Promoting Resilience in Children: Strengthening the human spirit.* The Hague, Netherlands: Bernard van Leer Foundation.
UNICEF and PCBS. 1999. *A Survey Assessment to Identify Risk Factors and Priority Needs for Palestinian Youth in Lebanon with Focus on Adolescent Girls.* Lebanon, November.
UNICEF. 2000. *The Situation of Palestinian Children in the West Bank and Gaza Strip, Jordan, Syria, and Lebanon: An Assessment Based on the UN Convention of the Rights of the Child.* Jordan.
UNRWA. 2001. *Registration Statistical Bulletin for the First Quarter 2001.* Department of Relief and Social Services, Amman: UNRWA.

3

Palestinian Refugee Children and Caregivers in Syria

Adnan Abdul-Rahim with the assistance of
Hala Salem Abuateya

Adnan Abdul-Rahim

I was born in Safad, Palestine, 1941. I was forced to escape with my family to South Lebanon in 1948, as a result of the Arab-Israeli War. We were forced to leave our camp and move to Tripoli, Lebanon and then we were later taken to Homs in Syria. We stayed there for two years in an old deserted French Army barracks and then moved to a village near Damascus.

I finished my elementary and secondary schooling in local schools and entered the University of Damascus in 1960. I took a BA in English Literature in 1964 and at the same time I started to work as a teacher in UNRWA schools. I continued my studies part-time and in 1969 I was awarded a Master's degree in Psychology of Learning. I then resigned from UNRWA when I got a scholarship to study for a Ph.D. at the University of Budapest, Hungary. I was awarded a Ph.D. degree in the Sociology of Education. My thesis topic was The Social Reality and Educational Goals of the Palestinian People.

I returned to Damascus in 1982 and joined the Education Department of the PLO in Damascus as the Director of the Kindergarten project in Syria. At the same time I worked as a coordinator of the UNICEF–Palestinian programme in Syria, which included training kindergarten teachers. In 1985 I joined the International League for Social Commitment in Adult Education and I became a board member, attending their annual conferences in Gutenberg, Managua, Amsterdam, Toronto, Derry, Tunis and other places.

I have worked for the Norwegian Applied Sciences Institute (FAFO) on a project about UNRWA services to Palestinians in Syria. I have written several books on educational topics and many articles in Arabic periodicals.

This chapter focuses on the impact of prolonged conflict and forced migration on young (children and adolescent) Palestinian refugees in Syria. The data provided in this chapter was conducted mainly in ten

Palestinian refugee camps in Syria.[1] The research sample included twenty households from different income groups, among which eighteen were Muslim and two were Christian. The study used a multidisciplinary and participatory approach in developing its main tool of investigation. A qualitative approach to data analysis was used to identify significant themes in the findings of this research. The main findings illustrate the importance of social identity among young Palestinians refugees in Syria.

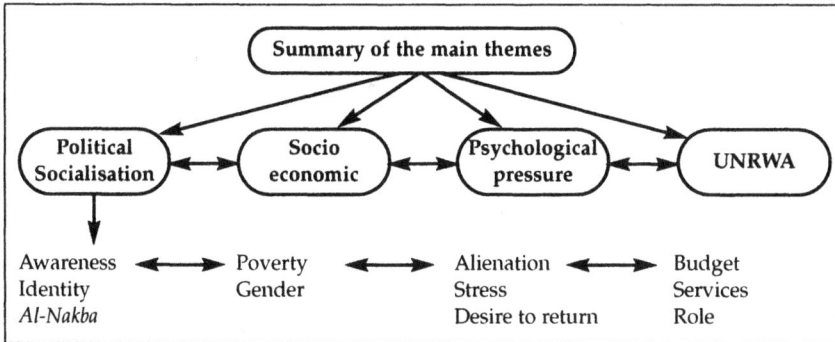

Figure 3.1 Syria: Summary of the Main Themes

Political Socialisation

This is Mohammad's story:

> Mohammad was born in a Palestinian refugee camp in Syria in 1984. His grandparents fled their homes in 1948, so that his parents were born refugees. Mohammad is confident and enthusiastic about his identity as a Palestinian and his homeland Palestine. His family is originally from Nazareth, located in the north of Palestine. He started to learn Palestinian history from the age of 6. He knew the history of his home town and its location on the map of Palestine; he also elaborated on the current Palestinian political issues. He gains his exclusive political knowledge from several sources, including his parents and grandparent who speak to him regularly about Palestine and through watching television; the teachers reinforced his national identity via writing essays on his home town in Palestine; also in his art classes, where students were asked to draw the traditional costumes of every town and village in Palestine. Mohammad views himself as a Palestinian refugee. He thinks that many Syrians believe that Palestinians sold their homeland and moved to Syria. His suffering started when his father tried to register him in the UNRWA school. He had to wait for more than two years to get UNRWA approval.
>
> Mohammad finished his primary education in UNRWA school and his preparatory education in a Syrian school. Later he joined a Syrian Vocation Training School to be trained as an electrician. Now most of his schoolfriends

are Syrians; they often ask him about his home town in Palestine and the possibility of his returning.

He joined a Palestinian Youth Organisation for one year. During his membership period, he learnt to dance *al-Dabka* and memorised some slogans and Palestinian songs. As a young man, he thinks life is harsh; he feels disoriented by not being able to exercise his rights in his homeland. He dreams of returning to Palestine and he believes that he can achieve his dream through hard work and good academic achievement. (HH8, G3, M)

The findings show that Palestinian children and young people in refugee camps in Syria have a wide social network of families and friends within and outside the camps. The social network of family, friends, schools, teachers and the youth organisations often influences young Palestinian refugees' political socialisation. Mohammad's story reflects some of these elements. It shows that family, school, peer groups and political parties are the main instruments for young refugees' political socialisation. At home, the young generation hear stories of their lost lands; through their parents and grandparents they learn the history of Palestine, the importance of political identity and the struggle for liberation. Our findings showed that the UNRWA and the Syrian school curriculum for Palestinian children in all levels had units on the Palestinian problem, the Arab–Israeli conflict, the history of the Zionist movement, the history of Palestine and the Palestinian struggle. Our findings demonstrated that many young refugees valued the contribution of these school textbooks to developing their political awareness and educating them about Palestine. Furthermore, the Palestinian teachers in the UNRWA schools devoted time, both during and after school, to Palestinian national education for pupils. For example, teachers encourage pupils to participate in festivities of the national days and exhibitions of folkloric customs; they also organise competitions on Palestinian issues. Suad said:

> In my school, all Palestinian students come together spontaneously to talk about Palestine and their life in the refugee camps. I do not understand why the Syrian students do not mix with us although we all studied the Palestinian case in the preparatory and secondary school. We also used to sing Palestinian songs in the school. Although I have a positive experience of school, I always considered myself a refugee who has no homeland, no sky and no clouds... I remembered the Prophet says 'no dignity to those who don't have land'. That is why I think we [Palestinian refugees] lost our dignity because we do not have Palestine. We should regain Palestine to have our dignity back even if we have to give up our lives in return. (HH11, G3, M)

Palestinian youth organisations also played an important role in educating children and young people through publications, training camps and public lectures. Many young Palestinians joined organisations that promoted social identity as Palestinian; however, some youth dropped out fairly quickly, as is shown in Mohammad's story. Active political socialisation of Palestinian youth was a theme we found throughout the data concerning nationalism. This finding is similar to that of Usher (1991), who argues that political socialisation is one of the principal features that characterise Palestinian children, especially refugees.

Major Political Events

Many Palestinian refugees in Syria have been in exile for more than fifty years. During this period, they experienced a series of political events (e.g., *al-Nakba* in 1948, *al-Naksa* in 1967) that further distracted them from their homeland (Palestine). Almost all the first-generation interviewees mentioned *al-Nakba* in 1948 as one of the major events in their life. They described their journeys of exile from Palestine into different Arab neighbouring countries; and they drew vivid accounts of war in 1948, as presented by Yessrah:

> The war began and the Jewish forces occupied large parts of Palestine; they were well trained by the British colonial power, while the Arabs were fighting with knives and simple rifles. Before the soldiers entered, they occupied the mosques' minarets and began shooting at the people. The Jews entered the village in two groups; the first one was responsible for kicking out the villagers to the shore, and the second one took care of hunting and killing the defenders of the village. They committed collective killing, imprisoned women; they gathered us all in a bus and took us to Faradees prison, where we stayed for 17 days. Later we were handed to the Jordanian army. (HH18, G1, F)

The journey of the refugees to exile was characterised by hunger, poverty and humiliation. Fuad shared his personal experience:

> We wandered around different villages; we stayed one week here and two weeks there until we were later deported to Bintjbail village in the south of Lebanon. The Lebanese army picked Palestinians from the streets and transferred them to Anjar. We were among the people who were transferred to Ba'lbek and we lived there for one year. In 1950, we arrived in Syria by train. We hired a small house, but soon after our landlord kicked us out because we were too large a family to rent his property. (HH 19, G1, M)

In 1958, Palestinians believed that the Egyptian–Syrian unity would liberate Palestine, but again their dream was short-lived, as that unity disintegrated in 1961. Many elderly refugees consider this long period of waiting for the liberation of Palestine as a time of burial, disintegration of their society and loss of their leadership. They saw the beginning of the 1960s as a turning point, with the emergence of the Palestinian resistance movements known as Palestinian Liberation Organisation (PLO), which aroused new hopes among Palestinian refugees. However, the defeat of the Arab Armies in 1967 increased the frustration among Palestinian refugees in Syria because many of those who were settled in Golan Heights or other neighbouring Arab counties after 1948 were displaced for the second time after the Israeli occupation in 1967. Subhi shared his story of displacement as follows:

> I remember how my family suffered when we were forced to migrate for the second time in 1967. I will never forget the horrible hours when we walked all the way to Jordan and then moved again to Damascus. I also remember my daily life in Jaramana, we lived there for a long time. During that period, my family was poor, therefore, I left school when I was in the primary stage and worked in constructions to help my family. I got married when I was 18 years old and could not afford my own place, thus I lived with my family. Later I joined the army, my wife worked as a servant in houses and later she worked as a labourer in the neighbourhood farms (HH8, G2, M).

Many refugees witnessed their children being killed in Jordan during Black September in 1970; they thought that Arabs hated them, and that they were not welcome anywhere, as Hamdan made clear:

> During the hard period of Black September 1970, I was in Jordan fighting with Palestinians; as a result I lost one of my eyes during the confrontations with the Jordanian army. I witnessed thousands of Palestinians being killed in Amman. I was very depressed seeing and knowing that other Arabs were watching us and doing nothing. (HH2, G2, M)

The October 1973 war against Israel encouraged many Palestinians to believe that their return to Palestine was possible. However, the Palestinian dream of liberation was short-lived, as the Arab armies were not capable of continuing the war. Some of those interviewed thought that the Palestinian resistance movement would be able to do what the Arab armies failed to achieve. But the inner conflicts within the Palestinian resistance movement were devastating and it became powerless.

The first Palestinian *Intifada* in 1987 renewed the hopes of many Palestinian refugees in Syria. They said it gave them a new meaning to being Palestinians. The third generation (children) had not been directly involved in many of the dramatic events of the Palestinian history. Through oral history, however, the tragic memories of exile experienced by the elderly generation were transferred to the younger generations, which reinforce their social identity. Tahani reflected on the tragic story of her grandmother thus:

> My grandmother informed me that her forced departure from Palestine was the hardest experience of her life. She told me many stories about lots of things

in Palestine, even the cows in our barn and how people used to earn their living by selling oranges. She told me how they were forced to migrate, and how people escaped from the massacres of the Jews and how they thought they would return to their homes soon. Before her death, she gave me a gown and she asked me to hide it to be used in collecting her bones and burying them in her own village in Palestine when we return. (HH17, G3, F)

Most of our interviewees expressed their disappointment at the recent Palestinian–Israeli peace process. They argued that the peace process did not offer the refugees the right to return from their exile. Moreover, many believed that the Palestinian National Authority (PNA) was selling their rights to return in exchange for a mini Palestinian state. With the current *Intifada* (started in September 2000) many young refugees are witnessing the Israeli army's cruelty against their kin in the West Bank and Gaza Strip live on television. They are taking part in demonstrations, marches and making donations, as a way of expressing their support.

Palestinian Identity

The overall Palestinian integration into Syrian economic and social life leads many to believe that the refugee camps in Syria are not ghettos. However, the identity of many refugees remains different from their Syrian counterparts and they could not be Syrian even if they wanted to be. Our findings showed that the semi-isolated refugee community enables refugees to live within their communities and maintain a life similar to that once experienced in Palestine.

As the social identity theory emphasises, often individuals' social identity determines their attitudes and behaviour towards others who are not within their social grouping. It also reflects the way in which people define their position within their community and their social roles. Refugees' awareness of their social-political identity becomes a defensive tool, and reflects the personalities of the individuals and their community. For example, many of our interviewees saw themselves as stateless, their identity humiliated and downgraded by their enemies and by some Arab communities.

The growth of resistance among Palestinian refugees emphasised the importance of their social-political identity. Our findings demonstrated that before the 1948 war many of the first Palestinian generation (grandparents) tried to defend their political identity and homeland, which was impossible considering the power, qualification and the overwhelming number of their enemies. Instead, many people escaped to protect themselves and their families; as a result they became refugees without the support of a social and political infrastructure. Home for many refugees meant regaining the components of their lost identity, stopping the stigma attached to being refugees and being able to lead a peaceful, social, rural life with common values and traditions. Sami said:

> Palestine is our homeland. If the old generations and Arafat gave it up to Zionists that doesn't mean that we surrendered. It is up to us the new generation to free Palestine and we will never forget it. Our life as you can see is a chain of tragedies and people dreaming of a shelter to protect them, beds that they can lay their tired bodies on and land to live in. We are all dreaming of living away from all the international and regional conventions or treaties that decide what our destiny will be without even consulting us. Our generation doesn't understand what the Oslo or *Sharam el-Sheikh* conventions are, we only have a simple dream to live decently, which is our natural right as human beings. We dream of eating, wearing clothes, going to school, being treated when sick and have a warm house in Palestine, this is whether the Zionists accept or not. (HH11, G3, M)

Our research team noticed that many refugees tried to reproduce their social values and the costumes that used to unify them in Palestine. For example, many people from the same original village or neighbourhood in Palestine live in the same refugee camp and/or marry within the same social network. The first-generation identity is coloured with memories of peaceful rural life and people they left behind. Many interviewees said that in Palestine they had been poor, but were proud of their dignity and their strong social network support. Refugees' refusal to accept an alternative homeland and their yearning for Palestine confirms a high degree of romanticism. Ismael said:

> We believe that Palestine was the land of our fathers and grandfathers, and will never give it up, no matter what they offer us as an alternative. Like the rest of Palestinians in refugee camps, I lived in alienation all my life. I was born in Damascus but I still consider Palestine as my country. I have always suffered from the crimes committed against our people. I heard that they will pay us a compensation. Do you think this money will be an alternative for our dignity, our martyrs' blood? (HH5, G2, M)

The second and third generation were born and brought up in the refugee camps in Syria and they did not experience life in Palestine. Many refugees lived in alienation, because the refugee identity was the only one they knew. The images of the refugee identity are 'poor', 'dirty' and 'dependent', which was hurtful for many refugees. Therefore, refugees tried to improve the negative image of the refugee identity by focusing on resistance and education. Moreover, family and friends, school activities and the curriculum provided young refugees with sufficient knowledge about Palestine, and reproduced and strengthened the social and political identity of young Palestinians in exile. The positive reinforcement of social identity assisted the young generation to create a sense of belonging to Palestine, as was shown in Mohammad's story. The young generation clinging to a Palestinian identity improved their self-esteem and confidence and redefined the social stigma attached to refugees. It could also be explained as a way of avoiding being called 'refugee', which reminded them of the unbearable life they are experiencing in the refugee camps. Ahmad shared his dream of going to his homeland as follows:

> I dream to go back to my village of origin in Palestine. I think that life is going to be much better when I live in my own village in Palestine. Our refugee camp here in Syria lacks everything, for example, there is not even a single garden; it looks like a desert. We are all unemployed and many Syrians call us poor refugees, meanwhile UNRWA is not doing anything to improve our situation. (HH8, G3, M)

Our findings indicated that many second-generation refugees left school and joined the resistance movement and became involved in political and military activities. Some developed hatred towards Jews, the Americans and the Arabs. A minority preferred to keep quiet and repress all their memories of the massacres and the defeats they witnessed.

Socioeconomic Pressure

This is Sa'ada's story:

> Sa'ada is an old lady. She moves slowly, her sight is weak and she hardly speaks. At present she lives next to her married son in one room with a small kitchen in one of the refugee camps in Syria. She was born in Palestine in 1914; she was brought up and lived in Al Qabba'a, Safad district. She was married at the age of 14, and she gave birth to three children including a daughter who died very young. She divorced her husband when he was in jail; her brother-in-law then took custody of the children. He moved them to be raised in his house. She heard stories of how her children were mistreated by their uncle's wife. But she could do nothing about that. She lost her children and she had nobody to support her. Then she moved to al-Dallatah, also in the Safad district. She worked as an agricultural labourer and sold green thyme. A year later she married Khalil, who was already married with five children and a sick [paralysed] wife. She lived with her new husband's family and gave birth to two children.
>
> In 1948 the Zionist forces attacked her village (al-Dallatah); many people were killed and injured and hundreds of men were arrested. Sa'ada fled the fighting in her village. She left behind everything she owned and sought refuge in the Hawran in Syria. In 1952 her husband died, leaving her with two young children. She found work again as an agricultural labourer. After a while she left the Hawran and went to Damascus to search for kin and people from her

village. She managed to get herself employed in the agricultural gardens of the Ghoutah on the edge of the city before it turns into desert. She would have to leave her one-room shelter at the very top of Mount Kassoun in the early morning and come back late in the evening. She would find her young children crying in the dark, as they felt very alone in their small house located in an isolated and remote area. After the end of her working day on the farm, she would gather some discarded onion, radish and marrow in a bag and sell them in the market in order to have money to buy some cheese and bread to feed her children and candles to light their room. Her children were provided with schooling from UNRWA. The school gave her children free education but she had to provide them with clothing and stationery. She could not afford the clothing and had to rely on some wealthy Damascene residents to provide her with second-hand shoes and clothes. In time, she saved some money and bought a room and made it habitable. Her children had to work during the school summer holiday in order to support their studies. One of her sons finished school, the other became involved in the Palestinian resistance movement.

Her eldest son lived in a small room which he constructed above her own. He worked as an X-ray technician in a public hospital. When he died, he left behind a wife and six children. Her second son is married with six children. He is not educated and he works as a casual labourer in a restaurant. He also rents a small shop to sell falafel. Sa'ada shares her room with her children and grandchildren. Today, they have electricity and water and the house is not so remote and isolated as it was in the past. But still people don't know each other. Now, when her grandchildren make their way to school in the morning, they buy bread and sell it in the neighbourhoods they pass to earn money to support the family.

Although she has lived in Syria for many years and her children are grown up, she still feels alienated and she hopes to die and be buried in Palestine. (HH11, G1, F)

The impact of socioeconomic pressure is high among Palestinian refugees. The story of Sa'da reflects some of these pressures. Our findings indicated that many refugees struggled economically. Many said that although recently there was an improvement to living conditions in the refugee camps, still they did not have enough public space, gardens, playgrounds and clubs for children. Therefore, many children continued to play in the narrow, dirty and dangerous streets of the camps, as illustrated by Ahmad:

Football is my favourite game; we play in the street of our camp because we do not have a playground to practice. People in the neighbouring houses often shout at us and order us to play away from their houses. We are always scared of being hurt by passing cars. (HH12, G3, M)

The findings demonstrated little socioeconomic and psychological differences between Muslim and Christian Palestinian refugees. However, there was a class difference in terms of the willingness to join the resistance movement. For instance, the children and young people of working-class Palestinians often joined the Palestinian military resistance movements, and hundreds of them were killed in battles against the Israeli, Jordanian and Lebanese armies. In comparison, the majority of the young generation of middle-class refugees participated in political and social activities of the Palestinian political parties.

Our findings clearly show that poverty has major negative effects on refugee children. Many leave school early and join the labour market to contribute to their families' low incomes. San'a said:

> I didn't live my adolescence the way that all girls do; I started working when I was 7 years old because my family economic situation was very bad. I used to sell cake in the streets to the workers. When I grew a bit older it was my responsibility to collect the aid ration from UNRWA centre in Jaramana Camp, and then go with my mother to buy some goods, which were often stolen by the workers in the streets. I used to go back home crying most of the times because the money I had to bring home went missing and I knew that my mother would beat me because of my negligence. (HH14, G2, F)

Those findings are in agreement with the UNICEF and PCBS report (1999) on the situation of Palestinian children in the refugee camps, which highlighted poverty and child labour among Palestinian refugees.

Among the young female refugees, a gender awareness of their social-political identity was partially illustrated. Many young women complained of not being able to establish friendships or relationships with men because of the conservatism and limited space within the refugee camps. Their complaints were understandable considering the sociocultural context of the Palestinian refugee community. Within this refugee community, social mixing between girls and boys is not socially acceptable and sexual relationships outside marriage are forbidden. This is connected to a social belief that women represent the family honour and sexual relations are illegal because they bring shame to the families. Samia said:

> As girls we are not allowed to mix with boys. I got married to a man chosen by my family when I was 14 years old and I was forced to leave school. Now I have four daughters and my husband is sick. When I dropped out from school after marriage, I stopped caring for anything and I couldn't distinguish between happiness and misery and my life turned into a series of misfortunes and disappointment like all other refugees. (HH7, G2, F)

However, some interviewees challenged this argument and insisted that their families treated girls equally. Manal said:

> My mother was educated and she never treated me differently than my brothers; we were all treated the same. I am the only girl and my mother respected me; my parents allowed me to exchange visits with my friends. My father kept telling me that I should have more girlfriends because they would be like sisters to me. My family also encouraged me to express my opinion. (HH6, G3, F)

Social expectations often differ by gender. Many young Palestinian females have to cater for their young siblings and help in the housework; for example, young girls are expected to take care of their younger brothers and sisters and help with the cleaning and cooking. In comparison young males act as heads of the household and are responsible for protecting female members of their families and also they instruct them on the socially accepted behaviour and norms. Halima said:

> I always helped my mother around the house and took care of my younger brothers and sister. When my mother died I was very young and became responsible for the whole family. I got married when I was 15 and had to take care of the two families. My husband was a great man; he worked in selling vegetables and fruits and he used to help me take care of my younger brothers and sisters. (HH14, G3, F)

The findings also showed that many female refugees gained a high social status through their active participation in the Palestinian resistance. Many young females were involved in the political activities of the Palestinian organisations and the resistance movements. Despite conservative attitudes towards women, the female political role was often socially recognised and appreciated by the community. However, our fieldwork notes indicated that in some very poor camps there are still gender discriminations and strong prejudices against the education, employment and social movement of females.

The interviewees thought that the percentage of early marriages among young people changed throughout generations, and the age of marriage for both males and females is rising. The reasons for the change might be connected to the hard economic conditions which forced members of families, including females, to work, the increase of educational level among the young generation, and the impact of the Syrian culture. Our findings were consistent with other researchers. Moreover, endogamous (cousin) marriage is still a dominant tradition within the context of some Palestinian refugee camps. Until recently, female marriage was the family responsibility and many girls complained that they were deprived of the right to choose their husbands. Comparing these young girls with their mothers and grandmothers showed that they seemed to enjoy more social rights, have higher education and participate in social activities. However, our findings showed that the illiteracy rate among females in the poorer camps was twice that of the males.

Psychological Pressures

This is Josephine's story:

Josephine was born in al-Ramleh in Palestine in 1926. She was the eldest among her siblings and her father died when she was a child. After her father's death, her mother was remarried to her uncle and they had six more children. Josephine was married when she was 14 years old to a Syrian who was chosen by her stepfather. She had nine children; four were born in Palestine and five in Syria. In al-Ramleh, her husband owned two big houses; one was rented and the other was used as a family house.

When *al-Nakba* of 1948 occurred, her husband was in Damascus while she was resident in the family home in al-Ramleh. Her husband was supposed to be returning within a short time, but the war started and she was without news of him. She heard that soldiers had attacked the Allad Mosque. She was very frightened at this time because she did not have anybody to protect her family. The Jewish militia who took over the town announced that all men and women should gather in the town's square. She was confused because her husband was away and her children were young, so she decided to hide with her children at home. One morning in early June, she heard somebody knocking at her door. Her children started to cry. She looked out of the window and saw more than twenty soldiers carrying guns; she did not know if the soldiers were British or Jewish militia. She opened the door and their leader approached her aggressively asking her what was she doing in the house. The other soldiers pulled her from the shoulders and forced her out of the house. She started to scream and her children ran and stood beside her crying while the soldiers stood laughing. She was very upset, lonely and confused. She didn't know what to do, where to go and who to turn to. The soldiers told her – as they laughed and made fun of her – that they would return the next day and take them all to hell.

She had a sleepless night. She hid the little money that her husband had left for house expenses. At about five o'clock the next morning the soldiers returned with a lorry full of Palestinian women and children all crying and praying to God and to Jesus Christ to help them. She saw the Star of Zion on the doors and the sides of the vehicle. The soldiers pushed her and her children violently into the vehicle. They drove them away; she did not know where they were going. After a few hours of horrendous driving, they were dropped off in the mountains. She spent the night in the mountains and the next morning they walked until they reached an area called al-Bira, where they stayed for a month trying to find a way to leave Palestine. She later learned that her husband had been arrested. She could not cross the border because her husband had their passports. After a month, they left al-Bira and fled to Amman with many other Palestinian refugees. In Amman, they were given shelter in a church where they remained for some time and her sons died after a fall and failed to get emergency treatment.

She crossed the Jordanian-Syrian border illegally and went to her relatives in al-Midan district of Damascus. She stayed there for a while and then rented a house in the old city. Her life outside Palestine was difficult and stressful; she could not answer her children's questions about their father's whereabouts. She prayed day and night for God to bring her husband back safe and sound. After two years her husband came back to Damascus and the family was at last reunited.

Once her husband was settled they moved into a much larger house in al-Joura quarter in old Damascus. Although the family was happy in this new house, still they considered that their stay in Syria was temporary and that they would soon be returning to Palestine. Some of her children did not attend the Syrian schools, because the family assumed that the children would waste their time as they would very shortly be returning to Palestine and be studying the Palestinian curricula. Recently, her husband died and now most of her children are married and live near her. A year ago, one of her sons died leaving her to look after his family. Although Josephine lives well in Syria, still she dreams of going back to Palestine. (HH20, G1, F)

As a result of wars and political conflict, several generations of the Palestinian refugees suffered from poverty, homelessness and displacement. Many families were scattered all over the neighbouring Arab countries without knowing what had happened to their beloved family members. Josephine's story presents some of these psychological pressures.

Our findings indicated that homeland and the right to return constituted the main psychological pressure on refugee families across generations. Many refugees yearn to return to their homeland in Palestine and therefore, the dream of return is very much alive in the minds and the hearts of many Palestinian refugees, especially the elderly generation who were born and grew up in Palestine. As Josephine's story demonstrates, many refugees were convinced that the only way to end their suffering was to return to Palestine and live a decent life with dignity.

Many of those elderly refugees still keep the keys to their houses and registration documents for their properties in Palestine. Few elderly refugees expressed their willingness to stay in Syria if they were to be offered the chance of returning to Palestine. Many members of the second generation were enthusiastic about the right to return to Palestine, although the majority of them were born in the refugee camps in Syria. The third generation's image of the homeland is communicated to them through the memories of their grandparents, parents and school textbooks, which create enthusiasm among the young generation for the idea of return. In addition, sometimes the unfriendly Syrian social surroundings influence young refugees, making them more determined to go back to Palestine. For example, many interviewees said that they were often humiliated by hurtful remarks directed at them by their Syrian hosts (e.g., 'inferior traders' and 'poor refugees').

Some of the third generation preferred to stay in Syria, even if they were given the option to return to Palestine. They felt that having been born there was significant. Mouayyad stated:

My father and me were born and brought up in Yarmouk camp, therefore, I feel I belong to this camp and not to Loubieh village in Palestine. If I have to choose between staying here in Yarmouk camp or return to Loubieh, I prefer to stay here in Syria, because I was born in this refugee camp, I went to the primary and the secondary schools here and I met all my friends. I know this place quite well and I do not feel that I have anything in common with Loubieh [my village]. (HH11, G3, M)

Most of the refugees we interviewed think that their return will not be possible in the near future, and that the liberation of their homeland is a hard task to be accomplished. Our findings agreed with earlier research of Al-Mawed (1999), which concluded that 95 percent of refugees stated that they would like to return to their homeland, and 63 percent expressed their concern over the peace process and thought that it could not bring the solution to their problems.

Poverty and displacement forced many refugee families to be split up, which increased the psychological pressure on family members. Some, like Abdallah, do not know where their family members are buried. He stated:

I do not know where my father's grave is, my mother is buried in Lebanon, and my son in Palestine, my other son in Amman, and I do not know if my younger son is dead or alive. (HH15, G1, M)

The majority of our interviewees were originally poor. But after fifty-two years of exile and hard work, many families had secured a sufficient standard of living. For example, currently, some refugees own properties and run small commercial businesses. Our findings showed that some refugees were wealthy and educated before they left Palestine, therefore, they were able to buy properties and seek employment. Some travelled to Saudi Arabia or Gulf countries to work for a few years and some collected small fortunes that enabled them to work in construction and buy properties and start small businesses in the refugee camps. However, the findings revealed that many of these rich Palestinians still suffer similar political and social alienation to other poor Palestinian refugees. Taimour, a rich refugee, illustrated these concepts:

It is true that we are living well, but we all suffered a lot when we were kids. I will always remember the way my schoolmates used to mock me because I am a Palestinian; they told me that we sold our land and properties to Jews to come to Syria. I was very hurt. I used to come back and ask my father if these accusations were true. Believe me, there is no difference between rich and poor Palestinians outside their country [Palestine]. We as Palestinians all agree that we must return, we are all called refugees and we are all treated as inferiors. I still believe that Palestine is the land of our parents and grandparents. Therefore, I will never give it up. (HH20, G2, M)

To sum up, our findings confirmed the hard impact of prolonged conflict and forced migration on the poor Palestinian refugees. The majority of Palestinian refugees were poor, subjected to stigma, suffering from political alienation, poor housing conditions, lack of space and entertainment. The stories of Josephine and Sa'da show that despite the differences in their economic background, they both felt inferior compared to their Syrian counterparts.

UNRWA and Palestinian Refugees

UNRWA was established in 1950 to provide Palestinian refugees with basic services such as health, shelter and education (UNRWA 1992). In addition to the Syrian government and the Palestinian resistance movement assistance, UNRWA is a major agency that plays an important role in the lives of Palestinian refugees, especially the young generation. Our elderly interviewees acknowledged their dependence on and benefits from the UNRWA, including regular assistance and food supplements to survive, especially during the beginning of their exile. The dependency of refugees is because of forced migration, as many refugees were poor, illiterate and unskilled, which made it hard for them to find employment and shelter.

The findings showed that many young interviewees had contradictory attitudes towards the UNRWA services. While they admitted their need of the services, its presence was offensive as it reminded them that they were dependent refugees. Most of the interviewees complained of the current declining standard of the UNRWA services, such as poor health services. Tahani said:

> As refugees, the doctors in the UNRWA clinics used to treat us badly. When our children needed treatment, we used to stand in queues in front of the UNRWA clinics for a long time, our children used to cry and moan because of the pain they encountered due to waiting for long hours. Doctors examine our children and prescribe a pill of aspirin that is usually used for headaches. What could we do? We used to give our children the pills knowing that our children will not be cured. (HH12, G2, F)

Many interviewees expressed their satisfaction with UNRWA educational services; they said that their children had their education in UNRWA schools and became successful adults. Many young interviewees liked UNRWA schools because the vast majority of pupils were Palestinians; many teachers taught them about Palestine's geography and history and about the Zionist invasion of Palestine. Hisham stated:

> Currently, I am studying in UNRWA school in my refugee camp. The pupils in my school are all Palestinian and my teachers educate me on Palestine. Although, I like my school and the pupils, but generally UNRWA schools often remind me that I am a poor Palestinian refugee child. (HH14, G3, M)

UNRWA services helped the first generation of Palestinian refugees to survive, but the second generation had to struggle hard to earn their living. However, members of the third generation wish to limit their dependency on UNRWA aid and services, although they realised that they had to depend partly on UNRWA social services, shelter, health and education. The findings revealed that it was always humiliating for refugees to stand in long queues waiting for their turn to receive food rations, medical treatment and other services provided by the UNRWA. Many never accepted the humiliating situation, but felt they could not change it.

Currently, UNRWA claims that a shortage of budget has severely strained its assistance to Palestinian refugees in Syria. Nevertheless, UNRWA continues to provide limited essential services in health care, education, infrastructure development and emergency relief. Many refugees understand the nature of the UNRWA budget problem and they related it to international politics. Abed argued:

> As refugees we are suffering. I am struggling to support my family especially after UNRWA stopped its support. They said that there was a shortage in the budget because some countries are not paying their share of debts to the Agency's funds. I know they are liars. America is behind it all. It is true that I quit school when I was in my fifth grade but I follow the news and I understand what is going on in the world. (HH2, G2, M)

Funding shortages forced UNRWA to limit hospital referrals and the duration of hospital care and social services. For instance, the number of people registered with UNRWA special hardship programme had increased by 7.2 percent to 28,513 in June 2001. The delays in funding prevented the Agency from providing emergency cash assistance in a timely manner to needy families. Furthermore, the serious problems of overcrowding in UNRWA schools has continued, with 94 percent operating on double shifts, the highest percentage in any of the Agency's fields of operation (UNRWA 2001). Many interviewees were aware that UNRWA is ready to withdraw and limit its services.

Many elderly refugees suggested that UNRWA should continue to provide its humanitarian services as a symbol of the UN's political obligations towards the Palestinian refugees as long as they are unable to return to their homeland. Many refugees have serious doubts about UNRWA claims of financial deficit; on the contrary, they believe that UNRWA reduced its services as a result of political manoeuvres by the donor states.

Coping Strategies of Young Palestinian Refugees

In Western societies, coping strategies are often connected to the individualistic approach, where individuals can seek help through professional channels, such as counselling. In comparison, the coping approach within the context of developing countries is more collective. Individuals are part of the community and they resolve their problems and get their support within the community network, since professional assistance is rarely available and is often downgraded by the community (Summerfield 1995). This indicates that, within the settings of developing countries, the social perspective is that the support of the family and the community is much more effective than professional counselling.

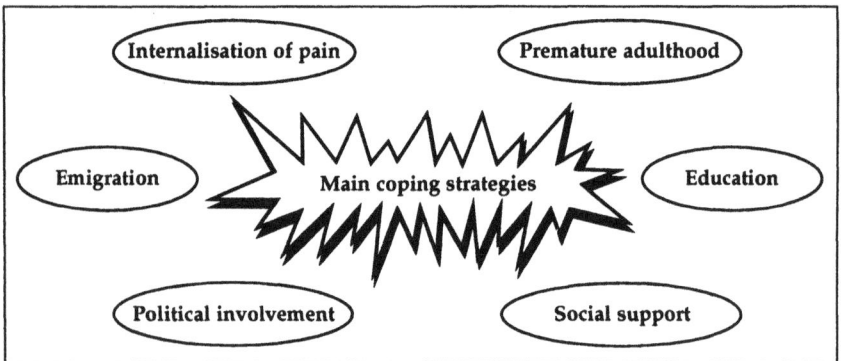

Figure 3.2 Coping Strategies among Young Palestinians in Syria

Refugees, especially the young generation, develop coping strategies to enable them to survive. For many Palestinian refugees, coping has meant more than just an acceptance of their hard reality, or a simple adjustment to difficult life conditions. On the contrary, it involves the development of resistance strategies against the difficult social, political and economic pressures. These hard conditions forced refugees to develop tactics to enable them to cope with difficult living conditions. The main coping strategies used by young Palestinian refugees are presented in Figure 3.2.

Internalisation of Pain and Social Support

Our studies showed that many young Palestinians in Syria suffer from painful experiences resulting from the forced migration of their parents and grandparents. Many interviewees admitted losing members of their families or friends and that they experienced poverty and difficult living conditions in the refugee camps. As a way of coping, many refugees internalised their painful experiences, suppressed their pain and continued their lives as normal. Hamad said:

> We were forced to leave Jordan in the early 1970s, so we went back to Sitt Zeineb where we lived for some time in a shelter built of mud and cloths. Our house collapsed later and my two young daughters were killed in the accident. Later, my oldest son was killed in a military operation; my other son was also killed and the third was wounded but survived. The death of my children made me very sad, but I learned to keep my sadness to myself. Now, my son is trying hard to educate his children; he teaches them manners, good behaviour and how to select the right friends. (HH1, G2, M)

Many young Palestinian refugees admitted to feelings of humiliation and inferiority, because life in the camps did not allow them a sufficient childhood. Also, many young people carried quietly the burden of the elderly generations of their parents and grandparents. Asa'a said:

> My grandfather told us about the Jews' occupation of Palestine, how my three uncles were killed in Lebanon fighting for Palestine and how he lost his eyes in Amman. I believe he is a hero, I feel sorry for him but what can I do? In this refugee camp, as you can see we have no activities, no playground, no sport clubs, or even a garden. How do you expect us to live our childhood; but we have to live with all this pain. (HH2, G3, M)

In Arab culture, the family provides traditional protection for its members and solidarity among them. Therefore, the strong network of family and social support is seen as crucial to the way in which young people cope with prolonged conflict and forced migration. The young refugees were born in exile; they never had the opportunity to visit Palestine. Nevertheless, many of them expressed their desire to live in Palestine. Abdulla stated:

> I am telling my children everything I know about Palestine. I am teaching them to love our homeland and to die for it. My grandparents fought for Palestine; I did too and I encouraged my son to join the Palestinian Liberation Army. I am very proud of him. (HH12, G2, M)

The findings indicated that the elderly often tried to persuade and reassure the younger generation that their refugee status was temporary and that one day they would return to their homeland. The wishful thinking of the elder generations seemed to help the young generation to cope with the hard socioeconomic and political pressures. Bouthaina stated:

I have never visited Palestine, but I love it. Thanks to my parents and grand-parents, they told us stories about Palestine, its amazing landscapes, mountains, valleys and rivers. They described it as the most beautiful country in the world. I am sure we will go back, that what our elderly generation promised us, we will have a homeland one day, you will see. (HH12, G3, F)

In sum, self-identification with peer groups who attend the same UNRWA schools were strong among the younger generation. Palestinian refugees tended to share with their peer groups similar political and social ambitions and aspirations. The association with the peer group reinforces the younger generation's feelings of belonging and established their social identity through comparing themselves with other people within their own groups. It also helped them to feel integrated in the community and develop a sense of social protection. The positive social identity assists young refugees to cope and lead a successful and semi-normal life.

Emigration

Emigration was not considered as one of the important coping strategies for Palestinian young people in Syria. On the contrary, the majority of the young interviewees preferred to remain in their refugee camps with their families. Omar said:

I feel I belong to Yarmouk camp, even if I am asked in the future to choose between staying in Yarmouk or any other place, I would say that I prefer to stay here. (HH6, G3, M)

Some interviewees considered temporary emigration to other countries for better employment, especially in the Gulf States, which enables them to improve their standard of living. Often immigrants return to the refugee camps to build houses and get married; some start small businesses. Fouad said:

I worked for some time in the Syrian Arab Airlines; then I quit my job and went to work in Kuwait for a few years to collect some money to improve my lifestyle. When I came back to Syria, I got married, built a house and worked in a textile factory where I stayed until 1995, then I went back to the Gulf for a few years and came back last year. Now I am considering going back to the Gulf for a short period to improve my family's standard of living. (HH19, G2, M)

Interestingly, many of the refugees returned to settle in refugee camps within their host countries: the explanation could be that some kept the dream of returning to their homeland alive. Hussein shared his working experiences in Kuwait as follows:

I was alienated twice, the first time was when I was born outside my country Palestine and the second time was when I had to leave my family and worked in Kuwait. In Kuwait I missed my family and my home Palestine. I felt very bad when I heard that the Zionist troops attacked South Lebanon, thus I joined volunteers to assist the Palestinian resistance without informing my family. After a short time I came back to settle in Syria as I am still hoping that we could go back to Palestine. (HH8, G2, M)

The findings indicate that there were a limited number of Palestinian adult refugees who emigrated to foreign countries looking for a better future. Some were hoping to get nationalities for their children to enable them to enjoy a better life than the one they experienced as refugees. Unfortunately, we did not find reliable figures to show emigration statistics, but our interviewees suggested that thousands of Palestinians emigrated with their families to Canada, Sweden and the U.S.A. Nevertheless this emigration does not suggest a significant level among the Palestinians.

Education

Education was viewed as a coping strategy for the vast majority of our interviewees. Through education many refugees were able to change their social status and use these accumulated educational skills as a tool to get them out of poverty. However, in some poor communities, such as Jaramana and Zeinab, higher education was not easy to achieve for some refugees because they were not able to support their children, and there are still negative attitudes towards girls' education. Therefore, currently the school dropout rate among children, especially girls, is high in the preparatory and secondary stages. Some young Palestinians who joined Syrian schools in the secondary stage suffered humiliation and alienation. The poor treatment meant that many children had to work hard to prove themselves in schools. Buthaina stated:

> Education for me was not easy, I had some difficulties in my schooling. I had a fight with the school director. The headmistress and some students laughed at me when I said that I am a Palestinian, and originally from Gjzem village in Palestine. I asked them why they were laughing and what is so amusing about being Palestinian. Many of my schoolmates told me that being a Palestinian means being a refugee and being a refugee indicated poverty, homelessness, being stupid and not good enough to study. But I know I had to stay in school and prove to them that I am not stupid and they were wrong. (HH2, G3, F)

During the 1970s and 1980s, many Palestinian refugees had free access to Syrian universities and some had scholarships from the ex-socialist countries, which enabled thousands of young Palestinian refugees to continue their higher education.

The majority of the elderly interviewees believed that the Arab defeat in the 1948 war was partly because the Jewish immigrants were better educated and more skilled than Palestinians. Therefore, many refugees urged their children to be educated using the UNRWA free education. Thus the level of education increased among the second generation of refugees. Sometimes it was recorded that the Palestinian refugees reached a higher level of education than the local citizens in their Arab host countries. The third generation followed the traditions of their parents and grandparents, and for many of them education is seen as a way to improve their living conditions and to confront the educated enemy. Nadia said:

> I know that our enemy is highly educated and well skilled. Therefore, we must use the same technique and knowledge while fighting them. I am convinced that we can win the war because we have the right on our side. I miss Palestine and I can visualise my return to it. I can achieve this dream by studying and working hard to serve the cause of Palestine. (HH20, G3, M)

Many young Palestinian refugees thought that a better level of education meant improving career opportunities. Many of our interviewees thought that academic qualifications could change the stigma attached to the Palestinian refugees. Mohammad said:

> We are used to being called poor and not good enough. However, many refugees are successful students, many managed to continue their higher education. Some became doctors, engineers and teachers in spite of their families' experiences of poverty, homelessness, violence and wars. (HH6, G3, M)

School drop-outs were due in part to poverty, hard conditions and the need for child labour. Thousands of children and young people who left school were young. A study conducted by the Palestinian Central Bureau of Statistics (PCBS 1998) added other causes, such as repeated failures at school, teachers' bad treatment of children, and a dull school curriculum and poor health. A UNICEF report (1999) argued that the school curriculum in Syrian schools does not respond to the individual needs of the children and that it is not flexible; children are still victims of corporal punishment and verbal abuse by teachers; the classes are overcrowded (e.g. more than fifty pupils per class); and schools lack basic facilities such as laboratories and libraries.

In summary, education for many young refugees does not only include knowledge and skills, but it also indicates a social status, prestige and survival. As refugees, they lost their lands and sources of income; therefore, education became their only means of earning a living and a mobile social skill, which can be implemented whenever and wherever convenient.

Premature Adulthood

Our findings showed that many Palestinians, especially the young generation, were not able to enjoy a normal childhood and regular schooling. This could be due to their hard living conditions caused by prolonged conflict and forced migration. Many young refugees adopted adults' responsibilities and behaviour – they developed a strong sense of social responsibility towards their families, especially when they witnessed their parents' struggle to cover basic family needs. Suleman said:

> As a child I do not have time to play or do anything children my age do. I am aware that my family are poor, and my father is half paralysed, therefore, I have to help my family, which is not easy. During summer holidays I worked with my father to help my poor family. But in winter, I have to go back to my school. I wish to grow up quickly to help my father in his work. (HH14, G3, M)

As a result of poverty, many children were driven to the labour market to assist their families. Many young refugees saw their work as a social duty to contribute to the limited family income and to gain some independence. Omar stated:

> My family are poor, thus I try to work in summer vacation to earn a living and to help my family. I try to contribute to my family's limited income, but they are not happy with that because they want me to continue my studies and focus on my education. I started working at the age of 13 years. Now, I am working, I can help my parents, I am not dependent on them anymore, I will give the money to my parents and kiss their hands. (HH6, G3, M)

Our outcomes confirmed earlier findings on child labour. A study conducted by the Palestinian Central Bureau of Statistics (1998) indicates that 8.17 percent of Palestinian children in the age group of 7–17 years old work either after school or they drop out of school. UNICEF (1999) and PCBS (1998) reports show that half of the children in the age group of 7–17 years old who dropped out of school are not engaged in any kind of economic activities, and they may constitute what are usually called street boys. Unfortunately, the interviews did not demonstrate the way these unemployed young people led their lives. However, the feedback during our dissemination workshop indicated that many young refugees adopted certain antisocial patterns of behaviour such as smoking, aggression, robbery, street fights, and drug abuse. Taking into consideration that the camps lack all kinds of basic facilities such as public parks, gardens and social clubs, we can conclude that thousands of young Palestinians spend their daily life in the narrow streets of the miserable camps; the others who have found jobs are victims of unhealthy work conditions that have a negative effect on their physiological and psychological growth.

Altogether they suffer difficult and unhealthy working conditions instead of enjoying a normal childhood. Many young interviewees did not seem to mind working at an early age, and they were proud to assist their parents and to share social responsibility.

Early marriage among girls and the traditional negative attitude towards girls' education influence the rate of girls dropping out of schools. The interviewees revealed that many of those females interviewed were married when they were 15–17 years old. Many young girls stopped schooling immediately after marriage, as was illustrated in the stories of Sa'da and Josephine. However, currently, the tendency towards early marriage is changing, the rate is decreasing and the marriage age for both males and females is rising. Interestingly, the findings revealed that some girls see early marriage as a way of escaping their family's control, to gain some independence and start their own family. This rosy picture of married life fits well with the social expectation of girls to be married. Also many families – especially among the poor section of refugees – marry off their daughters to reduce their financial and social responsibility, as such responsibilities are transferred to the husband and his family. Moreover, the findings showed that young males were overburdened with responsibilities. However, often they managed to adjust and cope with these harsh circumstances. Young refugees in Syria, unlike their counterparts in Lebanon, the West Bank and Gaza Strip, often manage to cope, because of the fundamental sense of social integration in the refugee camps.

Political Involvement

Some young refugees cope with their living conditions by being politically active. Through this kind of involvement, they try to prove to everybody – including those from Israel and the Arab countries – that they are more than poor young refugees. Many of them kept alive memories of their homeland, and were willing to struggle for the liberation of Palestine. Many joined militant groups thinking that such groups were struggling to regain their lost human rights and national dignity. For instance, hundreds of young refugees left school to join the ranks of the Palestinian resistance movement in Lebanon. Yousef described his experience:

> The liberation of Palestine is my top priority. I had to prove to everybody that we could do it; and we are more than just poor refugees. During my years of schooling, I had many problems with the pupils and the teachers at my school. I failed my exams, so I decided to quit school. I worked in several places and I was happy to earn my living and support my family. During the Israeli invasion of Lebanon, I joined the Palestinian liberation army, I fought in Beirut, and I am proud of that. (HH14, G3, M)

Many refugees fought in Jordan and Lebanon, and many were killed in order to end their prolonged migration and their status as refugees. Young refugees joined the youth organisation, where they practise political and social activities as a way of participating in the national struggle. During our fieldwork, many young refugees identified themselves by the original villages and towns in Palestine of their grandparents and parents, many of whom kept memories of Palestine in their minds and hearts and wished to return to Palestine. However, we noticed that violence around them had a negative impact on their daily lives, which deprived them the ability to enjoy a normal childhood.

Unlike the Palestinian young people in Lebanon and in the Occupied Territories, young Palestinian refugees in Syria did not witness internal forced immigration, as a result of a civil war or other wars such as the ones that occurred in Lebanon. On the contrary, for many young Palestinian refugees, the wars were taking place in the border around them, such as Lebanon. Although many of them lost members of their families (e.g., fathers and brothers), the majority were not subjected to continual direct violence like their counterparts in the West Bank or Gaza Strip. Therefore, it can be concluded that the Palestinian community in Syria is more settled and integrated into Syrian society. Palestinian young people are able to lead a relatively normal life and keep their status as refugees in Syria; meanwhile they keep alive their social and political identity as Palestinians.

The findings demonstrated that many young refugees were subjected to direct discrimination and prejudice from the official authorities, although it seemed that what hurt them most was the social stigma of being refugees, who were fully dependent on the UNRWA assistance. Nevertheless, many young Palestinians were still facing the same problems as the Syrian citizens, such as unemployment, unhealthy crowded houses, and hard economic conditions and the absence of entertainment institutions (e.g., sport and social clubs) to cater for their social and psychological needs.

Brand (1988) argues that Palestinians in Syria did not have the chance to organise their own local civil organisations. Interestingly, the findings indicated that many of the official social organisations that were established by the Palestinian Resistance Movement were not attractive for many young refugees. For a long time, UNRWA did not support social movements to enable young refugees to create their own organisations and institutions. Recently, however, the UNRWA slowly started to realise the importance of these grassroots organisations, and began to support the organisation of women's committees in all the refugee camps in Syria. These committees offer vocational training for young girls, and health, social and educational courses for refugees. Despite these changes, though, the majority of young Palestinians were generally supported by the traditional protection and guidance of their families and relatives, and they were often ignored and left without sufficient social and psychological support.

In summary, despite the hard conditions experienced by many refugees, many young Palestinian refugees in Syria do not show signs of collapse or anxiety. On the contrary, they have developed coping strategies that enable them to survive. Many young refugees internalised the pain that was experienced by their parents and grandparents and many of them focus on education as a way out of poverty. Interestingly, not many young refugees were willing to emigrate and many considered their refugee camps as their homes; this is because many of them were born and had their education and friends within the refugee camps. Many young refugees were involved in politics and participated actively in the different political activities within and outside their refuge camps. Young Palestinians developed a strong sense of social responsibilities towards their families and many joined the labour market at an early age to assist their family and support their education. In turn, these young refugees were supported by the strong social network of family, peer groups and friends.

Furthermore, young refugees continually kept trying to improve their standard of living and participate actively in the political life of the refugee camps in Syria. They were also aware of the development of the larger community in the Arab world and inside the Occupied Territories of Palestine. It seemed that their hard life did not lead them to develop anxiety or other psychological symptoms. The direct observation and the interviews reveal a genuine determination of young people not to yield to pressures, but to resist and overcome the hardships and problems they face in their lives. People cling to their social identity as Palestinians, which distinguished the lives experienced by their grandparents and parents in Palestine; they are also proud of their system of values and culture, which is considered as a safe social passage for many Palestinian refugees.

Summary and Future Outlook

The hard conditions in Syria forced the Syrian government to reduce subsidies towards public transportation and health services. This situation in Syria, in addition to the UNRWA budget shortages, created a negative impact on the standard of living of the Palestinian refugees, including the young generation. Currently, free general secondary schooling is not available for students who finish the third preparatory stage. Therefore, two-thirds of the high school students are forced to join one of the primitive vocational training centres (generally for those who get low grades in the school examinations) and consequently they are deprived of the right to continue their higher education at universities.

Interestingly, the findings revealed that the traditional social prestige associated with education was currently decreasing due to poverty and the increased unemployment among educated people. This leads many to expect the number of student drop-outs of schools to increase in the near future.

The young generation of Palestinian refugees in Syria suffer from the reduction of the UNRWA services, especially health and education. The deterioration of these services will lead to the deterioration of the living standards of the majority of Palestinian refugees in Syria, especially the underprivileged and deprived section of society which depends partly or fully on the UNRWA services.

The strategies of the Palestinian children and young people for coping with prolonged conflict and forced migration are becoming more difficult and complicated. This is because the infrastructure of many refugee camps is getting worse as a result of the increase of poverty and deprivation. Many refugee camps are overcrowded, housing conditions are below living standards, and there is a lack of basic services such as water and sewage systems in some camps. There are also limited spaces for private gardens or public parks to be used by children for entertainment. Moreover, there is a lack of clubs, cultural centres and public libraries for the young refugees.

These hard living conditions and limitations in the refugee camps have great negative effects on the young generation. Therefore, the international and local institutions are advised to focus on basic human rights and to provide and improve the services in order to influence the situation and behaviour of young refugees in Syria. Many young refugees continue to resist the socioeconomic and political pressures and still dream of returning to their homeland in Palestine. However, assessing the current international political situation in general and the Middle East in particular, it seems that the Palestinian refugees' dream of their homeland is vanishing gradually. It will be replaced by deep feelings of despair, anger and frustration. Therefore, it is difficult to imagine what kind of future is waiting for Palestinian young refugees. The discussion of the findings brings attention to the currently silent voices of young Palestinian refugees, and shows how they react and cope with their difficult living conditions, within their semi-isolated refugee camps and neighbourhoods in Syria. It also highlights the importance of recognising the difference that gender, social class and generation makes in learning how to live with prolonged forced migration.

Epilogue: Current Palestinian *Intifada*

The current Palestinian *Intifada* in the West Bank and the Gaza Strip, which started in September 2000, is considered by many interviewees as one of the most painful experiences of the Palestinian children and young people in Syria. Almost all the interviewees blamed the Israelis for the eruption of the current violence in the occupied Palestinian territories. Many of the interviewees thought that Sharon's visit to Al-Aqsa Mosque, the cruelty of occupation forces against the civilian Palestinian population, and the frustration of the Palestinians after ten years of meaningless peaceful negotiation are the main reasons behind the current Uprising. Currently, the majority of young Palestinian refugees in Syria are closely monitoring the daily tragic events in the media. The impacts of the current *Intifada* on Palestinian refugees in Syria are hard to predict now.

Anger and Frustration

Young Palestinian refugees were proud of the bravery exhibited daily on the television screens of the Palestinian children in the West Bank and Gaza Strip in facing the Israeli tanks with stones. Many felt sad and angry when they saw some of those children being killed by the Israeli troops. Many young refugees expressed their anger and frustration at not being able to participate directly in fights against the Israeli army – this is because they are separated by borders and distances including mountains and valleys, and because the Arab regimes have forbidden them to cross the border and fight Israel. Many of the young generation felt deeply motivated by the sacrifices of the children of the *Intifada*, and they show discontent at not being able to assist. Television pictures and media coverage of the confrontations between Palestinian civilians and the Israeli troops increased the Palestinians' hatred towards Israel. Interestingly, our outcomes showed that many young refugees, who were willing to immigrate or to settle in the refugee camps in Syria, were ready to fight for a liberation of Palestine and demand the right of return to their homeland Palestine.

Furthermore, the children from the refugee camps in Syria internalised the images of murdered children in Gaza and the West Bank; this increased their hatred towards the enemy and their frustration with the Arabs. Facing these new elements of hostility and isolation complicated the process of coping for young refugees in exile. It raised a mixture of feelings of fear, anxiety, frustration and helplessness that distinguished their lives in the refugee camps. The violent events of current Palestinian *Intifada* reminded many Palestinian children and adolescents in Syria of the original Catastrophe (*al-Nakba*) of 1948 and the Disaster (*al-Naksa*) in 1967. These wars resulted in making them and their grandparents and parents refugees. It also increased their hatred towards the Israelis, and reinforced their belief that the only way to end their exile and homelessness is through continuous armed struggle and not negotiation and diplomacy.

Disappointment

Our research showed that disappointment and shock was high among Palestinian refugees. The majority of the young generation were shocked and disappointed by the reactions of the Arabs and international public opinion towards the eruption of violence in Palestine. What shocked these young people most was the insignificant effort by the world community to stop the Israelis from murdering Palestinian children, the bombardment of private houses and the daily assassination of Palestinian political and militant activists. Many young refugees strongly believed that the Palestinians in the West Bank and Gaza Strip were not sufficiently supported. On the contrary, Palestinians were left alone to fight a well-equipped and skilled Israeli enemy without any support or assistance from the Arab countries. Equally importantly, many young refugees insisted on the importance of Arab direct intervention in the struggle against Israel.

Indeed, some young refugees accused the Arabs, especially the governments, of conspiring against Palestinians. Although many young refugees in Syria were disappointed by the Arabs and by international opinion, they also were sad and angry to see all the children and young people killed daily in Palestine. However, many of them wanted the Palestinian children to continue their struggle until they achieve liberation and independence of Palestine. The young generation's disappointment was eased knowing that the Palestinian children in Palestine were trying to accomplish what the adults failed to achieve. To be more precise, these young refugees believed that if their counterparts in Palestine continue their struggle they might be able to bring an end to the Israeli occupation of the West Bank and the Gaza Strip.

Solidarity

During the first few months of the Palestinian Uprising, the reported violent events created an atmosphere of solidarity, anger and restlessness among Palestinian refugees in Syria. This tense atmosphere dominated the UNRWA schools in general and refugee children's life in particular. Many schools were closed for a few days so that the children could participate in marches, demonstrations and public protests against the Israeli murders and cruelty towards Palestinians in the West Bank and the Gaza Strip. The majority of children were able to collect a small amount of money, which was given to UNRWA campaigns for the injured children and adults in the Occupied Territories, but many of them still think that is not enough and they should do more.

The current Israeli hostility against Palestinians in the West Bank and Gaza Strip recreated and maintained solidarity among Palestinians in Syria and with their counterparts in the Occupied Territories. It also strengthened their social identity as Palestinians who belong to one group of people inside and outside the Occupied Territories. Young Palestinian refugees in Syria often search for new coping strategies to deal with the effect of the unbearable situation inside the Occupied Territories. Meanwhile many members of the young generation are currently questioning the value of the peace process; they think it will never lead to independence or guarantee their right to return to their homeland, Palestine.

Note

1 Sincere thanks and appreciation are extended to Maria Salem, Fuad Suradi, Mai Barkawi and Manar Rabbai for their invaluable assistance in the field research as well as in the writing up of interviews. They gave most generously of their time and contributed significantly to the success of this project.

References

Al-Mawed, H. 1999. 'The Palestinian Refugees in Syria: Their past, present and future'. Unpublished research.

Brand, L. 1988. 'Palestinians in Syria: The Politics of Integration'. *Middle East Journal*, 4: 621–35.

PCBS (Palestinian Central Bureau of Statistics). 1998. *Palestinian Children: Issues and statistics*. Ramallah: PCBS.

Summerfield, D. 1995. 'Addressing Human Response to War and Atrocity: Major Challenges in Research and Practices and Limitation of Western Psychiatric Models'. In R.J. Kleber, B. Figley and B.P. Gersons (eds), *Beyond Trauma*. pp. 17–29. New York: Plenum Press.

UNICEF. 1999. *A Report on the Situation of the Palestinian Children in Syria*. August, Damascus.

UNICEF and PCBS (1999) *A Report on Children Labour in the Palestinian Camps in Syria*. Damascus.

UNRWA. 1992. *Basic Data on Palestinian Refugees and UNRWA*. October, Vienna: UNRWA.

———— 2001. *UNRWA Registration Statistical Bulletin*. Amman, Jordan.

Usher, G. 1999. 'Children in the Intifada: The Psychological Impact.' *Middle East International*, 26: 18–22.

4

Palestinian Refugee Children and Caregivers in Jordan

Randa Farah

Randa Farah
I am a Palestinian born in Haifa, when the State of Israel had already been established. My parents were both actively involved in protecting the rights of the Palestinians who had suddenly become a minority following *al-Nakba* or the 1948 war. In 1965 my family moved to the West Bank, which had been annexed by Jordan following the 1948 war. Two years later, Palestinians experienced another calamity, the 1967 war, when Israel occupied the West Bank and Gaza along with other Arab lands. Following this second major war, my family again found itself living under Israeli occupation.

I graduated from high school in Jerusalem and my family remained in the West Bank until the mid-1970s, when they moved again, this time to Lebanon just as the civil war began. In 1982 the Israeli army invaded Lebanon and entered Beirut in September. I fled Beirut as a young married mother on a cargo ship with my 3-year-old son and eventually immigrated to Canada.

In 1984, I enrolled at the University of Toronto's Anthropology Department and completed my thesis on popular memory and reconstructions of Palestinian identity. My fieldwork was conducted mainly in al-Baq'a refugee camp in Jordan. During that time, I carried out a study for the Canadian International Development Research Center (IDRC) on the impact of overcrowding in refugee camps in the West Bank and Gaza. I also worked as a researcher, mainly on the UNRWA-refugee relationship at the Centre d'Etudes et de Recherches sur le Moyen-Orient Contemporain (CERMOC) in Amman, Jordan, and then became a Research Associate at the Refugee Studies Centre (RSC).

Since 2002 I have been one of the research team leaders on a study of the impact of prolonged forced migration among Sahrawi and Afghani refugee children, directed by Dr Dawn Chatty and funded by the Mellon Foundation. At the RSC I also co-teach a short course on Palestinian Refugees and the Universal Declaration of Human Rights.

In 2001 I was hired as an Assistant Professor at the University of Western Ontario, where I currently teach in the Anthropology Department. My publications and lectures, at various universities in Canada and the U.S.A. reflect my areas of interest and to a great degree exilic life, namely, refugees and displacement, memory/history and identity, nations and nationalism and humanitarian aid.

This chapter[1] examines the lives and narratives of Palestinian refugee children and adolescents[2] living in a refugee camp in Jordan.[3] It deals primarily with how young people – like adults – are both products of history and society, as well as agents who reshape political, socioeconomic and cultural processes. Despite the larger collective experience of colonisation, dispossession and fragmentation, which they share with all Palestinians, most of the refugees who sought shelter across the River Jordan or the East Bank have acquired a special Jordanian-Palestinian experience, which will emerge in the chapter. Undoubtedly, examining this experience through the lives of children is of particular significance. Refugee children and young people, enmeshed in myriad social relations that cross generational boundaries, constitute the majority of the population and are actively contributing to the reshaping of Palestinian society and culture.

Equally important is children's participation in the political struggle. As agents, children have the ability and the right to formulate their political discourses and practices. When refugees are attacked, the whole community is targeted and children and young people are not spared military, political, economic or other forms of repression. Consequently, it should come as no surprise that children respond to those who kill, displace, injure or deny them (and their families and community) their rights. Indeed, some studies have shown that children and young people in certain situations cope much better when they participate in defending their community and when resisting oppression.

Historical Background

I went one day to the Ministry of Interior [in Jordan] to help my aunt get the right documents so she could go to *al-Hajj* [pilgrimage to Mecca]. The minute I went in, the man [the Jordanian official] told me [mockingly attempting to humiliate her]: 'Your face looks like that of a Gazan!' I answered him: '...God d— the uniform you are wearing... your rifle is longer than you, you haven't even shot a dog and now you carry a gun! Who told you to open the bridge [during the 1967 war]? If you hadn't it would have been better to die or to live there...!' There is a government official who said: 'We should deport all the Gazans and send them back naked!' God d— if I was there, I would have told him... 'This land was arid with nothing in it ... We came and built it and therefore you [Jordanians] today are able to sell and buy land, things and cars at the expense of [or because of the existence of] refugees and the Gazans! ... (Imm Azmi, HH2, G1, F)

Between 700,000 and 900,000 Palestinians found themselves abruptly acquiring a refugee status following *al-Nakba*, or Catastrophe, the term Palestinians use to refer to the war that led to their uprooting in 1948 and the total devastation of their society. Two years following the 1948 war, the West Bank was annexed to Transjordan and what later emerged as the Hashemite Kingdom of Jordan. The annexation of the West Bank dramatically expanded the constituency and territorial base of Jordan, a factor that played an important role in the particular shape of the Jordanian nation-state.

Following its annexation of the West Bank, Jordan extended citizenship and nationality rights to the majority of Palestinians, including refugees who had recently been uprooted from their homes and lands. Today, Palestinians with Jordanian passports represent the majority of the population. The demographic factor in favour of the Palestinians is a politically sensitive issue, to the extent that statistics revealing the number of Jordanian citizens with Palestinian origins are usually not available to the public and the justification is that such a revelation might incite ethnic conflict (Zureik 1996: 33).

Although the sense of Palestinian belonging to Jordan varies by factors such as class, generation and legal status and is influenced by the political context, Palestinians have maintained a sense of 'people-hood' and separate national identity. Moreover, Jordanian policies, mainly those that provide for preferential recruitment of Transjordanians in the public sector, aggravate the schism between the two communities (Brand 1995: 50–5).

The Oslo Agreement in 1993 and its collapse pushed to the surface the issue of identity in Jordan in relation to citizenship and national belonging. Questions pertaining to the future of the Palestinians invoked popular resentment among Jordanians and Palestinians alike. The Jordanians feared that Jordan would turn into the Palestinian 'alternative Homeland,' an idea propagated by the Israeli state, while the Palestinians were concerned that the Oslo negotiations would abrogate their right of return and force them to permanently resettle in Jordan.

Jordan is the host of the largest number of Palestinian refugees outside Palestine, estimated at approximately 3.7 million refugees registered with the United Nations Relief and Works Agency (UNRWA) in all its fields of operation, namely Jordan, Syria, Lebanon, the West Bank and Gaza.[4] There are approximately 1.6 million registered refugees in Jordan, constituting 32 percent of the total population. This figure represents 42 percent of the total registered refugee population in the region. Of more relevance to this chapter, the statistics indicate that over half the Palestinian refugee population (56 percent) are under the age of 25 (UNRWA 2000). Around 18 percent of refugees live in ten UNRWA camps established on lands leased from the government.

Over time and due to a dramatic increase in the population on the camp land area that remained legally fixed, the boundaries of camps have become very ambiguous, as inhabitants spilled over and formed new neighbourhoods in the vicinity. However, the socioeconomic status of those who live inside camps and those in close proximity is not very different, though the perceptions of 'inside' and 'outside' have political, social and cultural ramifications. According to UNRWA sources, the percentage of refugees living in 'camps' rises to 65 percent, if one is to include those who had moved into the immediate vicinity of the designated legal boundaries of camps (UNRWA 2003).

There were three major armed conflicts that led to the influx of refugees into Jordan. The 1948 war, *al-Nakba*, resulted in the displacement of an estimated 100,000 people who fled into Transjordan.[5] Four camps were established following the 1948 war, while the remaining six camps were erected as 'emergency camps' consequent to the 1967 war, when an estimated 400,000 people flooded into Jordan. For over half the population fleeing the 1967 Arab–Israeli war, this was the second displacement. Many of the 'second time' refugees had fled from camps in the West Bank and Gaza, such as Aqbat Jaber and Ain al-Sultan in Jericho, Fare'a and Balata in the West Bank and Maghazi and Rafah in Gaza.

A third exodus occurred during the Gulf War in the early 1990s, when approximately 400,000 expatriates were forced out of Gulf countries, mainly from Kuwait. Most of those expelled were Palestinians, many of them carrying Jordanian passports, who were classified as the 'Returnees'. It is important to note that a significant number of the Returnees had never lived in Jordan, having been born and spent most of their lives in Gulf countries. While working in the Gulf, the expatriates were an important source of remittances to Palestinian refugee families, as well as to Jordanians. Some 10 percent of the Returnees moved into refugee camps and/or needed UNRWA services, thereby changing their role from a source of livelihood to a burden on many refugee households. In addition, higher rates of unemployment were registered as a result of the large influx of Returnees into Jordan (Mrayyan 1994: 234).

The various categories of refugees have been granted different rights and obligations, privileges and prohibitions. For example, 'refugees' refers to Palestinians who originate in the areas occupied during the 1948 war, while the 'displaced' refers to Palestinians uprooted during the 1967 war who originate in the West Bank. There are several other such classifications, which makes it even more difficult for the refugee population to rally around collective demands. The 'displaced' are not eligible for all

UNRWA services and are registered by the Jordanian government. Those who fled the 1967 war from Gaza, many of them also 1948 refugees, also acquired a different legal status; the 'ex-Gaza refugees' are not eligible for Jordanian citizenship.

In addition to the three major wars, there were other conflicts that induced forced migration and internal displacement, such as the 1968 al-Karameh battle,[6] and the armed clashes in 1970–1 that led to the ousting of the Palestine Resistance Movement by the Jordanian government – along with a significant number of cadres – mainly to Lebanon. Consequently, the frequent relocation and uprooting resulting from armed conflict and the concomitant need to find shelter and livelihood characterises the trajectories of the vast majority of Palestinians, particularly refugees.

Literature Review

In the past decade, a growing body of literature on refugees and refugee camps began to emerge, propelled mainly by the peace process in the early 1990s. Consequently, this literature is generally policy driven and focuses on socioeconomic data and issues of 'integration'. An important research institute active in producing such literature is the Norwegian Institute for Applied Social Science (FAFO).

In addition, there is a growing number of reports produced by nongovernmental and intergovernmental agencies such as UNICEF and Save the Children Fund (SCF) with the purpose of implementing projects in poor neighbourhoods in Jordan. One example is the 'Family Planning' programme, which acquired different titles over time and in different countries, and which often conflicts with local cultures and histories. For Palestinians, having many children is not only culturally and socially significant, but it has a political dimension, whereby having many children is viewed as a response to the 'demographic battle' waged by the Israeli state. In addition, the consequences of international policies and programmes that do not respond to local needs compel many local NGOs to change their programmes to meet international requirements so that they will be eligible for funding.

There is a third body of academic literature on refugees and refugee camps, produced by individual researchers, scholars and research institutions. Again, most of this literature adopts a psychological, sociological or demographic approach at the expense of anthropological and participatory methods. The exceptions in this body of literature are individual studies and those produced by researchers such as work done by the Centre d'Etude et de Recherches du Moyen-Orient Contemporain (CERMOC) in Amman and Beirut.[7]

A review of the literature in the library at the University of Jordan showed that most of the existing literature on children and young people is found in the departments of politics (especially the relationship with Islamicist organisations), sociology (with a focus on violence), psychology, economics (unemployment and labour) or biology (behavioural and developmental stages). What is disturbing in these studies is the almost universal view that children, young people and youth are either responsible for existing social problems or are passive victims of corrupting and immoral trends and political movements; the studies usually direct the blame on globalisation, the West and political Islam.

Based on a preliminary review of the literature in Tunisian, Moroccan and Egyptian sources by the author, it is clear that the writings on children and youth seem also to fall within the aforementioned disciplines. A brief reading of some of the titles of articles and studies will clarify the point: 'Reflections on Religious Revivalism and Violence', 'Arab Youth and the Problems They Face', 'Youth and How to Utilise Free Time in the United Arab Emirates', 'Behavioural Problems and Alienation Among Youth in Kuwait'. A list of titles gathered by Ahmed Ebeid Abdel-Hamid Adawi and published in *Majallat al-Shu'oun Al-Ijtima'iyyah* (Journal of Social Issues) in 1995 includes the following headings: 'Islam and Youth', 'The Media and Youth', 'Alienation and Youth', 'Youth and Psychology', 'Youth in Political International Relations'.[8]

Methodology and Approach

As the research progressed, the voices, ideas and comments of subjects remoulded questions, themes and results. The foci of the study were children and young people, as well as adult members of the extended family, school staff and teachers, members of the community and representatives of various organisations and institutions. Thus, the research examined children within their communities and in the social and physical spaces within which they moved and lived, mainly at home, at school, in the streets and market place.

The Subjects and the Field: Marka Camp and Hayy al-Mahasreh

The in-depth study was conducted in Marka[9] refugee camp and most of the data cited here will be from camp refugees. However, another refugee neighbourhood, called Hayy al-Mahasra (al-Mahasreh quarter, which is not a camp), was also selected for comparative purposes, although this paper will not deal with this dimension. In addition, the conclusions and ideas that appear are also based on previous studies conducted by the author in refugee camps in Jordan, the West Bank and Lebanon.

Today there are around 40,000 people living on 917,000 square metres in Marka camp, which is 10 kilometres northeast of the Jordanian capital, Amman – the same land area allocated for the camp in 1968.[10] Most of the inhabitants originate from destroyed and depopulated villages in central and southern Palestine, mainly from villages in the districts of Hebron, Gaza, Bir al-Sabe', Jaffa, al-Ramleh and others. Upon its establishment, people attempted to reestablish family and village networks, thus the people of Dayr Nakhass lived in one area, al-Dawaymeh lived near the market area, people from the Jericho area in another, those from Ajjour also sought to cluster together and those from Bir al-Sabe' settled an area called al-Barr.[11] Over time, however, the areas have become heterogeneous, although clusters of extended families may still be found in the same area.

Unemployment, overcrowding and poverty are interrelated phenomena that aggravate the marginalisation of refugees in Marka and other refugee camps. Those who are lucky enough to find employment generally work in seasonal and daily jobs in the surrounding areas and factories; the income average is approximately JD 80–140 (Jordanian Dinars) per month for men and around JD 40–100 for women. Indeed, the inhabitants of Marka camp are a source of cheap labour for surrounding companies, such as the plastic, textile and paint factories. The most important social unit in Palestinian society is the extended family. Nevertheless, among the population studied and in addition to extended families, there are nuclear families, female-headed households and other living arrangements contingent on social and economic necessities. Although the socioeconomic status of households varies, the vast majority of the population is poor. Some members of a household have migrated or relocated outside, or simply moved from one place to another within the camp. In many households, there is no one source of income. Livelihood strategies are based on diversifying the sources, mainly as a result of a history of political and economic insecurity.

Most of the streets in the camp need repair, as do the water and sewer networks – the pipes often burst, creating puddles of dirty water. Overpopulation means that there is no space to erect parks or establish new playgrounds for children, or even to build new houses, except perpendicularly. Hence, camp streets and alleyways have become the play areas for the younger generations and are outlets for adults, especially for males. During the research period (1999–2001), there were problems with rubbish collection, which was not always picked up, thus increasing the level of environmental pollution – a significant point to raise considering that many children, some of them barefoot, play around rubbish bins. There are two markets in the camp, where many of the local entrepreneurs have transformed their housing units into retail stores, storage areas or mechanical repair shops. The main market is close to the entrance of the camp, while another, cheaper, market has evolved at the other end, sometimes referred to as the 'Gaza area'.

In Marka camp, there are several organisations, some of which emerged spontaneously and locally; others are branches of national, regional and international organisations. The Youth Club falls under the jurisdiction of the Jordanian Ministry of Youth, thus it is officially a Jordanian and not a Palestinian centre. UNRWA has several installations: two schools (one for males and the other for females) running on a double shift, a 'Mother and Child Centre', a Community Rehabilitation Centre (CRC) and a Women's Programme Centre (WPC). During the period of research there were very few programmes for children and young people, and none for young girls.

Categories and Instruments of Research

Twenty households were selected for an in-depth study, chosen to represent the heterogeneity within the camp. Therefore, households varied by economic status, their history and their employment trajectory, as well as by their place of origin. The research data was based on: (a) life histories and narratives of different generations of refugees; (b) a child-focused psychological intervention in order to find out from children what they consider sources of worry. (This involved 161 boys and girls in total); (c) structured and close-ended interviews; (d) group and individual discussions, mostly informal interviews. Participant observation represented an important dimension in the study. Research team members spent time in the camp, participating in and observing different activities in the streets, schools, households and centres.

Focus groups for children and young people of differing age groups were held both in the camp and in the Hayy. In addition, community workshops involving women and children were held in the camp. The purpose of the workshops was to engage the community as a whole in the study, and also to continuously update them on the research and results. Last, but not least, a review of the various publications, statistical reports and studies on refugees was conducted.

In the following section, I will highlight the major themes which emerged from the study and were voiced by children, young people and their caregivers. Similarly, coping mechanisms were extrapolated from the material gathered over the period of the research, which included research conducted during *al-Aqsa Intifada*.

History/Memory and Identity

A Dog in his Homeland is a Sultan! (Imm Awni, G1, F, HH15)

I was born in Bi'leen in 1930 and own there 300 *dunums* of land. I have the land deeds, the documents to prove land ownership. We used to plant wheat, barley, sesame, lentils, beans, hilbeh, figs, grapes and prickly pears. The first day of Ramadan in 1948, they attacked Tal al-Safi and captured it at the time of the *Shhour* (at dawn when Muslims break their fasting in the month of Ramadan). People ran away eastward toward Barquosia ... then al-Masmiyyeh ... Bayt Jibreen ... al-Faloujeh ... [lists many other villages] ... in Ithnah they [meaning we] stayed two years in the house of a person there. ... when a camp was built near Ithnah we went there ... then heavy rains forced us out and we were placed in schools and mosques for eight days... toward the end of 1951 we fled to Jericho [camps erected in the Jericho area] and stayed there until 1967... During the 1967 war, we fled to al-Karameh. (Kamel Abdel Rahman, HH17, G1, M)

The war of 1948 has left a deep rupture in Palestinian society and in the memory of individuals who lived through the traumatic experience of war and uprooting. Literally overnight, Palestinians were dispossessed of land and a way of life they had lived for generations. The political nexus and new geopolitical boundaries shifted radically and rapidly around them. Since then, these boundaries have continued to form an impenetrable barrier between them and their land.[12] Consequently, Palestinians embarked on rebuilding their society, torn asunder by exile, and their political identity in the context of exile and displacement.

There are many factors both internal and external – which are interrelated – that contribute to the reproduction of Palestinian identity. An important internal factor is the active will of the displaced population to resist resettlement and schemes to integrate them in host countries. Palestinian refugees embarked on a remarkable struggle 'against forgetting'. Indeed, the generations that had lived in Palestine passed on their memory of home and homeland to younger generations born in exile. The channels and spaces through which the attachment to Palestine as land and society were reproduced were not through formal or official histories.

Palestinians learned their histories and trajectories at home, in *hays* (neighbourhoods), at school (through Palestinian teachers who believed it their duty to teach them their history and beyond what the curricula required), in political organisations and social and cultural centres. As adults narrated, children listened, imbibing the stories and reminiscences of their elders, drawing images of villages, lands, of agricultural cycles, imagining heroes and victims and in turn reproducing these images in their own creative ways.

This reproduction of a Palestinian identity emphasised land and genealogy, which became the pivotal elements of the Palestinian political culture, and which pervaded the nationalist discourse in the absence of a Palestinian state. Interestingly, although most refugee camps were established near urban centres, including Marka camp, many refugees continue to describe themselves as rural and as *fellaheen* (peasants), despite the fact that the majority of those born in the camps may have rarely worked in the agricultural sector. Referring to themselves as *fellaheen* is a way to demarcate them as different from others, that is, from Jordanians, from city dwellers and nomads, thereby affirming a Palestinian identity and an attachment to the land. Seeking elements of differentiation is significant for Palestinian refugees, precisely because they share with the larger society around them much in common, such as language and religion – hence they emphasise differences to delineate the boundaries of a Palestinian identity.

A second factor that enhances a separate Palestinian belonging is the marginal status that Palestinians in general and refugees in particular occupy in Arab countries. As Hassan observes:

> We do not have any confidence in the Arabs and they are traitors, sometimes I am so depressed about it, I do not even want to talk to my children about what happened to my village Sajad in Palestine... I prefer to live in a tent in my homeland than a castle anywhere else... because I will always feel that the castle is not really mine. (Hassan, HHII, G3, M)

In general, many Arab countries, despite public announcements calling for 'Arab brotherhood' and 'unity', discriminated against Palestinian refugees (Takkenberg 1998: 131–71). In the narratives of refugees, there is always reference to bitter experiences including imprisonment, armed conflict, discrimination in employment and education opportunities and travel restrictions imposed by Arab states. Camp-dwelling and poorer refugees encounter discrimination because of their social status, including discrimination by middle-class Palestinians and those economically and socially advantaged. The aforementioned factors combined to reinforce the belief among refugees that they have been abandoned by Arab countries and therefore they have to fend for themselves in a hostile world. Odeh, a 15-year-old student from Marka camp, explains:

> When we go to Amman, policemen sometimes stop us and ask for our ID and when they discover that we live in Hitteen [another name for Marka camp], they take us to the station to see if we have any criminal record, only because we are from the camp. This happened to many people here, including myself. The policeman came and asked for our IDs [he was with friends], when they found we are from Hitteen camp they took us to the station and started to look up on the computer if we have criminal records. This is because we live in the camp and we are refugees. (Odeh, HH4, G4, M)

Three main elements characterise the narratives of the first generation of Palestinian refugees. First, the detailed description of the village of origin. In many cases narrators shift to the present tense, as if the village still exists, bringing it back to life with its landscape, changing seasons, colours, smells, the produce of each village, the 'peasant way of life' and their celebrations and commemorations. Invariably, there is a reference to the political history, mainly the British Mandate, particularly its repression of the 1936 Rebellion and its collaboration with the Zionist movement.

The second element that appears in narratives is the war of 1948, which attests to the violence inflicted by Jewish paramilitary organisations. The narratives describe how villages were bombed by Zionist paramilitary organisations, namely the Haganah, which inflicted terror against the inhabitants, usually besieging villages on three sides and forcing out the population through the remaining outlet. Those who refused to leave or who made an attempt to return were shot and killed.

The third part in the narratives pertains to the journey of exile itself and how the individual narrator manoeuvred through the larger historical and political dynamics. However, the experiences following their exile (i.e., of having to become a 'refugee') are downplayed by the first generation, possibly because during that time their lives were bereft of dignity and they felt the humiliation of needing humanitarian aid, of living in caves and tents and of lining up for rations. Consequently, the older generation tends to silence this experience publicly and they focus instead on the village of origin and the yearning to return. As Fatma said:

> Now I wish I would go back home and die in a bit of the earth of my land ... back home, we ate our own prickly pear, our figs, our harvest, your food and your drink was from your own land, your livestock ... this what they call 'cancer' we never even knew, we never went to doctors ... here we hate our lives, we are sick and tired of being outside our homeland... there is nothing like one's homeland and land and home ... here is not our homeland, they can expel us any time. (Fatma, HH12, G1, F)

The second and third generations focus on the refugee experience itself, with an emphasis on how they were able to challenge the hardship, acquire high education levels and contribute to the household income. Equally important in their narratives is their political participation and how they transformed the humanitarian and humiliating labels of 'refugee' and 'camp' into powerful political symbols of resistance and resilience. For the younger generations the return to their original village restores dignity and political rights. The following is a narrative of a refugee who was only 2 years old in 1948. Notice how she describes the land and the experience of uprooting, as she recalls her father's description prior to his death, as if she was there herself. Indeed, when narrating the story, Imm Khaled 'lived the experience'.

Also important to note is the reference in Imm Khaled's narrative to her childhood. Most of this generation refer to childhood in terms such as 'when I became aware of the world', a time when they were assigned particular tasks working alongside other members of the extended family, either in the field or in domestic chores. This perception of childhood is quite different from the Western concept of childhood, which is based mainly on biological developmental models. Another important point that emerges in the narratives is the contribution of women towards the survival of the family during those early years of exile.

My father ... maybe had 100 *dunums* of land, and this is only the vineyard ... this does not include the other agricultural land we owned. This is only the land where we had figs, grapes, fruits, olives, peaches. We used to plant and harvest in the land, thanks be to God [as if she was there]. We have wheat, barley, cows, sheep and our situation was excellent. We had land and we have the land deeds to prove it. My father brought these with him from Jerusalem and he used to hide them safely ... During the war we fled to Agbat Jaber [a camp in the Jericho area]. They put us in tents. Sometimes four families in one tent. This is what my father used to say about the fifties. At first they used to roam around under the heavens and the sky with no shelter, some days they were full, other days they went hungry ... the lice and fleas killed us ... how can there be cleanliness when there are four families living together? ... where should the girls and women wash themselves? Where would they bathe? How will they be able to unveil ... when you have sometimes 20 people in one tent, how will their hunger be satisfied? Some slept inside the tent and the men slept outside ... when I became aware, they [refugees and her family included] used to knead bricks, and each one was building a small room for his family and children ... I used to help my mother and carry the earth, mix it with water and hay, knead them ... we had no protection from heat or cold. There were no sewage networks. There was a washroom every 150 meters, we used to line up, one side for men and the other for women ... the washroom I remember had no door ... UNRWA did not give them [refugees] anything... UNRWA gave them a bit of flour, a bit of sugar ... but there were merchants who used to buy from us food items and sell and buy those ... because some people needed to buy for their children let us say shoes, or pants and this is how they acquired a bit of cash ... I was 17 when I was married ... people were so poor they did not have even bread ...

In 1967 I was living with my in-laws in Agbat Jaber ... when Israel began to bomb I was at my sister-in-law's house ... people were terrified ... they remembered the Deir Yassin massacre ... in 1967 we fled on foot with the morning prayers ... I was carrying my daughter ... we hid behind trees ... until we arrived in Amman, my daughter was seven months old. (Imm Khaled, HH4, G1, F)

The constant referral to the original village contrasted with the horrendous lives in the camps in the first few years following the 1948 war. This played an important role in instilling a Palestinian national belonging based on the village of origin. Second – and sometimes third-generation refugees are able to reproduce images of their villages of origin with meticulous detail. As for the fourth- and fifth- generation, a Palestinian belonging is expressed in a yearning to return, yet their knowledge of the village of origin and of Palestinian history is scanty, unlike older genera-tions. For example, Muhammad, a 17-year-old, responds to a question we raised:

Question: What do you know about al-Abbasiyyeh?

Answer: Nothing, I do not even know if it is on the map or not, I only know I am from there and that is all. (Muhammad, HH2, G5, M)

The first generation is passing away and today those who lived in Palestine and experienced the 1948 war are few. Consequently, children are not directly exposed to narratives and reminiscences as they used to be in earlier decades. In addition, the research showed that the younger generations face a dilemma due to the increasing ambiguity surrounding their history: they know they are not Jordanians, but are not very clear as to their Palestinian past and the trajectory of their families over the past five decades. However, there are still those whose grandmothers are alive and for Yaser, a 17-year-old student in Grade 10 (speaking in a boys' focus group, BFG), his grandmother is a central figure who passes down her experience:

My grandmother tells me about Palestine, she is like a dictionary, she has many stories to tell about Palestine. She always tells us about Palestine... I wish I could visit Palestine. There is no one in the camp who does not wish to visit Palestine, my grandmother tells me we are from 48, and there is also 64 [he makes a mistake, meaning 1967] she says those from the 67 territories are going to return but the people from 48 are not. My grandmother is from Marj Ibn Amer from Haifa, my grandmother always tells me about Marj Ibn Amer, and Haifa. She desires so much to return. (Yaser, BFG, Grade 10)

Omar, a 13-year-old, knows he is from Ajjour, a village in the district of Hebron, but does not know where it is and what district it belongs to, even when his older siblings are much more aware of this history. Omar says, 'I am from Ajjour [does not know the district or where it is/was]. My grandmother talks about it to my brothers and sister, she tells them they were forced out'. (Omar, G5, BFG)

Furthermore, the Oslo Accords signed in 1993 had a radical impact on refugee communities in Jordan and elsewhere. One of the fundamental repercussions of the peace process was the rupture in the PLO as a unify-ing political national reference and framework. The shift in the official national agenda of the Palestinians, mainly towards the building of a state on the West Bank and the Gaza Strip, left refugees feeling abandoned, marginalised and fragmented, without a unifying representative body to advocate on their behalf. Multiple references of identity and political expression have emerged since, including the various Islamic organisations, village associations, camp community-based initiatives, which provide alternative ways to keep the dream and right of return alive.

The television is an important source of news about Palestine and the political events there. However, the form and content of what is being shown differs from the oral narratives passed down by parents and grandparents. The official and public news do not bring back the original village to life, neither do they speak to each individual refugee and his or her particular roots back in Palestine. The oral narratives of parents and grandparents had the effect of clearly showing how the individual and collective histories are linked, as well as the private-public and the personal-political domains. Another growing medium through which the village of origin is kept alive is through personal videos developed by visitors who film their original village, then return to show it to others in the camp, particularly other village members. Odeh, a 17-year-old boy, explains:

> The mother, father, grandmother help you feel you belong and things have changed. We like to hear these stories about the past and how things used to be, about the vegetables, the lands, the environment. They say, the water from there tastes different in Palestine... Everyone dreams of returning to Palestine... There are people from our village who went back and made a film on the video... everything was different there, the vegetables, the fruits... (Odeh, HH4, G5, M)

Children's narratives on Palestine, like the generations before them, continue to refer to the land and its produce, thereby reaffirming land as the pivotal axis of Palestinian nationalism, even when the official Palestinian discourse following Oslo had shifted towards the state and the building of its institutions.

Political, Legal and Socioeconomic Discrimination

> Here they tell us you are from Gaza, our son cannot enrol in university and the other son cannot get a government job. We fled to Gaza in 1948 [and to Jordan following the 1967 war], we are not from there originally ... We suffered from some of the people of Gaza as well [local residents, that is, not refugees]. They used to look at a refugee and say *haram* [poor or pathetic] your face is like that of a refugee ... ! (Imm Awni, HH15, G1, F)

Refugees living in camps encounter discrimination at more than one level: as Palestinians, as refugees and as camp dwellers. Although most Palestinian refugees in Jordan have citizenship rights, in practice the Jordanian government favours Transjordanians in its employment and education policies. Furthermore, the legal and administrative segmentation of the population has had repercussions on the refugee community, including social relations. Some families will not favour a marriage with an 'ex-Gaza' man, whose economic prospects are deemed poor, and, therefore, they fear that he will not be able to support their daughter. In contrast, ex-Gaza women are encouraged to marry a man with full Jordanian citizenship, which is seen as an advancement in social status and future prospects not only for the bride, but also for her family.

Children and young people are conscious of the fact that they are 'campers', or *mukhayyamjiyyeh*, an experience invoking both denigration and pride. Depending on the context, a *mukhayyamji* may be granted the characteristics of strength and resiliency in having had to 'rough it out' in the camp and emerge as a political symbol of the Palestinian struggle. On the other hand, children are aware that in society at large they are looked down upon as socially inferior. Sa'eed, a 13-year-old boy complained: 'Many people from the outside think we are terrible and we are all bad. They call us *mukhayyamjiyyeh*. Even my sister's family, who live in Zarqa [a city in Jordan], they say that people in the camp are garbage, good for nothing and cows'. (Sa'eed, BFG, G5) However, an 18-year-old says:

> I like the environment in the camp, because of its social relations. Our area in the camp is one of the best. We play and sit together in the *hara* [quarter in a neighbourhood]. However, there are problems in the camp, such as people carrying knives, drugs, alcohol... but I love the camp, it would be hard for me to leave it, there are intimate relationships here. (Ali, HH11, G4, M)

The above quotation reflects the political malaise resulting from the Oslo agreement and the consequent crumbling of the PLO as a unifying nationalist umbrella. In a manner of speaking, the nationalist umbrella and political symbolism granted to refugee camps had been shattered, exposing the poverty in society, particularly in refugee camps (Farah 1997: 260–3). Yet, like the generations before them, many of the young people attribute their problems to their national belonging and to their status as outsiders in Jordan:

> I never visited Palestine, I yearn to return to my Homeland, because a human being far from his Homeland feels like a stranger. The stranger without his Homeland feels disgraced and people ostracise him from society. To live in dignity we must work on our land and build our country. (Latifa, HH19, G2, F)

Undoubtedly, economic discrimination is a problem that has ripple effects on the ability of the inhabitants to relocate outside the overcrowded camp area and causes different kinds of social stresses. Poverty forces many families to rely on children to help support the household, especially in cases of polygamous families, or when the father is ill, unemployed or disabled. This is the case with Mahmoud, whose family relies on the work of two brothers: 'My father is dead and my brother takes care of us, he is 22, he works in the Pepsi company and the other one works in the wool company, we are four girls and four boys'. (Mahmoud, BFG, G5, Grade 7)

In turn, working children are not always able to keep up with schoolwork, or even have time to play, because of the hours they spend at work. Around a third of the boys in Grade 10 in the UNRWA boys' school in the camp worked. Mahmoud works the year round, while others work during holidays or intermittently. When asked about his work, Mahmoud, a 17-year-old student, describes his daily routine as follows:

> I get up at four to pray, then I go to work until 11. After school I go home, eat, pray, etc. then I go to work until the evening. I work in an electricity company and in construction, I work with a contractor. I do not study, I come home watch TV and sleep. (Mahmoud, BFG, Grade 10)

The same applies to Sami, who explains why he cannot study:

> I work everything, electrician, plasterer, pipe repairs, painter, etc. I am 17 and a few months. My father is disabled... I am responsible for the house. I do not get good grades. (Sami, BFG, Grade 10)

UNRWA provides education from Grade 1 to Grade 10. Students then have the option of enrolling in government schools. However, the agreements between the Agency and host governments stipulate that UNRWA has to follow the curriculum of the host country in which it operates. The curriculum in Jordan, as in other countries where UNRWA operates, does not provide specific topics for Palestinian refugees. Of particular significance is the absence of history books on Palestine or the refugee experience and trajectory. Until 1989, the Jordanian curriculum included one book entitled *al-Qadiyyah al-Falastiniyya* (The Palestinian Question); however, this has been dropped since and has not been replaced.

Consequently, Palestinian children in Lebanon, Syria, Jordan, the West Bank and Gaza who attend UNRWA schools learn different histories, and here I am not referring to different Palestinian histories, which would be understandable, considering the specific experiences they had. The history books that refugee students learn from are the official history books on Jordan, Lebanon, Syria and the West Bank and Gaza. Even the Palestinian

Authority and its Ministry of Education has not been free to produce a national Palestinian curriculum, due to restrictions and censorship by the Israeli authorities, where periods in Palestinian history have been omitted, such as the experiences of destruction and depopulation of villages, the experiences of Palestinians in Lebanon and other important events for Palestinians.

The formal and informal education for Palestinian children has changed from an earlier era, when the political environment had encouraged teachers – credited for their commitment during those years – to educate students on Palestinian issues, even when it was not in the curriculum. In fact, there was a time when students sang the Palestinian national anthem in the morning, raised flags and commemorated and celebrated Palestinian events in UNRWA schools. However, the historical and political context has shifted radically since then, and UNRWA teachers are economically and politically more insecure than they were in the past. Consequently, many teachers are no longer willing to take the risk of going beyond what their mandate stipulates.

Physical and Social Spaces: *'No one listens and no place to go'*

Physical Space

> The houses are too narrow, there is overcrowding, our water is polluted, there is high unemployment and our streets are narrow. Also, the UNRWA clinic has no medicine and they treat patients badly. The schools, which do not even have proper desks, don't care about the students. Transportation is inefficient and unavailable for workers. The employees or garbage collectors do not work on Fridays, so the waste accumulates. The market is small and the gangsters attack shopkeepers with knives. Alcoholism is rampant and there is fear of the gangsters in the streets. As a result of overcrowding, there are many problems and it is difficult to maintain morals and traditions. (Kamel Abdel Rahman, HH17, G1, M)

The inhabitants of the camp remember a time when each family had some space in front of their shelters, which provided important outlets. An important function of this space was that children were able to play around their homes, thus relieving the shelter from overcrowding. Moreover, the space was often transformed into gardens, tended usually by women, and the vegetables provided basic food items for the household. The small space also allowed some families to rear domestic animals, such as goats and poultry used for domestic consumption. However, all this changed as the population grew and the need for new shelters devoured these spaces.

Consequently, today, the only outlet is the streets and narrow alleyways – generally speaking a male domain – while girls are encouraged
and in some cases required to stay at home. In schools, the classrooms are
overcrowded (in some cases over fifty students are in the same classroom), making it difficult for teachers to provide a proper learning environment or to control the classroom. The school buildings are run down
and, in some of the classrooms, stones replace handles and knobs to keep
the door closed. Desks and chairs are dilapidated, some are broken and in
some cases three students have to share desks made for two. The playgrounds are also too small for the number of students, causing fights over
spaces to play, especially since schools run on a double shift, which means
the earlier shift has to vacate immediately to make room for the next
round. Schools are in bad need of equipment such as computers and laboratory instruments and the libraries have few and old worn-out books.

In addition to street and neighbourhood corners, children and young
people play near rubbish dumps, cemeteries and little nooks in the camp.
Most parents cannot afford to give their children spending money or do
not allow them to leave the camp on their own. Consequently, refugee
children are unable to enjoy the centres provided for children and youth
in urban centres, such as in Amman, the capital, where only the more
affluent children can go. Overcrowding is a factor contributing to social
conflicts within the family, as well as among neighbours. Children and
young people complained that neighbours harass them. This is particularly true for girls, because they feel that neighbours 'gossip' and watch
them constantly.

> The problem I face has to do with the neighbourhood, there are a lot of young
> zu'ran [hooligans] and problems are frequent in our area. The other day it was
> so serious, they brought in weapons and it is very disturbing, we heard the
> police and the ambulance. (Samia, GFG, G5, Grade 7)

The same problem emerged in previous research conducted in the West
Bank and Gaza, where the ideal of 'neighbourly relations' in the camp
does not always apply (Farah 2000). Overcrowding has been the cause of
fights among neighbours over such issues as: building extra rooms in
ways that block the sun or impinge on their privacy; cleaning in front of
houses, which means that sometimes the dirty water seeps through a
neighbour's shelter; having young men harassing the girls next door, and
noise and interference. Yousef complained: "My sister had final exams,
we asked them to turn the radio down, and instead they turned it higher"
(Yousef, BFG, G5). For girls the situation is worse and parents, especially
mothers, feel the stress of having to cope with their children confined at
home, but mostly their daughters, who are not allowed on the streets.
Imm Omar remarks:

There are simply no spaces for the children to play, especially for girls. I some-times take my daughters to walk around the camp, and end up having to spend some money to buy them different things from the shops we pass by. In addition, we are often harassed, despite the fact that I am older and I am their mother walking with my daughters. (Imm Omar, parent, Marka)

The problem of physical space should not be underestimated; it applies to shelters, streets, schools, clinics, markets and other places in the camp. The repercussions of overcrowding affect all segments of the population, especially girls, many of whom spend most of their time confined within camp boundaries in their homes, schools, or with relatives and maybe neighbours.

Social Space

I am 12 years old, we live in a miserable family environment [she begins to cry] ... A suitor came for my sister, she is the one who forced her to marry, not my father ... she was the first in school, but my mother insisted she get married. The first suitor who came she forced her to marry him. She said, if she does not marry him, she will not marry at all, she will not find someone better ... My sister was 15 when she married. (Hanan, GFG, G5, Grade 7)

The issues of marriage, especially early marriage, children, divorce, polygamy and physical abuse, were major areas of concern, particularly to females.[15] Generally speaking, the family is cited as simultaneously the source of protection and oppression for many of those who were inter-viewed. In some of the households, polygamy leads to various conflicts; incidents of physical abuse were mentioned by women and children. However, the family remains a strong institution, especially since the state does not provide social, economic and political protection to the individ-ual; thus the family is the primary institution to provide the individual with support. Children and young girls and boys living in such families point to the stepmother or the second wife as the major source of trouble. Fathers, especially in the opinion of young girls, are blamed for taking a second wife. Samar explains her situation:

My father is married to another woman, my mother does not live with us, he divorced her and she lives with her family. This happened around five years ago, our life is full of debts. Every month or two months we go to see my moth-er for a day or two. The new wife has two girls... There are many problems with my father's wife and us, we are four sisters and a boy from my mother and she has two girls, so we are eight. There is a lot of stress, so there is never time or place to study. My sister is older, she is supposed to be in Grade 9, but there was a problem with my father's wife and she quit school. My father got her applications so she can at least go to study as a beautician, but my father's wife refused to allow that. You know, she began telling my father: 'Don't send her, she will start going out with bad girls, etc.' So my sister gets bored at home and she is not happy. (Samar, GFG, G5, Grade 7)

Suad, a Grade 7 student in Marka, said:

My father's wife – whatever she wants, she gets. She hates it when she sees us sitting with our father by ourselves and we are very afraid of her. Sometimes we do not dare tell our father the problems. At school, there are problems... especially teachers who discriminate when dealing with the students. We feel very lonely, no one cares. (Suad, GFG, Grade 7)

Almost all the young girls interviewed opposed early marriage and were aware that it is related to economic factors. Early marriage is often prompted by problems in the family and as such it becomes an escape mechanism. A third reason is the social and cultural stress on families living in overcrowded conditions, where gossip and the question of honour are important. Consequently, to ensure that their daughters are saved any 'reputation' problem, some families prefer to marry them as early as possible, as Samira, a student in Grade 7, said:

The other thing is early marriage, there are many families who face this problem. Many girls would like to finish school, but their parents do not allow them to finish. Even parents who are educated. Maybe because they have many girls eight or 10, or the girl passed through some 'honour' thing, so they want to get rid of her, so they force her to marry early. (Samira, GFG, G5, Grade 7)

An important issue for the girls interviewed is gender discrimination. In families, males have more privileges in terms of education and movement. Generally, fathers have authority over their wives and brothers over their sisters, even when the latter might be older.

At home, there is discrimination between girls and boys. Boys can go any time with their friends and come back at any time, but girls cannot do that, they are forced to stay home... If I go out anywhere, it is only if my brothers take me to my uncle's house. Picnics? Maybe once a year, they do not let us go out, there are only centres for the young men, but nothing for us. (Fatima, GFG, G5, Grade 10)

Indeed, discrimination experienced by female children and young people does not only mean the inability to move around within and outside the camp, but also involves having to carry responsibilities at home that boys do not. Cleaning, cooking, tidying up, taking care of younger siblings and older members of the family usually falls on the shoulders of younger girls. Abeer's chores are common to other female children and young girls: 'The first thing I do when I return home from school is change my clothes and help my mother in the kitchen, I clean the house and then I study'. (Abeer, G5, Grade 8)

There is no one explanation for why females wear or do not wear the veil, also known as the 'Islamic dress'. In one of the informal meetings at the Women's Programme Centre, a discussion on what constitutes an 'Islamic dress' revealed different explanations. Some women pointed to poverty, since not wearing it implies having to wear different clothes. Others point to the need to assert an Arab-Islamic identity to counter what they perceive as an aggressive western cultural assault in the region. However, there are some women who chose to do so without family pressure. Younger girls interviewed also differed in their attitudes. Some said they were forced to wear it and that they hated it, others said they believed it is their religious duty to wear the veil, or because they wanted to emulate their peers. Abeer, for example, explains: "My mother tells me to wear the veil, but I do not want to. I began wearing it last year ... My mother told me I couldn't go anywhere if I did not veil... I still do not like to wear it, because my friends don't wear it". (Abeer, HH19, G5, F)

The interviews and narratives reveal that female children and young people are very critical of discrimination based on gender and portray a high level of awareness of social constraints and restrictions that apply to them but not to males. Amer says:

> In regards to women's work, she must work and help her husband. However, I will not allow my sister to work, but in general a woman may work [meaning if she is married]. I do not allow my sister to leave home unaccompanied, either I go with her or my mother. Alone she does not leave the house! (Amer, HH19, G5, M)

Physical Abuse and Humiliation

> As the saying goes: 'If you want to hit, make sure you hurt, and if you want to feed, make sure you satisfy the hunger.' Here [in the camp] we are hit and get hurt, and our hunger is not satisfied. (Nidal, BFG, G5, Grade 10)

Almost all the generations blame the 'reckless youth' and the 'gangs' who 'carry knives and razors' for spreading fear and anxiety in the camp. However, abuse is not confined to youth or to the streets and exists in some cases within homes and in schools. All generations, both males and females, pointed out that violence is a real problem in the camp and that the streets are no longer safe. Naji, a 17-year-old student, summarises the issue as follows:

Here one cannot live without the knife, but if you have one there is a problem and if you don't it is a problem too. If you have one and the police catches you, you go to prison for God knows how long. If you don't you may be attacked. These problems can start in grade 5 and up. (Naji, BFG, G5, Grade 10)

Incidents of physical abuse, however, are blamed exclusively on the younger generations, who are accused of fostering an environment of anxiety, even when such abuse is also inflicted by adults. As Latifa, in her forties, said:

The youth are unruly and carry razors… The other day one of the 'gangsters' poured gasoline on a bus and burnt it. He was the ticket controller in a bus. The owner of the bus told him, that he no longer has a job for him. So, during the night, the young man went to the bus and burnt it. Now we live in fear in the camp. The main reason for this behaviour is unemployment, because the young men study but do not work. (Latifa, HH19, G2, F)

At school, students are angered by the frequency of beatings and by the poor quality of teaching. Moreover, many of the students do not inform their parents or adult caregivers of these incidents, fearing that they will be blamed for inciting trouble.

I am 13, the X and Y teachers do not make us understand anything. The X teacher says a few words and spends most of the time beating the boys who are making trouble in the back … Once the teacher hit me on my back really bad, and nobody did anything. If I tell my parents I get another beating. I can't concentrate when the teacher beats me like that. The neighbours throw stones sometimes. (Mahmoud, BFG, Grade 7)

For younger boys, older boys may pose as sources either of support and protection – for example, older brothers and friends – or of physical abuse:

Sometimes there are younger boys playing in the playground, older boys come and they have with them knives and razors and they threaten the younger ones and they take them and force them to do things they don't want. The boys do not dare to say anything to their fathers, because they will beat them also. (Yousef, Grade 10)

Beating is not uncommon in schools and most teachers use sticks or their hands. When questioned on this issue, teachers complain that they can not control the large number of students, except if they use the stick. This view was also expressed in the study conducted in the West Bank and the Gaza Strip. When I met with teachers in several UNRWA schools, I was clearly told that teachers have 'no alternative'; in fact, one teacher commented: 'Look, we were beaten in school when we were young, but we are okay!' Moreover, teachers point out that some of the parents accuse them of being lax and careless if they do not exercise tough disciplinary measures, including using the stick. One parent commented: 'The teachers are not good; the kids run away and are loose. My generation when we went to school we used to know what school means... I think government schools are better than UNRWA in terms of teachers and curriculum'(Raed, HH4, G2, F).

Young girls especially encounter discrimination and humiliation in school, usually based on academic achievement, so that those who have difficulties encounter worse treatment than the 'good students'. In addition, there is discrimination in treatment among girls:

> We have many problems in school, the teachers hit us a lot and mostly because of homework and if we do not do it, they punish us by making us stand by the blackboard. Sometimes the girls who do not know how to read, instead of helping them and teaching them how to read, the teacher gives them a zero. The girls who did not do homework are also given zeroes ... This is the reason why the girls do not do well in school, when they do not do well, they tell the girls they are 'donkeys' and they pressure them a lot. The X teacher is very, very harsh on us, she keeps telling us we are 'lazy, bad and instigators.' Once X [teacher] told the teacher [another] that the 'shoes' we were wearing are like 'our faces'. The daughter of the X can wear anything she likes and she gets away with everything, but if we wear clothes that we are not supposed to, or, for example, use nail polish, or wear colourful scarves, they give us hell. (Nadia, GFG, G5, Grade 7)

Almost all the interviewees were critical of UNRWA's services, especially in regards to schools and health centres. This situation is particularly difficult for refugees from Gaza, who are not eligible for any of the government services and rely primarily on UNRWA to fulfil their basic needs. As Sumayya observes:

> To complicate matters UNRWA diminished its services and there is no medicine in the clinics. We are denied basic services [Gaza refugee] by both the government and UNRWA. (Sumayya, HH12, G2, F)

The Future

Like all children and young people in the world, Palestinian refugee children dream of what they want to be and aspire for a brighter life than their parents were able to offer them. Yet, very few children expressed hope in future prospects, including their political future. Almost all the students doubted that the Oslo peace process, for example, would result in anything positive for them. Similarly, they did not believe that education would give them an advantage in terms of finding better jobs. In fact, children look around them and realise that unemployment levels are high and employment markets are limited.

> Teaching began to deteriorate in 1985 onwards. The economic situation became worse after that. If someone finished *Tawjihi* [General Secondary Education Certificate Examination] and his financial situation is bad, he can't go on to university anyway ... People think 'I will work for 80 dinars after I finish school, which is better than going for four or five years to university for nothing.' Even university graduates can't find jobs and it is worse for college graduates. (Ahmad, HH15, G2, M)

Therefore, many of the young people opt to stay at home, rather than spend a whole day working for so little. As far as the adults and care-givers are concerned, 'sitting at home' provided a great deal of 'free time', which lures the youth into 'all sorts of trouble'. The 'trouble' described includes the use of alcohol, drugs, smoking, sniffing glue and fighting.

Intergenerational Dialogue and Discord

The older generations think of children, young people and youth as being on the 'loose' and 'disrespectful' and point to a time when children obeyed their elders 'without question'. This applies to both males and females. The disagreements between the generations also emerge between young married women and in-laws with whom they often have to live, because they can't afford to live autonomously. However, younger women no longer believe that this is something they should do out of 'tradition,' as their mothers and grandmothers did. In the experience of the older generations, everyone worked on the land, including children and young people. As Imm Kamel puts it:

> In the past, the young used to respect their elders and to take them into account. Today they answer back rudely to their fathers... Now I worry for my children and I am scared when my son goes out... my daughters go out to visit their sister and only people that I know and like, because girls influence each other and can have negative influence on each other. (Imm Kamel, HH4, G1, M)

Similarly, Zahiyyah said:

> The youth of the past worked and were not familiar with 'unemployment'... Also, a son used to obey not only his father, but also his neighbour. Today, all the youth care about is clothes, perfumes, walking in the streets, carrying knives. These days, a person is a hero who dares to speak to his son or daughter

[meaning parents no longer have authority over their children]. The reason for all this is the absence of religion, lack of work and they are influenced by the things they see on television. (Zahiyyah, HH7, G1, F)

Indeed, Zahiyyah was not the only one who commented on the effect of the television on children and young people. Most of the interviews exposed ambivalence towards television programmes. On the one hand, parents and adults use the television as a lure to keep their children away from the streets; on the other hand, they worry that it is teaching their children 'corruption' and 'immorality'.

For their part, the younger generations feel isolated and have little to share with the older generations, except their refugee status. Children are constantly reminded of how their elder brothers, parents and grandparents suffered and struggled. From their parents or elder siblings they hear how the generations before them were able to make leaps in educational standards, despite the destitution of the first years of exile. Older siblings also have heroic stories to tell of a different political era, when the *fedayeen* (freedom fighters) carried guns and participated in battles for liberation. Thus, it is not surprising that the fourth and fifth generations refer to the camp as the 'forgotten village', reflecting their sense of isolation and marginalisation.

In the case of the first three generations, the gap was bridged by the shared experiences of displacement and the resistance movement. In other words, a 60-year-old man or woman could find a common platform and a dialogue based on the notions of exile and return with a son or even a grandchild of 20 years, who in the older generation's view was redeeming 'home' and 'Homeland'.

However, a discord is developing between the older generations and today's children and young people. In a manner of speaking, these younger generations have nothing to show for in the present: neither do they have a future through education that will eventually contribute to their households economically and socially; nor are they part of a larger Palestinian liberation movement. Moreover, they are not the children of the *Intifada*, who acquired heroic stature in Palestinian society; rather, they seem like their invisible and unrecognised shadow across the border, strongly linked, but unable to participate or support the way they would like to. Similarly, most of the children can not turn to their parents for support. Hence, the blame is directed both ways across the generations. As Jameel puts it:

The main problems we face is that parents do not take care of the adolescents and they do not understand their psychological needs and the developments they pass through... they are removed from the son or daughter. (Jameel Al-Rihani, HH2, G5, M)

Thus, children and young people are seeking a niche, a status and a role for themselves in society. This struggle for a social and physical space involves the creative appropriation of multiple discourses from their milieu. Children and young people today are creatively reshaping Palestinian culture, society and identity as they select and discard from a range of ideas, social practices and political and religious ideologies. These discourses cover Islam, nationalism and modernist visions of society. They critically engage ideas that flow from the television, from NGOs, state activities and policies, as well as from their local networks and their families and community.

More importantly, children and young people do not always see these notions as contradictory, between going to the mosque and praying on Fridays, for example, and using the mosque as a place to hide and secretly engage in all the things that adolescents like to do, such as talking about the recent events of the *Intifada*, and the girls down the street. Young girls also are critical and engage in 'local rebellion', such as resisting early marriage, wearing or not wearing the veil, but also speaking out about their rights to work, education and legal status. Children and young people, in other words, have their own way of living, acting upon and interpreting society and never passively or uncritically integrate these into their practices.

On another level, the very notion of stages in development, such as the categories 'adolescents', 'youth' and 'children' have become more prevalent in the camp, primarily due to the activities of international NGOs and state programmes. Indeed, an 'adolescent' category is meaningless for most of the younger generations, simply because they do not respond to the kinds of responsibilities or privileges associated with these categories in their lives. Similarly, for the older generations, these neatly organised stages did not exist. Yet, today, children and young people refer to these to claim their rights and they are not seen as contradictory to 'Islamic' or local ideals, but are being appropriated in ways that may benefit the community and its various interest groups.

It is probably safe to suggest that children and young people are viewed as anomalies that do not fit into local conceptions and categories, or for that matter, in society at large. As refugees, they are 'borderless' with no territory or state; as children and young people, they are also without borders in that they are neither 'dependent children' nor 'adults'. For the older generation, an 'adult' male was defined as such when he married, worked or joined the resistance movement. For females, marriage marked the transition from childhood to adulthood. Therefore, when 'children' or 'adolescents' cannot marry due to poverty, are unable to work due to unemployment or cannot join in the political struggle to liberate the land, they become 'undefined', and, in the view of the older generations, 'dangerously loose'. Thus, most adults complain that they are a group that need to be 'restrained' and – the Arabic word is symbolic in this context – *yindhabbu*, literally meaning 'brought into a physical place, usually the home'.

Maher also feels that the older generation is dangerously distant from them and is trying to keep control:

> The main problem facing adolescents is the lack of freedom to express one's opinion. Parents must allow the youth to express themselves and not to pressure them too much or to constantly place them under surveillance to a point that suffocates them, a person feels under constant observance. (Maher, HH3, G5, M)

It was noted earlier that discriminatory government policies and social practices entrench segregation and solidify the Palestinian–Jordanian boundaries. Equally important are radical political events and the eruption of conflict, which may have the effect of a lit match on dry land. This was the case during the *Intifada* in 1987 and today, as *al-Aqsa Intifada* spreads and Israel is reoccupying the West Bank and Gaza, refugee children and young people in exile have responded with a resurgence of empathy and anger.

Al-Aqsa Intifada

> Now when I watch the *Intifada* I want to cry and I think what can I do to help? If I could I would go there and fight ... I always say, let me just go for a week and see what I can do!!! I love and wish I could live in Palestine, in our country and among our people ... Even from here, our voices cannot reach them ... A month ago, all our relatives were hurt in one way or the other by what is happening there, I say to myself, there they do not eat for certain [they have no food]. Even the little children, they are scared ... Here, all of us are very sad. I was thinking, why don't we ignite an *Intifada* here in the camp? ... We are always switching from one channel to another... Sometimes you see us laugh, but inside we have deep sadness ... We always dream of returning to our Homeland ... Even little children now talk about Palestine all the time. Young children now feel for the children who are just like them and are being wounded. These days they sit in front of the TV to watch news on the *Intifada* instead of playing. (Suad, G5, F, 18 y.o.)

Television has become commonplace in refugee camps and a few families bought satellite dishes, the acquisition of which seemed to increase following the outbreak of the *Intifada*. Latifa says proudly:

> I always tell my children about Palestine, sometimes we discuss things and they tell me, we want to go to Palestine and carry stones ... we always follow the news, but the negotiations [Oslo] are useless ... we need an *Intifada*. (Latifa, HH19, G2, F)

Children and young people were particularly affected by *al-Aqsa Intifada*. Many of the victims of Israeli gunfire and bombing are children like themselves, some are village kin, relatives, or former neighbours; they see them being killed, throwing stones and protesting against a very powerful enemy that is armed with Apache helicopters, F-16 fighter planes and huge tanks. Consequently, it is not surprising that the *Intifada* in many ways speaks directly to them. At the girls' school in the camp, students held a strike against the administration and requested that a whole day be spent in remembrance of Muhammad al-Durrah, the 12-year-old boy who was shot in his father's lap. The administration agreed and the students held an exhibition of their writings, drawings and artistic work, which reflected how deeply the uprising affected them.

All the interviews with children and youth following *al-Aqsa Intifada* included feelings and interpretations like those of Suad, quoted above. In their narratives and drawings children portray images of death and resistance, ways of coping with danger and fear. The channels through which they express their views and feelings grant culturally significant meanings to the loss of life experienced so deeply at the community level. The idea of 'martyrdom' appears in the children's narratives, drawings and writings, a word that dignifies and bestows respect to those who were killed by the Israelis. Moreover, the word 'martyr' promotes the sharing of suffering experienced by the bereaved family at the community level, thereby easing the pain of parents and loved ones, by endowing death with a spiritual and religious dimension.

In coping with the *Intifada*, children and young people found ways to express their anger against repression and also their fears. They wanted to participate even within the confined spaces of the camp and hence in the small playgrounds of schools students refused to go to classes, unless they could dedicate a day for Palestine. Children's strategies for coping include resourcing available structures, such as they use to cope with the horrific events in the West Bank and Gaza. These strategies will be briefly overviewed in the next section.

Coping Mechanisms

Different Forms of Resistance

In our Homeland, twenty people shared one gun [they were disarmed by the British mandate and it was difficult to acquire weapons]. They used to fight with sticks ... How can we fight artillery or a tanker with a stick? Palestinians had no weapons. Israel is only a servant for America, America is the real occupier and the Israelis are servants of America. (Imm Awni, HH15, G1, F)

During the 1948 war, villagers tried to resist the armed attacks on their villages, even when the few and old weapons they owned were incapable of defeating the Zionist militias. When they failed to hold on to their land they were forced to flee in order to survive. Once in exile, they utilised different strategies to cope with displacement, such as joining the liberation movement. Equally important was the reproduction of a Palestinian identity to counter the Israeli policies of negation and the attempt to deny them a past in their land. Mahmoud, eager to show us how he held on to his land, brings the land deeds he had kept safely and says:

> I used to draw maps on the ground to show them [his children] where their original village is ... We are willing to die for Palestine ... especially during the *Intifada*. (HH17, G1, M)

The Extended Family

> I was three years old when my father remarried. When I was young I used to have a peddler's cart, which I used to sell ice cream. I made anywhere between one to one and a half-pence a day. My mother used to work in the fields so that she also could bring in some money to spend on the house... I struggled until I graduated and was the first in my class. (Hassan, HH11, G3, M)

The extended family is an institution that helped Palestinians cope with displacement. Children and young people helped in contributing to the household income and women played an important role in assisting the family to survive the trajectories of exile. The extended family provides refuge for those who are disadvantaged in society, such as the disabled, divorced women and orphans. Children and young people seek family members when in trouble. For example, many sleep over at their grandparents' house or another relative when there are problems at home.

Early marriage, though a source of stress for young females, is in many cases a form of coping, when young girls seek to escape from an oppressive family, as Fawziyyeh did: 'I accepted to marry him, although I did not know him, due to the difficult conditions we had in our house' (Fawziyyeh, HH8, G3, F).

Peer Support and Social Networks

> Sometimes I go to my friend, we bring books for the *tawjihi* class and discuss them [some students cannot afford to buy the books so they meet and help each other]. (Odeh, HH4, G5, M)

Rawan also says:

> I began talking to my girlfriend, who has a similar problem and whose father is also going to get re-married, and sharing my problems with her helped me. My girlfriend ran away from her home and went to her grandparents' house, she said she did not want her family anymore. (Rawan, HH8, G5, F)

Peer support is one of the most important factors that helps children cope. As refugees, they encounter similar problems at home, school and in society. When they face problems at home, such as in cases of divorce or polygamy, they cannot resort to the family and their peers become their solace, listening and sharing their problems and often providing them with advice. In school, peers get together either to deal with other students or to deal with the school staff. Again, within the camp and in the streets, they form networks of friendship and call upon each other in times of trouble.

Peer groups and friendships provide children and young people with a sense of strength, a feeling that they are not alone, and represent nodes or referral points upon which they develop their sense of self and identity. Within the peer group, children share resources and, in some cases, the peer group is the only network of support and comfort. There are several peer groups, many of them interact with one another:

> We put together a football team in our neighbourhood and we play with another team at the end of the camp ... if they win we bring them a medal, and if we win they give us one. (Odeh, HH4, G5, M)

Religion

> I used to give birth without anyone's help. I used to cut the umbilical cord and tie it in a knot, then get up and cook and bake ... God helped me, God was the doctor. (Imm Awni, G1, F, HH15)

> I go to the Islamic Centre for the Orphans; I go there every Wednesday and Sunday, they teach us Koran and Hadith, from nine to 11. Sometimes they take us on trips, Jarash and Aqaba. (Awni, BFG, Grade 7)

Religion is a resort and source of comfort to many of the refugees of all generations. Praying, going to the mosque or attending religion classes emerged in the interviews as sources that provide them with comfort, hope and a social occasion where they can meet friends and catch up on recent news. Some of the Islamic organisations offer material support and services, which are important at a time when UNRWA's services have deteriorated. In light of *al-Aqsa Intifada* and the killing of so many children and young people, some children turn to religion in order to cope with the traumatising experiences.

Physical Strength

This applies mainly to male children, who emphasised that they need to protect themselves either by carrying knives or by physical strength. Samer is encouraged by his father to learn street fighting to defend himself:

> I am 16 in grade 10; there are many problems in the camp. My father is capable and comfortable [materially], but because there are so many problems in the camp, he wants to teach me how to street fight. (Samer, BFG, G5, Grade 10)

Physical strength also allows the older boys to protect their younger siblings in school and in the streets. For girls, rather than physical strength, coping often means having the ability to verbally 'answer back', stand up for oneself.

Severing Relations or Avoidance

> I do not like to interfere [in the sense of having close relations] with the neighbours. (Imm Khaled, HH4, G1, F)

> I ignore the person who takes drugs as the saying goes: '*Ibi'd 'an al-sharr we-ghannilu*' [meaning stay away from trouble]. (Bashir, HH4, G4, M)

This strategy is used to avoid problems (this is particularly the case with families that have young unmarried girls, where the neighbours have young men). It also applies to younger women and men who said they avoid the 'hooligans'. Avoidance is an important strategy in overcrowded places. Therefore, to achieve some level of distance, families often cut themselves off, thereby avoiding constant interference and visits from neighbours.

Conclusion: Children and Adolescents as Agents

Displacement, poverty and the sense of imprisonment in the confined spaces of the camp have led many children and youth to feel their camps are 'places of misery'. Yet, they challenge the social, political and physical structures – the family, school authority, the state and their marginalisation – and carve out spaces as their own. Most importantly, they are not passive recipients in history, rather they creatively appropriate and discard from the multitude of discourses around them, thereby contributing to the reproduction of Palestinian identity and culture. Palestinian refugee children are not victims of 'brainwashing' by Islamicist groups, as the Western media portrays them, rather they mix and integrate, reject and reproduce, reinvent and reshape ideas and social norms.

Children and young people challenge the physical and social confines of their space and reinscribe them as their own, including the formation of informal networks, which allocate areas where they play, fight and forge friendships. As they seek spaces, they sometimes have to challenge regulations, for example, climbing over school walls when authorities are not around to have a soccer match or fighting with another group for space. School staff comment that their authority is slowly being undermined by students who 'answer back.' They also find corners in camps, where they engage in 'clandestine' relations, revealing that females are also engaged in challenging authority and 'tradition': "Once there was a small alleyway near our neighbour's house, there were three boys and three girls, they were kissing and doing things like that" (Nader, BFG, Grade 10).

The education system is an important issue that emerged, primarily the inability of children and young people to acquire proper education, including knowledge of their own past and refugee trajectories. The knowledge of one's past is important and will enable children and young people to participate more fully in society and as equal members who have a right to a past. In previous decades, education was a form of coping strategy and children worked hard to acquire degrees so that they could redeem both the nation politically, and the family economically. Today, the political crisis in Palestine and the economic depression in the region has reduced the significance of education as a strategy of coping and resisting marginalisation.

Displacement from the land and the 'peasant way of life' meant that the older generations can neither pass on their agricultural skills, nor can they pass on the land to their children. In fact, the generations born after *al-Nakba*, instead of inheriting the land from their parents, found themselves in a position where they had to actually redeem the household from poverty and destitution. While patriarchy is prevalent, children do not 'fear and obey' their elders the way their parents and grandparents claim they did.

Finally, processes of change in social and cultural norms intensify when communities are suddenly uprooted. The new host society and urban setting in Jordan allowed for modernist concepts to be disseminated publicly: in schools, the media and not least by international organisations implementing programmes based on targeted segments of the population, such as 'women', 'children' and 'adolescents', which has an impact on world views and local discourses. However, this is occurring in a society that does not have modernist institutions and that cannot fulfil the promises made to children and youth, whom they address as the 'future of the nation'. Poverty and lack of opportunities and political disenfranchisement continue to afflict refugees.

Perhaps more significant is the political impasse, which Palestinian refugees have lived with for over half a century. On the one hand, they hold on to their political and legal rights as declared in UN General Assembly Resolution 194 (III), which calls for their right of return to their homes, compensation and restitution; simultaneously, they seek ways to improve their daily social, legal and economic lives in host countries. This in summary has been the struggle of refugees in exile, including children and young people. Tragically, as is the case in the West Bank and Gaza, their struggle can lead to violence and death by more powerful actors. Yet, what is important to highlight is that neither geographical nor generational distance from Palestine leads to the disappearance of the 'refugee problem' and their integration in host societies. To use Sayigh's (1994) title, they have 'too many enemies!'

Notes

1 Special thanks to the research team members for assisting in the project, namely, Suzan al-Salhi, Hassan Mohammad, Jihad Ghosheh, Yousef, Basima and Susanne. I am also grateful to many of the UNRWA staff who extended their assistance and support. In particular, I would like to thank Maha Abdel-Hamid Rantissi, Matar Saqer, Randa Halaweh and Fuad al-Shawwa. I am especially grateful to Suzan al-Salhi for her special contribution during the last phase of the research and her invaluable assistance in interviews and the transcription of tapes.

2 The terms 'child' and 'adolescent' are used in this chapter to correspond to the title of the book. However, in Palestinian society, as is the case in many other societies, human development stages are linked to social and economic responsibilities and not to age.

3 The chapter builds on several years of research (1994–9) during which time I was conducting fieldwork in Palestinian refugee camps on popular memory and reconstructions of Palestinian identity for my Ph.D. thesis. The thesis relied on the life histories and oral narratives of three generations of refugees, both as a methodological approach and an object of study.

4 This figure excludes Palestinians who are not registered with UNRWA. According to official Jordanian figures cited in Zureik (1996), the number of Displaced Persons in 1994 who were not registered with UNRWA totalled 500,417 persons and the number of Displaced Persons carrying Israeli permits – a category referred to as 'Latecomers' – totalled 88,211, while deportees were estimated at 12,500. Again this figure excludes Palestinians who did not register with the Agency and are not regarded as displaced (Zureik 1996: 23).

5 This figure excludes those who sought refuge in the West Bank and Gaza.

6 Al-Karameh was the first time that an organised Palestinian resistance movement, with some help from the Jordanian army, clashed with the Israeli

army. Although the Palestinians were defeated, their ability to fight and inflict losses on the enemy boosted morale among Palestinians and in the Arab world, especially since it closely followed the Arab defeat in 1967.

7 For example, Bocco (2002).

8 The titles were translated by the author. The annotated bibliography mentioned by Ahmed Abdel-Hamid Adawi is found in *Majallat al-Shu'oun al-Ijtima'iyyah* (1995), 46: 207.

9 Marka camp is also known as Hitteen or Schneller. The latter name is used by the older generation and refers to the man who funded the Schneller rehabilitation school in the area.

10 Some of UNRWA's figures show a total of 65,000 people, 50,000 of whom are registered; however, this figure includes people who live around and near the camp, rather than inside, but they utilise UNRWA's services in the camp.

11 Ajjur, or Ajjour, al-Dawayimah and Dayr al-Nakhass are villages that were destroyed and depopulated as a result of the 1948 war. They belonged to the Hebron district. Beer al-Sabe' is the Arabic word for Beer Sheba in al-Naqab or Negev.

12 For more on this topic see Farah (1997).

13 Deir Yassin is a village in the district of Jerusalem, whose civilian inhabitants were massacred on 9 April 1948 by the Zionist Jewish paramilitary organisations, the Haganah, the Irgun and the Stern. Among the leaders of the latter two militia organisations were the former Prime Ministers of Israel, Menachim Begin and Yitzhak Shamir.

14 See also Sayigh (1979) on how the first generation of refugees in Lebanon compared and contrasted their present lives to their original homes, villages and towns.

15 In this research, 'physical abuse' is used as a general term that includes beating, physical fights and sexual abuse.

References

Bocco, R. 2002. *Le Royaume Hechémite de Jordanie 1946–1996: Identités socials, politiques de développement et construction étatique*. Paris, Karthala: Amman et Beyrouth, CERMOC.

Brand, L. 1995. 'Palestinians and Jordanians: A crisis of identity'. *Journal of Palestine Studies*, 24(4): 46–72.

Farah, R. 1997. 'Crossing Boundaries: Reconstructions of Palestinian Identities in al-Baq'a Refugee Camp, Jordan'. In R. Bocco, B. Destremeau and J. Hannoyer (eds), *Palestine, Palestiniens: Territoire national, espaces communautaires*. pp. 259–99. Amman and Beirut: CERMOC.

——— 2000. *A Report on the Psychological Effects of Overcrowding in Refugee Camps in the West Bank and Gaza Strip*. Paper prepared for the Expert and Advisory Services Fund, International Development Research Centre (IDRC), available on http://www.arts.mcgill.ca/MEPP/PRRN/farah.html

Mrayyan, N. 1994. 'The economic impact of the Gulf Crisis in Jordan'. In S. Shami (ed.), *Population Displacement and Resettlement: Development and Conflict in the Middle East*. pp. 234–5 New York: Centre for Migration Studies.

Sayigh, R. 1979. *Palestinians: From Peasants to Revolutionaries*. London: Zed.

——— 1994. *Too Many Enemies: The Palestinian Experience in Lebanon*. London: Zed.

Takkenberg, L. 1998. *The Status of Palestinian Refugees in International Law*. Oxford: Clarendon Press.

UNRWA 2000. *Report of the Commissioner-General of the United Nations Relief and Works Agency for Palestine Refugees in the Near East, 1 July 1999–30 June 2000,* General Assembly, Official Records, Fifty-fifth session, Supplement No. 13 (A/55/13).

——— 2003. *Jordan Refugee Camp Profiles,* http://www.un.org/unrwa/refugees/jordan.html

Zureik, E. 1996. *Palestinian Refugees and the Peace Process.* Washington, D.C.: Institute of Palestine Studies.

5

Palestinian Refugee Children and Caregivers in the West Bank

Salah Alzaroo

Salah Alzaroo

I was born in Hebron. I was 6 years old when the June 1967 war started. My family decided to flee to Jordan and on the way I saw military operations and some of the consequences of war: the dead bodies spread in the roads and the fields. It was the most devastating experience of my childhood. Six months after the war, my father decided to bring us back to Hebron. The economic situation was very difficult and people had nothing to feed themselves. I became a street pedlar selling sweets, bread and beans and, as a consequence, I became famil- iar with every street and corner of my city, Hebron. I enjoyed my elementary education in my beloved Osameh Elementary School, which was later occupied by Israeli settlers and became a settlement in the heart of the Palestinian popu- lation in the city.

It was not easy for me to see the settlers invading the city, occupying its heart and swallowing it up piece by piece. As a child, I was not able to understand why the settlers, strange in both their clothes and attitudes, behaved in very nasty ways. The religious and historical explanations that I heard from the adults did not make sense to me. I was witnessing daily the settlers' harassment of my people: they used to put road blocks to disturb normal Palestinian life, shoot at roof-top water heaters, burn cars, smash windows, destroy crops and uproot trees, harass merchants and owners of the grocery stalls in Hebron mar- ket, and attack olive pickers in their fields, killing and wounding them, stealing their crops and destroying their trees. It was clear to everybody, including me, what the aims of the settlers were.

After finishing my school education in Hebron in 1979, I went to Jordan, entered the University of Jordan in Amman and finished my BSc in Political Science and Economics in 1982. I came back to the West Bank in 1984 and found myself in an Israeli detention centre because I had been active in the university student union. They arrested me late at night. During the interrogation period my hands were tied up and cuffed painfully, and my head was covered with a sack. They forced me to stand in painful positions for prolonged periods, to stay awake for many nights, they splashed cold water on me in very cold weather, and they pushed my head in the toilet bowl and flushed it. In addition, there were the beatings, the death threats, the cursing and the degradation. This period was a severe assault on my dignity and my humanity.

Despite that, I never thought of revenge. I always felt that the only way out of this disastrous situation was through dialogue and peace. However, believing in peace does not mean that we should give up our rights, accept injustice or stand powerless without being able to protect our women and children and above all our humanity.

When I got out of detention, I worked for the Palestinian Polytechnic University as a lecturer, researcher and director of its Department of Continuing Education. During this period, I published many books and papers and organised community-based courses and outreach activities. In 1994 I was awarded a British Council scholarship to study at the University of Warwick for an MA in Continuing Comparative Education. I completed this and then went on to complete a Ph.D. on the role of nonformal education in Palestine. During this time, I worked as a Research Fellow on an EC-funded regional network in the area of reproductive health. In 1998 I returned to Palestine and the Department of Continuing Education. Since 2000 I have been seconded to work as the Vocational Training Senior Officer within the Ministry of Labour of the Palestinian Authority.

> I wish peace would spread all over the world not only between leaders but also between nations. I wish there were no wars or deception. I wish there were good leaders. I was wondering how we are going to live in a just world without having honest leaders.
>
> Palestinian girl, 19 years old, al-Aroub refugee camp

This chapter focuses on the impact of prolonged conflict and forced migrations on the young Palestinian refugees who live in the West Bank. The research team[1] conducted this study in al-Fawwar and al-Aroub refugee camps. The research sample comprises forty interviewees from thirteen households, of whom seven are from al-Fawwar refugee camp and six are from al-Aroub refugee camp.

Life in Palestine before 1948

Most of our interviewees fled from southern Palestine, and the majority of them were living in rural areas and working in agriculture in Palestine. Their lifestyle was very simple and traditional. An elderly man from al-Aroub camp said:

> We were shepherds, we ploughed, harvested, threshed wheat and picked olives. We were farmers. We didn't plant grapes, we planted barley, corn and

wheat. God blesses these three seeds. There was milk, yoghurt, oil and cheese. I was taught by a person who used to receive an amount of corn or wheat in return for teaching me. There was no money. We used to exchange wheat, corn and barley. (HH10, G1, M)

Ajour was big, the population was 10,000. It had a school till the 7th grade. There were 18 families in Ajour and 18 *Mokhtars*. Land was divided into 18 parts and each *Mokhtar* used to divide the land for the members of his family. It was similar to socialism. The one who is born gets land and the ownership stopped when he died. The wife got a share of the land if she married in Ajour but she didn't get a share if she married outside of Ajour, that's why people preferred to marry off their daughters in Ajour and polygamy was common. (HH3, G1, M)

The Journey into Exile

The refugee family was transplanted from their original context to a new and unknown setting, resulting in a state of continued vulnerability. The journey usually took them through several places until they reached the camp, and some families experienced years of displacement. A first-generation male from al-Fawwar camp said:

> I lived with 200 people. I was 20 years old. At 10 o'clock Jews entered and occupied the village, the girls and boys were at school. At night they hit a lot of people. They used to threaten us with shooting if we stayed. The second night more were beaten and threatened. So people went to the Red Cross and asked to leave because Jews wanted to kill us and there was no security. The driver asked us to load up everything in the car then tied it up with a rope and I left with two elderly women. After one month, people left Tarqumi and we left to Loza ruins. Then we went to Alsafla well camp and Ezn. Then UNRWA moved us to al-Fawwar and we lived in tents until 1958. Then they built houses for us... Our property remained in al-Falujeh. My family left everything behind. They only carried some blankets on two donkeys. and we left in October. It was cold. We took our herds with us then we sold them to get money. The first years were very difficult and people sold what they had. There was water in al-Aroub and a spring in al-Fawwar. That is why they chose these two areas to put people. We were subjected to false propaganda that we were going to return to our villages. (HH2, G1, M)

The first and second generations of Palestinian refugees are strongly affected by moving from their place of origin to their place of exile. The separation from their natural environment and from their relatives is an emotional burden they all share. They are affected by the violence they and their families have been exposed to, the deep mourning they and their parents felt when leaving everything they ever loved, and the difficulties they faced in the new situation they have been forced to escape to. Not surprisingly, all the first-generation interviewees mentioned the 1948 emigration as the most difficult and painful experience they had ever had. A first-generation woman from al-Fawwar camp stated:

> In 1948 the village was without weapons. The people of Zakaria and Tel Alsafi left at the time the Deir Yassin massacre happened. People slept two nights in the mountain. Jews entered with tanks. They killed a mother and her blind son. They killed her behind her house. My family left to Deir Nakhas and they slept under an olive tree. Then Jews occupied Beit Jebreen and Deir Nakhas so they left to Ezn village. We lived in an orchard under the trees for five or six days. Then we went to al-Rihia village and lived in a cave for 10 years. It was damp and without water. Then the Red Cross gave us a tent and we lived in it for two months till we were given a house with two rooms. (HH1, G1, F)

A third-generation woman from al-Aroub camp stated:

> We opened our eyes to misery and disaster in 1948. We used to play in our childhood, but all our life we have remained refugees. We have been suffering since 1948. We have spent our life talking about our homeland, which we miss and will never forget. (HH11, G3, F)

The second generation have witnessed the 1956 and 1967 wars, the Israeli occupation, and the first *Intifada* (1987–94). Therefore, many of them became politicised and frustrated. In fact, until the beginning of *al-Aqsa Intifada*, the third generation showed little interest in politics but this situation subsequently changed dramatically. In general, children and young people who have had one or more of their family killed or injured during the confrontations with the Israelis show more interest in politics. A first-generation woman from al-Aroub camp said:

> During the 1967 war we were in Jordan, living with my brothers. I have seen the effects of the 1967 war. It was a big shock. I witnessed the displacement of thousands of Palestinians. I couldn't believe what I saw. We used to listen to the radio. On the third day people from Jericho arrived in Amman. They crossed the border by foot and they told us what had happened. It was a very hard time. (HH11, G1, F)

A second-generation woman from al-Aroub camp stated:

> I was young when I participated in the *Intifada* [the first *Intifada*], then I became afraid of it. My brother Ameen was imprisoned administratively three times and my eldest brother was imprisoned before the *Intifada*. They came at night to arrest Ameen. He was held in Alnaqab and in al-Dahariya prisons. We used to visit him there. We were very happy to see him but troubled by the bars that separated us. My mother used to spend the whole visit crying. Visits to

Alnaqab prison were forbidden but my mother used to send him letters. (HH9, G2, F)

A third-generation woman from al-Fawwar camp said:

My two uncles have been in prison for a long time. My uncle Ismail has been there for three years and he is suffering from kidney problems so he only eats brown bread. My uncle Arafat became psychologically sick. I used to visit my father during his arrest in Hebron prison with my mother. Once, after I had been screaming, my mother pleaded with the soldiers to let me take cigarettes to him. So they allowed me to stand for a couple of minutes inside the prison gate. They called me 'Handbag' because I was always with my mother. (HH2, G3, F)

Life in the Camp

For children born in the camps, the world of the refugee camp may be the only world with which they are intimately familiar. Many of the refugee children stressed that they felt safe inside the camp. A young girl from al-Fawwar camp said:

My family is here. The camp is better than many places. It is safer and there is no crime here. People's relations are normal but my mother says it was better in the past. When I visit my brother in prison, I feel that I am not living. I see all the beautiful places on the road. It is better than here with a lot of green areas. I know the camp is not my place but I belong to it. (HH3, G3, F)

Many interviewees considered their relationships inside the camp to be excellent. They thought that social relations between people were positive and intimate: for example, nobody attacked anybody, they shared food and there were few differences between people of different origins. Nevertheless, the narrow streets of the camp and the overcrowding was felt to be a major problem – they felt there was no space to breathe. A second-generation man from al-Aroub camp stated:

People's relationships are very good. We are the only family from Iraq al-Mashiah in our neighbourhood and there are ten different families but thank God nobody ever hurt anybody. Once a bad person needed blood because he had been in an accident but everybody went to donate blood for him. This camp has a large number of institutions. A youth club was formed here. I don't wish to go out of the camp unless to go back to Iraq al-Mashiah. We own land in Hebron. We visit it occasionally. We can build a house in Hebron, but we don't want to because the people here are compassionate and co-operative. (HH4, G2, M)

People inside the camp reported that they had learned how to live together despite the difficulties they experienced, such as water shortages, destroyed streets and infrastructure, problems of sewage and rubbish disposal, overcrowding and the absence of entertainment facilities. A second-generation woman from al-Aroub camp said:

> Overcrowding makes us very close to each other. Sometimes I listen to the neighbour's radio and I ask them to turn the volume up. Sometimes I smell the food at our neighbours and we share it. But when a problem occurs, we hear them shouting in their homes. The most important problem is the size of the place. Children can't play. People ask their neighbours to keep their children at home. There are problems of transport inside the camp and a shortage of water. People who live inside the camp are forced to walk because there is no transport inside the camp. (HH9, G2, F)

A first-generation man from al-Aroub said:

> I don't like the camp at all. There is no social security. My wife and I are very old and there is no proper health care. The clinic doesn't give us what is necessary. There is no government, no sewage facilities, a lot of insects and a shortage of water. Nothing is good although people are good to each other at weddings and funerals. (HH13, G1, M)

Almost all the children had been born in the camp, although some of them had had to confront death before understanding what life is. These losses affected the children in different ways and degrees depending on their age. A young girl from al-Fawwar camp said:

> A lot of journalists came to our house. I came back home with my uncle. My friends said: 'Why are you not crying? Your brother has died as a martyr.' I didn't know what 'martyr' meant. I went home, my aunt was crying, and I knew that he had died. I cried and my mother cried. My father was in prison then. (HH3, G3, F)

Most of the refugee children had experienced discrimination either through being refugees or through being female. Some of the children had noticed how some people outside the camp treated them. Sometimes neighbours and/or schoolteachers outside the camp treated them badly and they were unable to understand why. This feeling of discrimination has been passed from generation to generation and has become very rooted. Some mentioned that teachers discriminated against girls in school; many teachers swore at girls and called them idiots. A second-generation woman from al-Fawwar camp said:

> Girls in the camp are oppressed. Nobody asks their opinion about their life. I know about girls being forced to marry their husbands without their opinion being asked. (HH6, G2, F)

Many interviewees said that they sensed the discrimination against them when they went outside the camp; for instance, when a girl married someone outside the camp and when young girls went to schools outside the camp.

Many interviewees accused teachers of being discriminatory when dealing with students. They mentioned that teachers blamed students from the camp for making mistakes and they discriminated in their marking of work in favour of the non-refugees. Many young interviewees wished that their teachers were less aggressive and that they wouldn't discriminate between students because of their place of residence or status.

Many interviewees mentioned the lack of ownership of property in the camp and how this affected their image, and some referred to discrimination by other resident Palestinians against refugees. An elderly man from al-Aroub camp said:

> If I want a loan from the bank, I need to provide security in the form of property. We don't own anything. We don't have any land. Today, we don't even have any dignity which is perhaps more important than anything. The people of Hebron used to say, "your face is like the face of a refugee." We call ourselves 'gypsies' because we don't have any property or land and we don't have dignity. (HH10, G1, M)

Many of the children emphasised that violence is very common at school. A young male student from al-Fawwar camp said:

> My father sent me to school but I made a mistake in the alphabet and the teacher hit me so I ran away and never returned. Once I couldn't memorise a verse so the teacher hit me with a pipe which had a piece of metal inside it. I was very angry at the teacher. (HH5, G3, M)

A young girl from al-Fawwar camp shared her experience as follows:

> I don't like the teachers in the school. They are biased. For instance, nominations for trips to America and France are always given to the teachers' children. I used to be in section A in school, but I was moved from my section because I got a higher mark than a teacher's daughter. They wanted her to be the top of the class. I refused the transfer. My Aunt and the officer of the camp tried to intervene but the head teacher insisted on transferring me. She expelled me from class because I held her hand when she tried to slap me. She said I am impolite and I should go home. I stayed at home for a couple of days. Then the

head teacher said I would stay in section B for only a week but I am still there. (HH2, G3, F)

Some of our interviewees mentioned that in the past some girls did not finish their higher education because their parents were against the mixing between sexes in universities. However, recently, more girls are completing their education. A young girl from al-Fawwar camp said:

> There are differences between my thinking and that of my parents. When I am bored I like to go out of the house but my mum prefers me to be at home. I can see the discrimination between boys and girls. Boys can spend 24 hours outside the house but we stay at home. It is true that it is better for girls to stay at home but it is boring. I participated in the summer camp in Ramallah because my Dad was there. At first I was hesitant to participate in the camp because it was far from my family but I love people. I stayed for a couple of days but I cried every day because I was away from my family. (HH3, G3, F)

Education: a Tool for Oppression or Liberation

Education is not neutral for it always has a political intention, either for the domination of people or for their liberation. Graham-Brown (1991) noted that education has often been a tool of repressive regimes whilst also being the vehicle for the oppressed to protest against their oppressors. Harber (1991) identified three broad ideologies of political education: the conservative, the liberal-democratic and the radical. In the conservative approach, the intention is to use education to reinforce, support and legitimate the existing system of government and, in particular, political regimes and their policies. It tends to devalue the discussion of controversial issues and the possibilities of alternatives or reform. The liberal approach stresses the individual's ability to make up their own mind after consideration and discussion of the relevant evidence. Finally, the radical approach attempts to remodel society in a certain ideological direction via education. The emphasis is generally collective and cooperative.

From the beginning of the twentieth century, Palestinian education was influenced by all three approaches. The oppressor, represented by the ruler or governmental body (whether the British Mandate, the Jordanian and Egyptian administrations or the Israeli occupying Civil Administration), emphasised the conservative approach by perpetuating economic and social stratification, and dehumanising and taming the Palestinians in order to maintain the status quo. On the other side stood the oppressed (the Palestinians inside and outside Palestine). They focused on the liberal and, to some extent, the radical approach. This was translated into the adoption of different kinds of nonformal activities, intended to promote social change and the liberation of Palestinians and their land.

Consequently, confrontations on education between the Israeli occupying authorities and the Palestinians were rife in both the occupied Palestinian territories (West Bank and Gaza Strip) and inside Israel itself. The Israeli government figured out the importance of education for the Palestinians, especially the refugees. Unsurprisingly, therefore, the Israeli government obstructed the delivery of education. The development of an educational infrastructure for Palestinians who were under its occupation in the West Bank and Gaza Strip was not a priority for the Israeli government. The Israeli authority provided minimum funding, which barely covered teachers' salaries. It ignored the increasing lack of school buildings, equipment and furniture (Alzaroo 1988).

Frequent closure of the Palestinian education institutions was a common policy adopted by the Israeli authorities in the occupied West Bank and the Gaza Strip. During the first *Intifada* (1987–94), for example, all Palestinian education institutions were closed for periods ranging from two years, in the case of the West Bank schools, to more than four years in the case of some universities. Even the kindergartens were included in the military closure orders. Many of the schools were used as military camps and detention centres during the closure period (Alzaroo 1989; Ramsden and Senker 1993).

Teachers in the occupied West Bank and Gaza Strip were subject to various oppressive measures, such as compulsory retirement; redundancy on political grounds; arbitrary transfer to remote teaching posts; suspension of teachers' grades and professional allowances; deduction of pay following strike days or closure of schools; low salaries; the hindrance and obstruction of their professional development; and the prohibition of teachers' unions. Students were also subject to Israeli repression, such as expulsion from schools for political reasons, arrests during general certificate examinations, arbitrary transfer, prohibition from travelling abroad, and detention and imprisonment (Alzaroo 1988).

Curricula of the West Bank and Gaza Strip in the three education sectors were subject to restrictive Israeli control. The Israeli authority initially tried to impose Israeli curricula, as it did with the Palestinians who lived inside Israel itself. However, this failed due to Palestinian resistance. Thus, the Jordanian curricula in the West Bank and the Egyptian curricula in the Gaza Strip (which was in use before the occupation) were reinstated but with strict censorship by the Israeli authority (Alzaroo 1988).

The Israeli authority excluded or distorted any text or word referring to the land, history, geography, people and literature of Palestine and the Palestinians. Classroom maps were required to show Israel instead of Palestine. Quranic verses, poetry and history on the struggle against the aggressor were deleted. Even texts or sentences mentioning Arab unity or the struggle against imperialism were deleted. In addition, about 4,000 books in different fields were prohibited (Alzaroo 1988). There were no criteria fixed by authorities, but any book in the colours of the Palestinian flag, published by a Palestinian publishing house or discussing the question of Palestine was prohibited. The rule was that every book should be outlawed until permission was granted for its use (Ramsden and Senker 1993). As a consequence, the school curricula in the West Bank and the Gaza Strip were almost frozen from 1967 onwards. Textbooks were not attuned to the national identity or to the specific socioeconomic needs of the Palestinians, but rather often contained inaccurate and outdated information (Alzaroo 1988).

Formal education for Palestinians was altogether irrelevant, out-of-date and inequitable and as a result Palestinians focused on nonformal education to make up for the inadequacy of the formal system. The nonformal education (NFE) programmes included:

1. Educational programmes, such as adult literacy, preschool education, vocational education, teacher training, special education, continuing education, distance education, political education, and summer camps.
2. Health programmes, which included health policy and awareness, nursing, midwifery, health care, preventive health, environmental awareness, continuing professional development training for doctors, and clinical supervisors, school health education and first aid training.
3. Development programmes, such as training the trainers, income-generation projects, technical programmes, tourist industry, secretarial training, and sewing and design.
4. Arts programmes, including painting, design, flower arrangement, ceramics, music, theatre and photography.
5. Rural development, such as agriculture programmes, farming and food processing.
6. Business programmes, such as management, financial management, marketing, accounting, journalism and media, counselling, statistics, executive secretarial and communication.
7. Athletic programmes, like sports activities and scouting.
8. Human rights and information.
9. Women's programmes focusing mainly on gender consciousness.

The providers of NFE were the political parties and movements, the NGOs, the charitable societies, women's institutions, religious institutions and the higher education institutions.

Significance of Education for Palestinian Refugees in the West Bank

The findings of our study revealed that despite the special context of education in the West Bank, it was still regarded as a 'good' thing *per se*. Our data strongly suggest that the experience of displacement and prolonged conflict is a decisive factor for pushing Palestinian refugees towards education. Education has both helped refugees to adapt to their new life in exile and kept alive the prospects of returning home. It is no surprise that refugees attached great significance to education. For them it was a survival strategy. The quotations below highlight how education constitutes a significant coping strategy. A second-generation woman from al-Aroub camp said:

> I like education. In order to survive you not only have to eat and drink, but to study as well. I am the youngest of eleven brothers and sisters – imagine eleven people wanting to eat and sleep: it is difficult. However, my dad tried his best to give us the chance of education and our financial situation did not prevent anybody from having an opportunity of having an education. (HH8, G2, F)

A young girl from al-Aroub camp said:

> Education is very important in our lives. The first thing people ask is, "What qualifications do you have?" (HH12, G3, F)

A first-generation older man from al-Aroub camp said:

> If I was the Minister of Education, I would make education compulsory till university. (HH11, GI, M)

The following text, which is part of an interview with a young refugee girl, shows how education is one of the main concerns for Palestinians.

Q. What would you like to accomplish?

A. The biggest concern is finishing my law studies and becoming a lawyer. I want to defend people who have been unjustly treated and give them back their rights. I want to be independent.

Q. What distinguishes your family?

A. My grandfather and his brothers were educated. Their father was blind but educated. He used to memorise the Quran. My father was always interested in our education and I had to be the first in my class. My mother failed history in her general exam and my grandfather begged her to resit the exam but she refused to and got married. My mother says that this was the biggest mistake of her life because the certificate is a weapon and without it there is no value for a girl in our society. If I got 18/20 in an exam, my grandfather felt upset... We are facing a difficult situation and my mother wants to work; her chances would be better if she had her certificate. My mother likes our marks to be in the nineties so that she can be proud of us. (HH11, G3, F)

In the group interviews in the two camps, the majority of the eighteen participants identified education as their first personal priority; building a house came second and then getting married. When they were asked about their future career choice, they identified education-related careers (pharmacist, chemist, teacher, journalist, engineer, English lecturer, accountant).

The perceptions of the refugees about education affected their social life. One might expect that because of the economic difficulties, money would be a priority for them, or looking for a wealthy husband. However, Kuroda's study of 234 young people aged 14–17 in Jordanian camps suggests the contrary. In answer to the question 'What would you ask for if you had Aladdin's lamp?', only one person said 'money' (Kuroda 1972: 326). The data collected in our study confirmed this, as the following statement from a second-generation man from al-Fawwar camp illustrates:

We had a rich relative and I once asked my sisters if they would accept him [as a husband] but they said they would decline because he was not educated. (HH5, G2, M)

When interviewees were asked what they taught their children, many mentioned the fear of God and the value of education. This explains why Palestinians frequently express concern about their education system and accuse the Israeli government of undermining the educational achievement of their children, especially during the first and the current uprisings.

Education as a Coping Strategy

It is argued here that education for Palestinians in general and for refugees and their descendants in particular is being used as a unique tool for nation building in three ways. Firstly, it is a remedy to overcome the consequences of the Palestinian disaster in 1948 and the subsequent displacement. Secondly, it is an incentive for political, economic and social mobilisation. Thirdly, it is a tool for identity building.

Education as a Remedy

A consequence of the 1948 displacement has been that educational provision for Palestinians has often been 'remedial' or 'compensatory'. Sayigh (1995) stressed that for Palestinians, having an education was seen as a temporary replacement for a homeland that had previously supplied prestige, status and a passport. On the other hand, they realised that building Palestinian identity and unity, achieving the goal of return and enhancing skills would require a great focus on education. This could explain the 'Palestinian phenomenon in education'. This refers to the jump from one of the lowest rates of educational attainment before 1948 to one of the highest after two or three decades.

Our interviews revealed that refugees put great emphasis on education after 1948. The informants still recalled clearly the characteristics of the education system before 1948. Access to education at that time was limited, especially for girls, but it has improved since then. An elderly woman from al-Fawwar camp said:

> My father bought me the school uniform and the other school supplies but then he ripped the uniform off because a young man told him that if I learnt the alphabet, I would write letters. When I remember this now, I swear at this man. I wish I could read so I can read the Quran. (HH4, G1, F)

Many said that they wished they could finish their education; also many mentioned that there was gender discrimination against girls in education, therefore many females were not able to attend schools. An elderly woman from al-Aroub camp said:

> Boys used to continue their education but not girls. Girls used to study the Quran, while older girls used to get married. I recall that girls would stop going to school when their monthly period starts because they felt shy. I reached the sixth grade. There were eight girls in the class. In the harvest season, the girls would stay at home to look after their younger sisters and brothers while some parents went to Jordan or Egypt for work ... After the harvest season girls came back to the class. My father begged me to continue in the ninth grade but I dropped out because I had my period. I felt I was a mature girl studying among young kids. In the past, education was better than today. After I left school I stayed at home. From 1958 to 1972, I was sewing, bringing water and fuel from outside and making bread. (HH11, G1, F)

Education for Palestinians was used as a remedy to make up for the loss of land and property; as a way to understand precisely what had happened and why; to rescue what was left and to rebuild themselves; and to stand up for their rights. In other words, and using Freire's (1987) famous phrase, they used 'the words to understand the world'. An elderly man from al-Fawwar camp stated: 'Education is our shelter. We do not own lands, farms, factories or any businesses' (HH9, G1, M), and a young girl from al-Fawwar camp said:

> We are nothing without education. Education gives value to humans especially us the Palestinians. We are without money or support and we have no choice but education. (HH2, G3, F)

In addition, many international agencies and NGOs used education as a major tool in their rehabilitation programmes to help Palestinian refugees deal with the suppressed trauma that often affects refugees and the daily anxieties of an insecure existence.

Education as an Incentive for Political, Economic and Social Mobilisation

After the major population dislocations in 1948, Palestinians in general, as Haddad (1980, cited in Harber, 1991) stresses, came to regard education as a form of portable commodity that could not be taken away by any party. Many reasons prevented them from building their infrastructure and so they tried to build themselves through education. Thus, education became a primary means of economic success, social integration and an avenue of political liberation. It was a way of gaining control over their fate, a chance to build a future and escape from passivity and dependence. It was, above all, the most decisive factor for change. Therefore, Palestinians tried to gear their education system to contribute directly to an effective national reconstruction process.

At the economic level, as Abu-Lughod (1973) pointed out, education was valued for the hope it gave of economic security in circumstances where political security was not to be had. It was a way of escaping the hardship of the camps. Mahshi and Bush (1989) noted that the traditional value of education, especially formal schooling, has strengthened over time. Formal education was perceived by the Palestinians as a means of searching for a white-collar job with steady income and to enhance social status. A young man from al-Aroub camp said:

> You should learn the history and the geography of your country. You should also learn languages so you can travel and mathematics to deal with people. (HH8, G3, M)

A second-generation female from al-Aroub camp stated:

> My father considers education to be very important. He believes that in these days if you do not study, you will die of hunger. A person with no certificate will face hardship. (HH9, G2, F)

An elderly man from al-Aroub camp said:

> Nothing is better than education. For 38 years, I imprinted my thumb when I received my salary. This really embarrassed me. I lost many work opportunities because I couldn't read. (HH3, G1, M)

It can be argued that although education is linked to economic revenue, Palestinians had not given great attention to the relationship between education and economic variables. It is true that they focused on education in the 1960s and the 1970s when simultaneously there was a huge demand for employees in the Gulf States. However, they also pursued education in the 1980s and the 1990s in spite of the high rate of unemployment in the West Bank and Gaza Strip. Obviously, the relationship between education and economics exists in all societies and Palestinian society is no exception, but Palestinians ignored or overlooked this relationship. They invested resources in education voluntarily and without expecting any direct economic return.

This happened for several reasons: firstly, Palestinians value education highly; secondly, they have nothing to lose – they realised that keeping their children busy in schools and universities was better than leaving them hanging around in the streets with nothing to do; and thirdly, Palestinians have never fully funded their own education system. Usually, the contribution of local funds is very little. The dominant authority often funds the governmental education. The UN funds the UNRWA schools, which are open and free to all descendants of refugees until the last two years of high school. Even private and higher education is heavily dependent on external aid.

The social role of education was seen not only as an important part of changing social attitudes and aspirations, but also as important for placing people into particular roles in society. Education, since it aims at producing more competent, better informed and more understanding people, has implied within its goals the possibility that its activities will indirectly cause social change in the society inhabited by those who undergo it. A young girl from al-Fawwar camp said:

> Education develops the mind. It gives value to human beings. My aunt was the first student in the West Bank in her General Exam but now she is a teacher and she got married. I am scared of being like her, get tired then marry… My parents encourage education; they feel it is important for girls. (HH3, G3, F)

One of the social consequences of wide access to education in Palestinian society is a lessening of the gender gap. Education affects the eligibility of girls for marriage, since those with little formal education have more limited chances. However, a high level of education for girls is also an obstacle to marriage. An elderly woman from al-Aroub camp stated:

> Education is very important especially for girls. Girls must have education even if they will end up in the kitchen. Children who are brought up by educated mothers will be in a better position to face the problems of life. (HH12, G1, F)

When interviewees were asked what distinguished their families many said education, especially for girls. A second-generation female said:

> All the girls in my family are educated and so we are different from other families. In my childhood I did not think about studying but since I have joined the university I would like a Master's degree. I feel that through education, I will develop high self-esteem. (HH8, G2, F)

Palestinians have used education to raise public awareness, to enable people to critically understand their reality, and to liberate themselves economically, socially and politically. It seems clear that the greater the length of one's formal schooling, the more likely one is to be a participant and the better one's understanding of political issues. However, it is an illusion that education *per se* will create revolutionary change in the awareness of the individual. Education could deepen the awareness but it does not necessarily produce it. People must be educated in a particular way before they can stand up for their political rights and appreciate freedom, democracy and human rights.

Through education, in particular nonformal education, Palestinians inside Palestine and in exile have tried to create a critical awareness of political phenomena by opening discussion and analysis of a range of evidence and opinions. They realised that education is one of the primary tools without which they cannot liberate their land. For them schools and universities were not only educational institutions but also political establishments. An adult man from al-Fawwar camp stated:

> I believe that the way of liberating Palestine is through science and learning, therefore I intensified my study hours during the *Intifada* and came top of my class for the first time in my life. (HH2, G2, M)

A second-generation woman in al-Aroub camp said:

> The first *Intifada* destroyed us. They used to come to school and ask us to go out for demonstrations. We did not mind because we used to leave school. The severe consequence of that is a generation of illiterates. There was a high rate of school drop-outs. Everyone should have worked to control schools because getting us out of schools is the aim of the Zionists. It was the camp youngsters who asked us to go out for demonstrations. (HH8, G2, F)

For many interviewees the struggle against occupation and for libera-tion is not only limited to the armed struggle – the good educator can also be a militant whose actions are in line with a political and revolutionary stance. A middle-aged man from al-Fawwar camp argues:

> I didn't keep quiet. Participation in the struggle is not necessarily with a sword or a bullet or a stone. Fighting can also be with words. (HH4, G2, M)

Education played a major role in the Palestinian liberation movement. During the Occupation era, the Palestine Liberation Organisation (PLO) encouraged the establishment of higher education institutions and, as a consequence of PLO financial support to higher education institutions, tertiary education was, in the main, free for the majority of the Palestinians in the West Bank and Gaza Strip. The flowering of a new gen-eration of university graduates created two main outcomes for Palestinian people. One is the social and economic mobilisation and the other is the emergence of a young local leadership.

During the first *Intifada*, political education was given priority in non-formal education. The aim was to develop individual and collective awareness so as to achieve emancipation by using educational resources and activities for organising and mobilising the population to challenge the occupier and confront its policies.

The providers of nonformal education made a distinction between learning and schooling and argued that learning takes place outside schools. This emphasised the importance of nonformal education activi-ties such as 'Popular Education', which spread widely when Israeli authorities closed all the Palestinian schools during the first *Intifada* for many years.

Another example of these nonformal programmes was 'Prison Education'. The prison educational programme was implemented for Palestinian prisoners in the Israeli prisons in spite of strong Israeli objec-tions. The Israeli authorities in the early years of occupation banned Palestinian prisoners from using pencils and paper. Only after very long and hard hunger strikes did the prisoners win the battle and were gradu-ally able to use pens, pencils, paper, books and newspapers, as well as receive a certain amount of carefully censored radio broadcasting. As a consequence, the prisoners established a library in every prison and organised literacy classes, language courses, awareness-raising sessions, political discourse and orientation workshops, as well as classes for the young prisoners to prepare them for the General Secondary Examination. Furthermore, the prisoners succeeded in building an information system network to exchange information between the rooms, and between pris-ons and their families and political leadership outside the prisons and in exile (Qazzaz 1997).

Education as a Tool for Identity Building

The role of education here was to create the fundamental background necessary for the full participation of every Palestinian in the development of Palestinian identity and community, whether inside Palestine or in exile. In order to maintain traditional songs, sing the national anthem, salute the national flag and say the national pledge regularly to restore pride in their cultural heritage, they have to be literate. Therefore, many Palestinian educators have argued that Palestinian formal education could not contribute to identity building because it has been controlled by the oppressor for so many years. Fasheh (1990, 1992, 1995), for instance, has argued for 'community education' rather than 'formal education' as a means of identity building. He noted that much of the effort to reform Palestinian education has focused on the visible level (building schools, recruiting teachers). All of these elements are important, but they will not work without investment in the more fundamental invisible (human and cultural) levels.

Fasheh argues that under present conditions, when Palestinians are denied control over their natural resources and offered only loans for survival from the World Bank, the only hope for Palestinian people lies in the investment in the invisible, that is, the human treasure (mainly children and youth) and the cultural treasure:

> [C]ultural products and cultural producers should and could be the basis of our economy. We have almost all the ingredients necessary to excel in this type of production: a common language; common history and culture; common land; common needs and realities; and a common destiny. Such products and producers are much harder to destroy; they are built on what we have, and they do not produce a spiral increase of debt. Moreover, they are a natural accompaniment of learning environments. (Fasheh 1995: 68)

He stresses that Palestinians have not only to end the occupation of their land, but also the occupation of their minds through their daily practices: in their conversations, dialogues, activities, cultural expression and cultural products:

> Ending the occupation of our minds means rediscovering ourselves, our voices, and the internal strength in our people and our communities. It means seeing the value of our experiences and our culture. It means ending fragmentation, factionalism, cultural dependency, and the competing with one another over small and symbolic gains. It means feeling happy and proud of being Arabs, disregarding the racist and poisonous messages that the Western TV, journalists, academics, and experts try to spread around the world against Arabs and Muslims. It also means defining ourselves as Palestinians, as Arabs, and not as underdeveloped or as developing. (Fasheh 1995: 69)

In community education, people are creators and not receivers. Community building means developing an institution's environment and individual capacities. An integral part of community building at the invisible level is the 'cultural product', which serves as a source of economic return and can also inspire feelings of self-worth, both at the individual and national levels (Fasheh 1995).

The Effects of *al-Aqsa Intifada*

The current *Intifada* has had a strong effect on Palestinian society in the West Bank and Gaza Strip, especially on children and young people, and has had a devastating effect on the two camps in the study. In the al-Fawwar refugee camp, three people were killed, of whom one was 16 years old. More than sixty were injured (one of them lost both eyes) and about 120 young people were arrested. The camp was under siege from the beginning of the *Intifada* and the Israeli army shelled the camp many times. In addition, there is a big Jewish settlement at the rear of the camp and there are military checkpoints in front of the camp. All this makes daily life inside the camp extremely difficult. In the al-Aroub refugee camp, four people were killed, one of whom was 14 years old, eighty were injured and about seventy people were arrested. In addition, more than 500 people who used to work in Israel became unemployed.

In both camps, a large proportion of children and young people were exposed, directly or indirectly, to violence in several ways. Firstly, children participated in or observed the confrontations between the Palestinians and the Israelis; they watched the shelling and demolishing of houses, uprooting of trees and destruction of roads and general infrastructure. Secondly, they have experienced provocation and humiliation during their daily journeys to school or at military checkpoints. Thirdly, many people watch the developments on satellite television stations. The confrontations between the Palestinians and the Israelis have dominated television stations, especially local ones and the satellite television stations of Arab countries.

Despite their economic difficulties, the majority of families in the camp have satellite dishes and digital receivers that allow them to watch tens and even hundreds of satellite stations. This phenomenon did not exist in the first *Intifada* (1987–94). The themes that emerged from the group interviews conducted in the two refugee camps, after six months of the *Intifada*, concentrated on the issues presented in Figure 5.1.

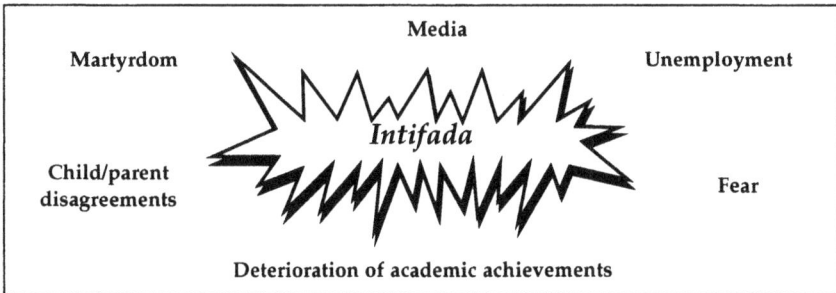

Figure 5.1 The West Bank: Summary of the Impact of the Current *Intifada*

Unemployment

There is unemployment and other economic difficulties. In order to control the *Intifada*, Israel stopped giving 120,000 Palestinian workers access to work in Israel. It also imposed a comprehensive siege around the Palestinian cities, towns and villages, which affected the local economy badly. According to reports by the Palestinian Ministry of Labour, the West Bank's unemployment rate in 2001 reached 48 percent. This situation put great economic pressure on the population, especially the refugees. A young woman from al-Fawwar camp stated:

> The current *Intifada* destroyed my dreams. I was dreaming of becoming a journalist in the future, but now my economic and social situation will not allow me to do that. I know that the economic situation is very bad so I did not ask my family to buy me any new clothes for the Eid holiday. (Girls' Focus Group (GFG, G3, F)

Some university students stopped going to universities because of financial problems. The daily wage for workers was 100 NIS (US$ 23) before the *Intifada* but in 2002 it is only 30 NIS (US$ 7). Before the *Intifada*, 451 people from the camp worked in Israel. The majority of them no longer do so.

Fear

Many of our interviewees expressed their fear of soldiers. A young man from al-Fawwar camp said:

> I do not leave the camp because I am afraid of soldiers and checkpoints. I am scared because soldiers have shot many people without reason, some of whom were in their own homes. (BFG, G3, M)

Many interviewees said that the pictures shown on television of injured
and disabled people were terrifying. Others said that the effect of being
close to Israeli settlements was scary. Another young man from al-
Fawwar camp said:

> There is a settlement at the back of the camp and the people in the camp feel
> that the settlers will attack at any minute. The people of the camp are alarmed
> and they have put stones on the top of their roofs to defend themselves. Since
> the beginning of the *Intifada*, I no longer leave the camp. (BFG, G3, M)

Some interviewees said that they even stopped going up to the roof of
their house because of the risk of being injured or killed. A young man
from al-Fawwar camp said:

> Before the *Intifada* I used to go to Hebron by myself. Now I cannot even go to
> the gate of the camp. We stopped going out for picnics because we are fright-
> ened. (BFG, G3, M)

Many interviewees said that the girls of the camp were terrified because
of rumours that the gas the Israeli soldiers were using against demonstrations had an effect on female fertility. This rumour sparked panic in
the whole camp. Every time a girl was injured in the camp, families
would try to transfer girls away from the confrontations.

Deterioration of Academic Achievements

Our findings suggest that the educational achievements of most students
have deteriorated because they have participated in confrontations with
soldiers in the daytime and spent the evenings watching confrontations
on television. Also students lost many days of schooling. A young man
from al-Aroub camp said:

> Students have lost more than 25 studying days since the beginning of the
> *Intifada*. This has been the result of teachers being unable to reach the camp and
> also due to confrontation. The students have become more interested in poli-
> tics. Before the *Intifada* few people participated in throwing stones at soldiers
> but now the majority of the students do so. (BFG, G3, M)

Many students complained that because of current political events they
could not concentrate on their studies. A young boy from al-Aroub camp
said:

> Because of the *Intifada*, we cannot concentrate on our study. It is difficult for me
> to follow the class and pay attention to my teachers. We have lost interest in
> studying and we just watch the news. (G3, M)

Child/Parent Disagreements

Our findings show signs of disagreement between children and their parents over their participation in the current *Intifada*. A young boy from al-Fawwar camp said:

> My father used to forbid me to participate in the confrontation against the soldiers because he does not agree with the *Intifada*. For him, the whole matter is just a play and people should not sacrifice themselves for nothing. I am always challenging him and reply that if people sacrifice themselves in this life, they will be rewarded on the Day of Judgement. Anyone who loses his life will be a martyr. (BFG, G3, M)

The findings indicate that there is a tendency for parents to forbid their children to participate in the confrontations. However, the children and young people have different views and many believe that they are not scared of death. A young boy from al-Fawwar camp said:

> My father encourages me to participate in all national activities but my mother hates it. She does not want me to die. However, she changed her mind when the soldiers shelled the camp. She asked me to go and participate in confrontations. She said, 'it is better for you to die in the confrontations as a fighter than dying at home.' (BFG, G3, M)

Many interviewees said that there is an increase of free time due to the closures. A young girl from al-Fawwar camp stated:

> The increase of free time because of the closure has led to a lot of tension in the relations between my brothers and sisters. Sometimes we fight with each other. The siege imposed on our camp, indeed on Palestine, has hindered our work opportunities. (GFG, G3, F)

The findings show that parents have become more anxious and the boys and male youths have become more aggressive towards the girls. Many think that this may be a consequence of the bad economic situation and the psychological pressures. A young male from al-Aroub camp said:

> It is only natural that my dad does not encourage me to participate in the *Intifada*. I do not allow my younger brother to participate but I go. (BFG, G3, M)

Some of the young people said that they noticed that relations between them and their parents were tense because of their differing views about the *Intifada*. Many said that although their parents did not allow them to participate in the confrontations, they do so behind their parents' backs.

Martyrdom

Our findings show that the concept of martyrdom seems to be strong among Palestinians in the West Bank, especially young refugees. Many young people expressed their willingness to die for their country. Some said that their families did not encourage them to participate in the confrontations, thus many of them were secretive about their activities. Many were considering being martyrs. A young male from al-Fawwar camp said:

> In the beginning my father forbade me to participate in the confrontations. He subsequently gave in and I started to participate. Now, my parents forbid me from going to the gate of the camp where the soldiers are standing because they do not want me to be killed or injured. I do not feel frightened. My belief in God's will is so deep. But let me tell you something, most of the children of my age and other young people in the camp are aspiring for martyrdom. I would like to be a martyr, but I do not want to be injured or disabled and be dependent on others. (BFG, G3, M)

Some young girls express their willingness to participate in the confrontations and to be martyrs. A young girl from al-Fawwar camp stated:

> As a girl, I would like to participate in throwing stones at soldiers. I would like to be killed and become a martyr. I have on three occasions arranged with some of my schoolmates to go to the confrontation points after school and throw stones hoping to be killed and become martyrs but they often changed their minds. I would like be a martyr so much because our living circumstances are not pleasant at all. We are suffering a lot. Martyrdom is more appealing and a better option than this unworthy life. (GFG, G3, F)

Some young people thought that the *Intifada* would continue and they were willing to die as martyrs. Many said that living in fear forces young people to martyrdom. A young male from al-Aroub camp said:

> Let me tell you something, living in fear and in humiliation forces us to think about martyrdom. The *Intifada* has to continue and I am ready to be one of its martyrs. (BFG, G3, M)

Media

The effects of the media coverage of the current situation are immense. Our findings show that many people, especially from the younger generation, watch the confrontations live on television. In addition, many young people have nightmares and their educational achievements have deteriorated because they spend their time watching television and devote less time for studying. A young boy from al-Fawwar camp stated:

I have nightmares almost every night as a result of the TV pictures and reports. My family, like other families in the camp, spend a lot of time watching TV and switching from one TV station to another. I think that this is one of the significant reasons explaining why our educational achievement has deteriorated. On the other hand, there is a positive side to the media coverage as the national songs raise our morale. However, sights of the injured and disabled people make me afraid all the time. (BFG, G3, M)

Many children said that they were shocked by all the violent events they witnessed on television screens. A young boy from al-Fawwar camp pointed out:

As a result of watching too much TV, my results at school fell. The media coverage strengthened the *Intifada*, displaying live pictures on TV stations, which showed the killing of the child Mohammed al-Durah in Gaza. This picture shocked Palestinians and the world. Nowadays the best TV station for the Palestinian children and youths and even for the adults is al-Maner TV Satellite station [the rest of the group confirmed this]. (BFG, G3, M)

Many children said that the current *Intifada* was making them fearful and many said that they were experiencing sleeping difficulties. A young man from al-Fawwar camp said:

The media coverage instils fear in my family and me. Before the *Intifada*, my 5-year-old sister used to go to bed at nine o'clock in the evening. Nowadays she stays awake till one o'clock in the morning because she is afraid of the shelling. She thinks our house will be destroyed and she will get killed. However, I think that the positive point about the media coverage is that other nations all over the world can see the reality of Israel before their eyes. (BFG, G3, M)

Conclusion

As a result of prolonged conflict and forced migration, many Palestinians were transplanted from their original context to a new and unknown setting. The result was a state of continued vulnerability. A child whose family becomes displaced or is forced to flee into exile is profoundly affected in wartime since displacement is threatening to the well-being of children. It also threatens learning, socialisation and cultural continuity. Displacement is also associated with a decline in traditional intra-familial authority structures and informal mechanisms for adoption and shared childcare, and it disrupts traditional survival skills. See Figure 5.2 for a summary of our main findings.

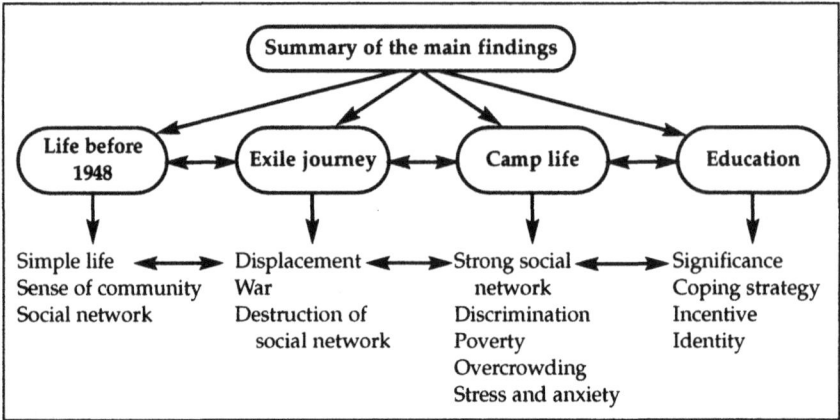

Figure 5.2 The West Bank: Summary of the Main Themes

The first and second generations of Palestinian refugees are strongly affected by moving from their place of origin to their place of exile. The separation from their natural environment and from their relatives is an emotional burden they all share. They are affected by the violence they and their families have been exposed to, the deep mourning they and their parents felt when they were forced out of their beloved places and the difficulties they encountered in their host countries. Therefore, it is not surprising that all the first-generation interviewees mentioned the 1948 emigration as the most difficult and painful experience they ever encountered.

The second generation have witnessed the 1956 and 1967 wars, the Israeli occupation and the first *Intifada* (1987–94). Until the beginning of *al-Aqsa Intifada* in 2000, the third generation showed little interest in politics but this situation subsequently changed dramatically after 2000. In general, children and young people who have had one or more of their family killed or injured during the confrontations with the Israelis show more interest in politics.

For children who were born in the camps, the world of the refugee camp may be the only world with which they are intimately familiar. Many of the refugee children stressed that they felt safe inside the camp. People inside the camp reported that they had learned how to live together despite the difficulties they experienced, such as shortage of water, destroyed streets and infrastructure, sewage problems, garbage, overcrowding and the absence of entertainment facilities.

The refugee children experienced discrimination outside the camp very dramatically. The feeling of discrimination has been passed from generation to generation and has become very rooted. Many of our interviewees emphasised that violence is very common at school but not at home. The study reveals that the gender gap is narrowing and that currently young women have better opportunities than their grandparents had.

Our data strongly suggest that the experience of displacement and prolonged conflict is a decisive factor in pushing Palestinian refugees towards education. Education has both helped them adapt to their new life in exile and kept alive the prospects of returning home. Many Palestinian refugees view education as a unique tool for nation building in three senses: firstly, it is a remedy to overcome the consequences of the Palestinian disaster in 1948 and the subsequent displacement; secondly, it is an incentive for political, economic and social mobilisation; thirdly, it is a tool for identity building. Therefore, it is no surprise that refugees attached great significance to education.

Finally, it is evident that the current Palestinian uprising (*al-Aqsa Intifada*) has had an immense effect on refugee children. In both camps, a large proportion of children and young people were exposed, directly or indirectly, to violence through their participation or observation of the confrontations between the Palestinians and the Israelis and the provocation and humiliation experienced during their daily journey to their schools or at the military checkpoints, or even as a consequence of watching the confrontations on satellite TV stations.

The current *Intifada* has impacted on every aspect of daily life. Increased unemployment has resulted in economic difficulties for many households. Children are experiencing increased fear and stress, and there is a deterioration in school attendance and educational achievement. There are disagreements between children and their parents concerning their involvement in confrontations, an interest in the concept of martyrdom, and the media coverage on satellite television stations of the *Intifada* has had a disturbing and radicalising impact on children and young people. At the time of writing, the war in Iraq and continuing fighting in the West Bank leaves the children and young people of the West Bank facing continuing prolonged conflict.

Note

1 The author would like to express his appreciation to the research team of Maesa Irfayeh (research assistant and interviewer), Hisham Sharabati (interviewer), Ilham Ayoub (interviewer), Tahani Alzaroo (translator) and Ahlam Iqrea' (typist) for their hard work and commitment to this project.

References

Abu-Lughod, I. 1973. 'Educating a Community in Exile: The Palestinian Experience'. *Journal of Palestine Studies*, 11(3): 94–111.
Alzaroo, S. 1988. *Education Under Occupation*. (in Arabic). Hebron: University Graduates Union, Research Centre.

——— 1989. *Education Under the Shadow of the Intifada*. (in Arabic). Hebron: University Graduates Union, Research Centre.

Fasheh, M. 1990. 'Community Education: To Reclaim and Transform What Has Been Made Invisible'. *Harvard Educational Review*, 60(1): 19–35.

——— 1992. 'West Bank: Learning to Survive'. In C. Poster and J. Zimmer (eds), *Community Education in the Third World*. London and New York: Routledge.

——— 1995. 'The Reading Campaign Experience within Palestinian Society: Innovative Strategies for Learning and Building Community', *Harvard Educational Review*, 65(1): 66–92.

Freire, P. 1987. *Literacy: Reading the Word and the World*. South Hadley, Mass., U.S.A.: Bergin and Garvey.

Graham-Brown, S. 1991. *Education in the Developing World: Conflict and Crisis*. London and New York: Longman.

Haddad, Y. 1980. 'Palestinian Women: Patterns of Legitimisation and Domination'. In K. Nakhleh and E. Zureil (eds), *The Sociology of Palestinians*. London: Croom Helm.

Harber, C. 1991. 'Schools and Political Learning in Africa: Themes and Issues'. *Compare*, 21(1): 61–71.

Kuroda, Y. 1972. 'Young Palestinian Commandos in Political Socialisation Perspective'. *Middle East Journal*, 26(3): 253–70.

Mahshi, K. and Bush, K. 1989. 'The Palestinian Uprising and Education for the Future'. *Harvard Educational Review*, 59(4): 470–83.

Qazzaz, H. 1997. '*Adult Non-Formal Education in Developing Countries: The case of Palestinians in Israeli prisons*', D.Ed. Dissertation, School of Education, University of Leeds, U.K.

Ramsden, S. and Senker, C. (eds) 1993. *Learning the Hard Way: Palestinian Education in West Bank, Gaza Strip and Israel*. London: World University Service.

Sayigh, R. 1995. 'Palestinians in Lebanon: Harsh Present, Uncertain Future'. *Journal of Palestine Studies*, 25(1): 37–53.

6

Palestinian Refugee Children and Caregivers in the Gaza Strip

Abdel Aziz Thabet and *Hala Abuateya*

Abdel Aziz Thabet

I am a Palestinian whose family were originally members of a Bedouin tribe of the Nagab. They left the Nagab like so many others and settled in Rafah where I was born and grew up. I then moved to Alexandria in Egypt to study medicine and upon qualifying, I worked in Libya as a doctor from 1982 to 1986. I subsequently studied psychiatry in Vienna from 1987 to 1990. I returned to the Gaza Strip and worked in the community mental health programme. In 1993 I studied for a Diploma in Child Psychiatry in England. I have worked as a psychiatrist both within the Ministry of Health and for the Gaza Community Mental Health Association. I am committed to developing community-based psychiatry in multidisciplinary teams. I recently completed a Ph.D. at the University of Leicester in 2003. I have published extensively on the topic of post-traumatic stress amongst Palestinian children. I am a member of the Faculty of the School of Public Health of Al Quds University and am closely involved in the management and teaching of the Masters in Public Health that is taught in Gaza.

Hala Abuateya

I was born and brought up in Ramallah in Palestine. I am the oldest of two brothers and two sisters. Between 1983 and 1987 I studied for an undergraduate degree in sociology and psychology at the University of Birzeit. During this time I represented my university at several international events and shared the difficult experiences of Palestinian students under the Israeli Occupation. From 1987 to 1998 I worked as a researcher and trainer at the Institute of Community and Public Health in the University of Birzeit. My task was to build bridges between the University and the local community. During this time I gained both practical experience and wide theoretical knowledge on how to deal with complicated issues of public health within the Palestinian community, such as the perception of disability and the understanding of health and illnesses.

In 1990 I was awarded a three-month scholarship from a UN-sponsored Women's International Cultural Exchange Programme (ISIS) to do an International Diploma on Communication and Documentation in Chile and the Philippines. My time outside Palestine was critical. Listening to other people's experiences of poverty, struggle and liberation made me reconsider the uniqueness of the Palestinian experiences of forced migration, war and political conflict. It also made me realise the commonality of suffering across cultures, religions, social classes and gender.

In 1991 I won a scholarship to do a Master's Degree in Health and Development at the University of Leeds in England. During this time, I explored the principles of primary health care and its importance in rural development, especially in the developing countries. I wrote my Master's dissertation on the role of community health workers in primary health care. In the late 1990s I received a British Council scholarship to complete my Ph.D. at the University of Bristol in the U.K. In my doctorate research, I investigated the connections between political conflict and violence among Palestinian secondary school students. I integrated social identity and social learning theories into my theoretical framework to analyse and explain my research outcomes.

I am currently working as a research associate in the Greenwood Institute of Child Health at the University of Leicester, where I am investigating the connection between ethnic diversity and children's mental health. I have several research interests, including violence in schools, youth and violence, the impact of political conflict on people's behaviour, and disability and mental health. I am also interested in research methodology and project evaluation.

This chapter focuses on the effect of prolonged conflict and forced migration on Palestinian refugee children and adolescents living in the Gaza Strip. The research used a multidisciplinary and participatory research approach and was conducted[1] in three refugee camps and two urban settings in the Gaza Strip. This chapter presents the voices of children and young people who are facing and coping with the direct and indirect impact of forced migration and prolonged conflict. We consider coping strategies as a combination of problem-focused and emotion-focused styles in dealing with chronic social adversities in our society, which include the long-term effect of trauma combined with the low socioeconomic status of families. Children and young people are trying to use normative adaptive defence mechanisms to overcome their problems. They use coping strategies to develop positive thinking and behaviour accepted by Islamic society.

Displacement and Conflict

The Palestinian refugees' journey to exile started in 1948 as a result of the creation of Israel. The journey of displacement continued in the 1967 war between Israel and some Arab neighbouring countries including Jordan, Egypt and Syria. Almost all the interviewees, especially the elderly generation, provided detailed stories describing their journeys to exile and their experiences of displacement. *Al-Nakba* (Catastrophe) in 1948 was the event that precipitated the journey into exile and altered life irrevocably in terms of place, status and security. There were also other wars subsequently that affected these families and many of them experienced repeated traumatic episodes through encounters with the Israeli troops occupying the Gaza Strip. Abu Mohammed remembered his experiences of being arrested by troops:

> During the 1948 War, the Jews told me to accompany them to the house of activists. When I refused they asked me to stand by a wall. They were ready to shoot me but one of the officers came and saved my life. I was arrested and held in an ice-cream factory before being transferred to El-Arish in Egypt with 200 other people in one bus. It was intolerable. Jewish soldiers threatened us with knives. I was afraid but I assured my colleagues that the Jews would not kill us. It was psychological warfare. I remember in the El-Arish prison how the Jews took one of my friends and killed him in front of my eyes. I was interrogated and I stayed in prison for 32 days. They then took us to buses without telling us where we were going. As far as we knew we could have been going to our deaths! We reached Gaza and went on to Bureij on foot. We kept looking behind us and thinking they will shoot us. When I reached home I hardly recognised my own children. (HH12, G1, M)

In the 1967 war between Israel and some Arab countries (Jordan, Syria and Egypt), Israel occupied the whole West Bank and Gaza Strip in addition to parts of some neighbouring Arab countries. Palestinians were subjected to a second forced migration and displacement. *Al-Naksa* increased the number of refugees not only within the borders of the West Bank and Gaza Strip but in other neighbouring Arab countries such as Jordan, Syria and Lebanon. Abu Ahmed described his experiences of being arrested:

> At the beginning of the occupation in 1967, the Jews called me to meet with them and I went three days after being notified. Soldiers attacked me with guns; my wife was with me; they pushed her out of the way and interrogated me. They asked me to talk in Hebrew or English but I could do neither. They brought me an interpreter and asked me to sign a paper; I refused and the interpreter supported me. They released me after six hours and I found my wife waiting for me. She did not believe that I would be released alive. (HH11, G2, M)

The 1973 war between Israel and neighbouring Arab countries raised the hopes of many Palestinians. At that time, many people thought that the Arabs would liberate Palestine and they could go back to their homes. But their dream did not last for long because the war ended and their situation remained unchanged. The Israeli military invasion of Lebanon was another dramatic event in Palestinian history. The invasion caused a destruction of the Palestinian resistance in Lebanon and many Palestinians were displaced for the third time. Munir said that in his opinion, the Lebanon war was another catastrophe for Palestinians and Arabs are to blame for the Palestinian problems.

> The Israeli invasion of Lebanon in 1982 and the migration of the Palestinians from Lebanon to a different Arab world were other catastrophes which shocked us. Palestinians believed that there was a plot stemming from the removal of Palestinians from Jordan and then from Lebanon. Arabs were the cause ... they started by pushing Palestinians from Jordan and then from Lebanon. Syria and the other Arab countries are the cause of the problems. During the Israeli invasion of Lebanon, I heard about the death of my brother in Lebanon, who covered three times the withdrawal of his colleagues in the war ... in the third time, he was killed on the Israeli Lebanese border. (HH6, G2, M)

The Gulf War had direct and indirect effects on Palestinians both inside and outside Palestine. This is because many were forced out of their jobs and houses in the Gulf countries and Kuwait. During the Gulf War the majority of Palestinians supported Iraq with high expectations that Saddam could liberate Palestine. People's hopes were raised when Saddam fired a few rockets at Israel. Again the Palestinians' dreams of liberation were short-lived, as the Gulf War ended without the liberation of Palestine. Ahmed said:

> During the Gulf war, we hoped that Saddam would attack Israel. We were happy in the beginning and proud as Arabs. He said he would destroy Israel and he attacked it using rockets and missiles. At the time of the war, I hoped to be a bird flying to Iraq. Israel and America are strong by the weakness of the Arab countries; they are after Arab resources especially the oil. (HH7, G2, M)

The beginning of the peace process between Israel and the Palestinians in the early 1990s was a turning-point for many Palestinians. Abu Ahmed said:

> I did not believe in the Oslo agreement. The people who want Oslo did not read the Koran. El Bagara verses mentioned that the Jews like to argue. Jews will never give anything to Palestinians. We should have the force and power. They only know the language of power. Our prophet Mohammed said that the stone will talk, the conflict will continue; there will be no solution through Oslo. (HH8, G2, M)

This section shows that the Palestinians' journeys to exile started in 1948, followed by the 1967 war and the 1982 Israeli invasion of Lebanon. The prolonged conflict and forced migration raised the political awareness of Palestinians.

Political Awareness

All generations were aware of Palestinian political conditions. Politics and political issues are part of the daily life of many Palestinians, including those who lived in refugee camps. Heavy Palestinian involvement in politics is connected to the intensive media coverage of the situation, and the activities of many political parties in recruiting from the younger generation. Many young people showed their full awareness of the political conditions. Salwa, speaking in the girls' focus group (GFG), reflected on the causes of the current *Intifada*, the destruction of the Palestinian infrastructure and the reaction of people:

> *Al-Aqsa Intifada* erupted because our fighters wanted to defend the Al-Aqsa Mosque... Our struggle against the Israeli occupation is escalating. We increased the attacks against our enemy, the Israelis lost their minds when their people were injured and killed... they became like wild wolves smashing everything without mercy or sympathy. For example, soldiers destroyed land, uprooted olive and orange trees, demolished private houses and buildings while people were asleep and left many people homeless or living in tents. The Israeli military closed our roads and tightened the siege on our areas. Sharon increased the destruction of our lives, the displacement of our people and tightened the military siege on us; he is still the Prime Minister of Israel. We will continue our military operations, which scare the Zionists... our people continued their struggle to defeat the Zionist enemy and to rebuild our Palestinian State and raise our flag high. (GFG, G4, F)

Many young participants were able to connect the political situation with poverty. Nuha, in her description of the situation in the Gaza Strip, said:

> I think that the future of Gaza is not good. Gaza is a very limited area. We have nothing. When people are hungry they react. Poverty causes most of our problems. Money can solve most of my problems, but there is no money. What can I do? I tried to work but there are no jobs around here and it is difficult for me to work and study at the same time. (HH12, G3, F)

For many Palestinians, their experiences with the Arab leaders were disappointing and frustrating. Many participants reported being suspicious of the motivations of the Arab leaders. Abu Mohammed highlighted this issue thus:

> To tell the truth I did not believe in the Arabs; no one can solve the Palestinians' problem other than Palestinians. The Arab and international efforts often hurt the Palestinian cause. In the 1973 war we classed it as a real war and a real win after crossing the Suez Canal. Once the war ended, we saw it as a foreign plot. I remember how the Jews occupied Gaza and Sinai. As Palestinians this action did not surprise us. It was a plot to kill us, all of us! The Lebanon war and the

PLO withdrawal from Lebanon was another plot from America in agreement with Israel to scatter the Palestinians. In all these events the Arabs left us alone and without support. (HH6, G2, M)

Confrontation

Confrontations with the Israeli troops are one of the main features of life for many Palestinians, especially refugees. Almost all the interviewees admitted involvement in confrontations during different periods of Palestinian history. For example, while the younger generations provided detailed stories of their participation in confrontations with the Israeli troops, the older generations remembered the confrontations with the Jewish paramilitary groups and the British troops before 1948. Abu Bassam's memories of the confrontations between the Jewish community and Palestinians are a good example of the latter:

> The Jews were in the Negba settlement, they attacked our villages daily; they destroyed homes and killed people. Several times, we approached the British army seeking protection. They gave us 10 guns and gave the Jews cannons and tanks. In 1947 the Jews occupied the village and I was the responsible man in the village. I was an officer for the revolutionaries. I met with an Egyptian officer in the area of Abdes, who brought us assistance. The Egyptian officer and his soldiers attacked the Jews and liberated our village. I still remember the names of those people who fought with us in Palestine. (HH12, G1, M)

Some elderly participants (grandparents) mentioned the growing tension that erupted between the Palestinians and the Jewish community; military confrontations started between Palestinian fighters and Jewish paramilitary groups. The fights increased and reached their peak in 1948. Those who were involved in the confrontations were known as *wateneen* (nationalists) or *thouar* (fighters). The British tried to separate the two communities; they supported the Jewish community and in doing so they isolated the Palestinians. Palestinian society supported and respected the nationalists. Abu Mohammad remembered the confrontations before 1948 as follows:

> In Salama we were nationalists. My uncle was one of the nationalists. The British authority sentenced him to death. Revolutionists were hiding in our groves. We were trained on how to use guns. My father gave me a gun to carry at the age of 15. I participated in many battles in Jafa. The route from Jafa to Gaza was very difficult. Planes attacked us and the Jews attacked Jafa with mortar cannons. The troops attacked us for two months. I met up with a friend of the family who told me where my family were but unfortunately they had already left that place. Consequently, I lived in Rafah with another family and there I remained without work for sometime. (HH12, G1, M)

Al-Nakba for many interviewees represented memories of the confrontations between Arabs and the Jewish community, the creation of Israel, killing, forced migration and displacement of Palestinians. Abu Mohammed remembered the confrontations during *al-Nakba* as follows:

> When the British army withdrew on 15 May 1947 and declared the independence of the state of Israel, the Jews celebrated and this provoked the Arabs. The Palestinians killed a Jewish man, and subsequently other Jews living in the settlement, which was situated higher than our village, started attacking our village. The inhabitants of Salma sold their wives' gold and bought guns and cannons with the proceeds. They placed the cannon in a high place and one Palestinian, who worked with the British army, fired the cannon. The confrontation continued. We killed a couple of Jews and they killed a few of us. *Shabab* [youth] told the inhabitants of the village that they would attack the settlement and set it alight. This is what happened: women carried a cupboard containing one of the Jews killed in the village and we brought three Jewish men and three children. We killed the men and released the three children to Mr. Mosa Abu Hashia who negotiated with the British army to lift the siege on the village. The inhabitants protected Salma. There was a home outside the village but the Palestinian family living there left it. Later on one of the Jewish army troops occupied the house for a while. Another Jewish troop came and not knowing who lived there, surrounded the home with mines and bombarded it, killing all its inhabitants. After the attack on the settlement which destroyed the cannon and killed the Jews in the settlement, the British army gave the Jews weapons such as cannons instead of guns. They attacked the village destroying half of the buildings and killing many people. The inhabitants of Salma were forced to leave in trucks to the Lod and Ramla. I did not migrate because I was in Jafa visiting my brother-in-law. (HH12, G1, M)

The political activism of the younger generation was clearly shown during the first (December 1987) and the second (September 2000) Palestinian Uprisings. The first *Intifada* was a popular movement against the Israeli systematic aggression towards Palestinians. It lasted till the beginning of the peace negotiations between Israel and the Palestinian authority in the early 1990s. As a result of the *Intifada*, hundreds of Palestinians were killed and thousands were wounded. Mohamed described his family experiences during the Intifada:

> During the *Intifada*, soldiers came to our home in the early morning and got me out to read the slogans on the walls. This was despite the fact that the soldier was a *Druze* [Muslim sect] and he knew the Arabic language better than I did. He asked me who wrote the slogans and I said I did not know. He called me a liar and beat me. I remember the curfew, unemployment, sleeplessness and soldiers knocking on doors at night. I was beaten in front of my wife and children. Once I was severely beaten by soldiers, I went home crying and I had pain all over my body. (HH12, G2, M)

Many interviewees said they were beaten or had witnessed others being humiliated or beaten by soldiers. Sami shared his family's experiences with the Israeli soldiers during the years of the Uprising:

> I hate Jews. I am scared of them. During the *Intifada*, I watched the Israeli soldiers ask an old man to clean the ground in the Palestine Square in Gaza City known locally as Sahet Taxiat. Jews made all people hate them. One day during the *Intifada* I saw soldiers beating my mother; I cried, shouted and tried to help but I could not. The Jews beat my mother and me because she tried to help two children escape from the soldiers. I saw one of the soldiers try to shoot her with a gun. The soldiers occupied the roof of the house to control the area and they brought many children to the roof to beat them. At night we could not sleep because of the crying of boys on the roof. I saw how soldiers pulled the children, injured, on the stairs. My children thought that by throwing stones we would regain our land. (HH6, G3, M)

The early involvement of youth in political activities encouraged many of them to be independent, gain self-confidence and take on more responsibilities. Some participants presented the positive side of the *Intifada*, which brought unity to the Palestinian community. Mohammed said:

> The *Intifada* is the best thing that Palestinians had in their life. *Shabab* of the *Intifada* solved the problems among the people. All types of people participated in *Intifada* to express their feelings without fear. As a youth, I participated in the confrontations and felt like the other *Shabab*. During the confrontations, I saw some Israeli soldiers running away from children. The *Intifada* broke the fear barrier. The different political factions worked in unity and everyone worked in harmony. There was cohesiveness in the Palestinian society. I had high self-esteem. (HH8, G3, M)

Many young people admitted their active participation in the street confrontations of the current Uprising. As a result of their involvement many were subjected to high levels of stress and anxiety. Many girls coped with the stress by weeping, feeling helpless and hopeless. San'a said:

> One day I participated in a demonstration near Kfar Darom settlement. During the confrontations, I saw young children weeping and many *Shabab* were injured or killed. I had the urge to attack those Jews. I felt helpless, hopeless and hurt; my tears were the only friends I had, so I started to weep. My father comforted me by explaining the Palestinians' situation; he took me to the beach, which lessened my tension and sadness. (GFG, G4, F)

Participants from all generations spoke of the political socialisation of children. Many children hear stories of their lost homeland from parents and grandparents. They also see the news of confrontations in their neighbourhoods and hear details of the debates and discussions on political issues. This intensive political socialisation is reflected clearly in children's games: many children play games that reflect their living conditions. Sa'id described the games he played during his childhood:

> The game we played as children was 'Arabs and Jews'. In this game the Arabs would attack using stones and the Jews would retaliate with guns. Children were divided in those who played the role of Jews while others were Arabs. Children who represented the Jews in our games were those who assumed the power and were stronger, while others chose to represent the Arabs and refused to be part of the Jewish group. Our games had violent elements; I thought that it was a useful training for the future. In our play it was always victory for the Arabs. (HH6, G3, M)

Political socialisation and awareness encouraged many people to participate in confrontations. This participation fed into the growing resistance among Palestinians.

Resistance

The current Palestinian youth are experiencing the unworkable and blocked peace agreement, the tight Israeli military closures of the Palestinian self-ruled areas, the unbearable living conditions in the refugee camps and the eruption of the current Palestinian Uprising in September 2000. Almost all the interviewees agreed that young people are being subjected to intensive sociopolitical and economic strains. Currently, many participants are witnessing and living through horrifying violence, such as killings, assassinations, bombardments and demolition of property. Such horrific events encouraged many people to resist. Tariq explained:

> I can not explain or describe the horrifying situations I witnessed or experienced. I witnessed the killing of many people. For example, I saw a terrifying killing of a man in my neighbourhood; soldiers dragged his body in the street. It was awful. Meanwhile, the Arab leaders are not doing anything; they do not care even if hundreds of Palestinians are killed. We will stay in our land and fight for our principles to liberate Al-Quds [Jerusalem] and sing the songs of liberation of Al-Quds and the Al-Aqsa Mosque. I will fight for Palestine and my principles. (BFG, G4, M)

According to the elderly interviewees many children have lost their childhood as a result of war. This finding is in line with some studies from South Africa, which viewed children there as the lost generation or children without a childhood (Mercy and O'Carroll, 1989). However, many young people started to resist the occupation. Abu Sami remembered his childhood during the 1967 war:

Wars turned children to adults. During war we did not have a childhood, we were not children, we felt like adults. For example, in the 1967 war we hid in our neighbour's home among the sheep. There was a rumour that people found with guns would be killed. People escaped to Nusierat. I remember how my cousin went to attack a tank with a gun and his mother went running after him shouting for him to come back. He screamed at his mother saying, 'I should go. I have a gun. I am a brave man, not a woman.' I remember many Palestinian heroes who have stood to fight tanks with a gun. (HH9, G2, M)

The young generation talked about extreme actions being taken to liberate Palestine. Such actions included martyring operations, which are often presented in the media as suicidal operations. Currently, the culture of *al-Istishehad* (martyrdom) is getting stronger among the generation who were children during the first Uprising in 1987. Ahmed said:

I saw the ruination of land by bulldozers, the destruction of beautiful houses to increase the size of settlements. Most of the children in Gaza suffered from the Zionist bombardment. I will defend my country and homeland. We will stay and die as martyrs till we liberate Palestine and Al-Aqsa. If they fight us with their planes and tanks, we will defend ourselves by faith and unity. We killed many occupiers by martyr operations. The fear of these operations has made soldiers more aggressive and they react violently. I participated in funeral ceremonies for martyrs. I feel proud of them; I want to do the same and die for the cause of Palestine. (BFG, G4, M)

Feelings of safety and security are rare among Palestinians, especially in the young generation. Many young people internalised their feelings of frustrations and anger while others feel that adults fail to protect them. To overcome such feelings, many young people participate in street confrontations. For instance, the findings showed that many young people were willing to be martyrs to defend the cause of Palestine. The Gaza Mental Health Centre, in their studies among Palestinian young people, raised this point (Qouta et al. 1997). People's willingness to die is accompanied by the growth of feelings of nationalism and a sense of national and social-political identity. Samir said:

The Zionist Sharon entered Al-Aqsa and shot Palestinian people. Later on, *al-Aqsa Intifada* erupted. Many people were killed and injured. The Israeli army destroyed houses, confiscated our land and killed our children like Mohammed El Doura while he was in his father's arms, who was severely injured in trying to protect his son, but he could not. The Jews are heartless and merciless. Also, the killing of Eman Hejou, who was killed in the bombardment of Khan Younis, her body and shape were terrifying. The Israeli army also closed the roads, which led to lack of food and drink. We will struggle till we liberate Palestine and raise the Palestinian flags on Al-Aqsa Mosque. When the Israeli army destroy our land, I will defend it and kick them out. I will kidnap their soldiers and tell them I will kill them if they do not leave. If they agree to leave I will release their soldiers. (BFG, G4, M)

Many participants, especially children and adolescents, mentioned humiliations inflicted by Israeli troops. Sami said:

> The Israeli army creates a terror for our innocent children who were taken away from their mothers' warm chests. The Jewish Zionists have tried hard to destroy us [Palestinians]; they created terror for our children. The *qafla* [group] of the martyrs increased daily; there are at least three martyrs per day. The Israelis have continued to offend and humiliate us, uproot our trees, destroy and bombard houses. I remembered how Jews deliberately brought female soldiers to humiliate Palestinians. At the Erez checkpoint the Israeli soldiers continually humiliated us, for example, they say you are a *himar* [donkey]. (BFG, G4, M)

The findings show that people's feelings of abhorrence, anger, frustration and revenge created high levels of resistance as a way of coping with the violent situation. The first and the current Uprisings show that many young people are willing to die; they refuse to withdraw or to watch their communities being uprooted again. In reflection of his experience of the first *Intifada*, Iyad said:

> During the *Intifada* in 1987, the feeling of hate towards Jews was high and the call for revenge created a feeling of resistance. When university and school students hear the sounds of military jeeps, they leave the university and school in order to throw stones. (HH6, G3, M)

Participants showed an increase of hatred of Israelis – many of them refer to Israelis as Jews – because of the hard experiences with the Israeli troops. Abu Omer described his feelings towards Israelis:

> We imagined Israelis as an army without families. I hated the Jews more and more after the 1956 war. How these human beings killed and destroyed our villages; how these people took our land. We shared our tents with insects, bugs, fleas and lice. I hate them and told my children to hate them. Jews have long hated Arabs. This hatred stems from the time when Isabel [the Palestinian woman] married a Jewish king and played an influential role before the Jews burned Isabel and the king. (HH8, G2, M)

Some participants, especially women from the elderly generation, said they were scared of the tanks and the killings. Um Roshdi said:

> During the 1967 war I was scared of them. They had tanks and aeroplanes. My father and uncle had guns. We heard the shooting from the tanks. I saw the fear in my parents' eyes. I was afraid of losing my father and living alone. We raised the white flag without resistance! (HH12, G2, F)

The long conflict and continuing confrontations between Palestinians and the Israeli troops left strong negative images of the Israelis. Hate of the enemy is another element that was raised frequently by the different generations of interviewees. Salim's response to hate was:

> I hate Jews, and I know the Jews hated the Arabs. Jews revealed this feeling in buses, for example. They did not sit near Arabs and in some restaurants they did not allow the Arab to work in the restaurants. I worked in Israel as a labourer and the life of a labourer in Israel was very difficult. Jews undermine and humiliate us. (HH6, G2, M)

In summary, the above narratives show the political awareness of the interviewees in the continuing confrontations. There is also evidence that Palestinians from different generations participated actively in the resistance movement. These findings fit the image of Palestinian youth who are known to be active participants in resistance. This is unlike other war situations world-wide, where children and young people are often passive or victims of political conflict (Barber 2000).

Sociocultural Structure

Each generation has developed some coping strategies to deal with changes and the stressful events they encountered while trying to overcome and cope with some emerging problems. This section includes four main themes: destruction of the social network, social change, gender discrimination and education.

Destruction of Social Networks

Al-Nakba in 1948 caused major destruction of people's social and family networks; many Palestinians suffered as a consequence of not knowing what happened to members of their families, neighbourhoods and villages. Abu Mohammad presents a picture of continual uncertainty:

> I remember feeling frustrated because I had no money, no family and no friends. I walked and walked and suddenly I found myself among Egyptians in Egypt-Rafah. One Egyptian welcomed me and helped me. He asked me to bring my family and gave me a camel. I worked with the Egyptians for two and a half months and then I heard that people from Jafa, Lod and Ramla were living in Bureij military British camp barracks. I went to Bureij and found my family. I started off living in the barracks but I later bought a tent and lived in the tent with my wife. I subsequently had a room made of mud, which was built by UNRWA. (HH6, G1, M)

Many people heard horrifying stories from neighbouring villages and they feared being killed, therefore they left the majority of their property behind, carrying very little with them. As Abu Bassam's account of displacement shows, many families were divided:

> My wife and my son were evacuated to Hamama and I remained in Bet Affa. At that time the Jews attacked KoKaba Square and Bet Affa was separated from the other villages and towns. It took 15 days to get from Hamama to Majdal, then on to Herbia and finally to Gaza. We had only one horse, one mattress and sheets. My family was at Bet Affa and they moved to Falouja. During the siege of Falouja, the people used all the stored wheat to make bread. The people from Bet Affa bought wheat and made bread for those in Falouja. Many women threw away their things so that they could carry their babies. I saw one woman putting her clothes and baby aside so that she could run. She later went back to carry him. When we reached Gaza City, we lived in a tent in Rayes land. I sent people to collect my family from Falouja. I did not see them for five months. We left our homes barefoot; with no clothes; we had nothing at all. (HH12, G1, M)

Interviewees characterised life in the refugee camps as hard and unbearable due to poverty, unemployment, hard living conditions and total dependency on United Nations (UN) donations. Abu Bassam presented his family life in the refugee camp:

> We lived for six months in the Sabra area and then we moved to the Bureij camp with most of my family. Our families settled in the Bureij and Nuseirat camps. We lived in a military camp barracks. There was no privacy; there were 15 families in each of the barracks. Later, we erected a wall so we could have some privacy but the wall fell on my children. In the beginning life was difficult. We used blankets as clothes and then we wore second-hand clothes distributed by UNRWA. We received dry rations and tins of beans from UNRWA. The wall dividing our place in the barracks in the Bureij camp fell and injured two of us. The women re-built it. We played football with a ball made of clothes. My clothes were often dirty from playing in the mud. My father would beat me over the state of my clothes. There was no water to clean our clothes at that time. We collected water every day. I used to carry the plate of bread on my head from the bakery. The school class was very crowded with 55 pupils in a dark place. Despite my age, I was obliged to work and help my father as well as attending school. We were totally dependent on UNRWA aid. There were communal baths in the camp with hot water and soap. (HH12, G1, M)

Um Rushdi described the poverty in the refugee camps which forced her to work in order to assist her family:

> We were poor, I had to work with my husband. I helped my husband in the factory on an unpaid basis. The male income is insufficient to meet the needs of the family especially when the family size is 7–8 persons. So, women work from sunrise to sunset. Inside the house I shared with him the home affairs but for outside affairs I did not share the workload. (HH8, G2, F)

In coping with refugee camps many interviewees of the grandparents' generation mentioned their acceptance of God's will and being tolerant. Abu Mohammed thought himself lucky for being educated and for having a job:

> After *al-Nakba* we went back home and we had nothing; I had to live with my wife in a tent. It is too much to tolerate. We accept God's will. If I had no UNRWA job, my living conditions would be totally different. I am a lucky man. I think before I act. I am an educated man. I am a sports man. I always organise my work and the work of those around me. I had a good social and economic position as an UNRWA staff member compared to the other refugees. People were jealous of me. (HH6, G1, M)

Other generations were born and brought up in the overcrowded refugee camps. They heard stories from their parents and grandparents about life in Palestine. In the early days of the migrations some elderly refugees were able to visit their property in Palestine. In comparison, the young generation were aware of the current level of destruction caused by the daily confrontations in their surroundings. They described in detail examples of killing and bombardment. For example, Maha said:

> During *al-Aqsa Intifada*, I saw the destruction, bombardment, and killing of Mohammed El Doura in his father's hands. I saw the bombardment of houses in Khan Younis and Deir el Balah. The soldiers first threw a light bomb and then the bombardment. I saw the destruction of roads. Once I went to Khan Younis and saw the tank standing on the road preventing people from crossing. I saw pictures of Eman Hejo, a five month old girl sleeping in her bed; after Jews shot and killed her. (GFG, G4, F)

In the early years of the Israeli-Palestinian conflict, many Palestinians refused to buy land or to move out of the refugee camps. The refusal was based on the belief that refugee camps were a temporary arrangement until the end of the war, at which time people could go back to Palestine. Abu Bassam said:

> We did not buy any land because we thought that the war would end within three months and we would go back home. We had hoped to go back to our land but the wars in 1956 and 1967 destroyed our hopes forever. (HH12, G1, M)

Social Change

The forced migration resulted in some social changes to the structure of the family and the society. The findings show the increasing awareness of young people of their social and cultural identity; many youths participated in organising festivals and cultural events within and outside their camps. Elder generations (first and second) complained about the sensitive relationship between residents, who are known as *mowatneen* (residents), and those who live in the refugee camps, who are known as *laje'een* (refugees). Many highlighted the tension between the two groups. The word 'refugees', according to the interviewees, represented stigma, shame, poverty and homeless people. Such negative images had long been felt by many refugees. The younger generations of refugees (third and fourth), by focusing on education and resistance, turned the word 'refugee' from a shameful stigma to a positive symbol that was rewarding and made them feel proud.

The first Uprising united Palestinians and strengthened their sense of national identity; different generations participated actively in social and political activities. Firstly, many political parties developed social activities, such as the women's movement, voluntary committees and students' movement. Secondly, the active participation of youth and young people in street confrontations allowed them to actively and openly express their anger and frustrations. For example, many of them played the role of protectors for their local community and they participated in solving some internal problems between families.

Early marriage for girls seems to be a common practice among many Palestinian refugee families, especially those from Gaza. Many interviewees felt that early marriages increased because of the *Intifada* (Hammami, 1992; Manasrah, 1989). According to the interviewees, the reasons for early marriage are: firstly, some families' fear for their daughters' honour and reputations, which is connected with the fear of mixing with boys in the demonstrations or being arrested by the Israeli troops; secondly, many families are poor, therefore, marrying off a female member of the family means fewer people to feed in the household; thirdly, some people think that a woman's place is at home to take care of the family – thus they should be married and by doing so families transfer a woman's responsibility from her father to her husband. Interestingly, many interviewees viewed early marriage as a way of protecting females, so that their husbands became responsible for their safety. Samar said:

> I remember the start of the *Intifada*. I remember how my classmates were forced into early marriage. This is because of their families' fear that they will mix with boys or Jewish soldiers ... All these factors pushed people to arrange early marriages for their daughters. (HH12, G3, F)

In early marriage, generally, girls are not consulted; on the contrary, often they were forced out of schools into arranged early marriages. The marriage of girls is the decision of their family – mainly male members – therefore, they are not allowed to reject or object to their family's choice. Samia shared her early marriage experience as follows:

My father did not consult me when my husband asked for my hand in marriage. I agreed to marry upon the wish of my father... My mother-in-law told my mother that she wanted me for her son. My mother told her that I was young and knew nothing about marriage. My mother-in-law said that she would teach me. This was how I came to be married; so simple! Since my marriage, I have suffered a lot from my mother-in-law. (GFG, G3, F)

Another social change was in young people's relationships with their families. Many interviewees see the relationships as tense and challenging, while others are aware of the different generational expectations. Samar said:

I am aware that my father's mentality is different to mine, he is often nervous but he did not impose his opinion on us. My father is a difficult person. He had a difficult life. He was an orphan. My father and his two brothers are working in Israel. He sponsored my university education. He is frustrated because he did not complete his studies. (HH12, G3, F)

Gender Discrimination

Palestinian society is a patriarchal and authoritarian society. In such societies, males have unlimited freedom while females are kept away from social life outside the family. The findings show that some families perceived boys as responsible for their sisters' movements and behaviour, even if the father is still at home or the sisters are older than them, and boys have the dominant role in society. In comparison, girls are viewed as weak and needing protection; their social movements are restricted. Therefore, girls have to be accompanied by their brothers or other elderly women whenever they go outside the house. Neveen said:

Parents prevent us [girls] from going alone outside the house; this is because we could not protect ourselves. When there is a party, my father prevents me and my sisters from attending. We feel that culture and tradition make us very tied. Boys have more freedom than us. Once we arranged to have a good party for one of my friends; on the day of the party, I called my father at home. He refused to allow me to go. I cried and avoided him for sometime. (GFG, G4, F)

Some families believed in restricting female freedom in terms of access to a social life, education and employment. This is connected to the strong social beliefs that present men as breadwinners and heads of households, while women are housewives, child carers and care providers. Sadika said:

My husband Mohammed brings all the necessary things for the home and all the money is with him. I have no money. My husband cares too much about his money; all that he wants in life is to collect more money. I do not mind that, I am a housewife, I take care of the family. (HH8, G2, F)

In general, within the Palestinian struggle women are often presented as the mothers and sisters of the fighters; their role is limited to protecting youth during the confrontations. However, the traditional image of women is currently changing; many women are educated and working, and more are participating in the confrontations. For instance, some interviewees argued that there is no difference between males and females in society; each gender gets what they deserve. Shaaban said:

There are no differences between boys and girls. Everyone benefits from life according to his efforts. My oldest daughter finished her university education. One of my sons is an agriculture engineer, one has a Ph.D. in nursing, and one is a physician and his daughters are at secondary school. (HH8, G2, M)

Education

Generally, education is valued highly in Palestinian society. Many Palestinian refugees in Gaza Strip see education as a way out of poverty and as transferable skills that can be used whenever and wherever convenient. Many interviewees thought that focusing on education was a way of coping with their hard economic, social and political conditions. Education was affected during the Uprising by the Israeli closures of schools and academic institutions. Many students participated in violent incidents around schools without the knowledge of their parents. Hani participated in confrontations despite the disagreement of his family:

During the *Intifada*, the Jews provoked the students on their way to school. In one year we only studied for three days due to the curfews. I would occasionally participate in the *Intifada* activities to the disappointment of my father and grandfather. If they discovered my participation they would beat me. All the people in the camp would hear me crying from the beating. They were afraid of revenge from the Israelis. They wanted me to go to school but I hated school. I quit education and worked in construction. My grandfather taught other people who became doctors, engineers, etc. But, he could not educate his own sons and grandsons. (BFG, G3, M)

The Israeli soldiers targeted schools and students, especially those located within the refugee camps; many of them were closed for long periods of time, and many of the confrontations occurred within and around schools. As a result of confrontations many schooling days were lost and many students were left with minimal literacy skills, while others left to join the labour market. Husam said:

Education before the *Intifada* was excellent, but the *Intifada* spoiled the education process. Jews closed the schools and attacked the pupils. In one year the secondary school was only open for a few days. How could we succeed? We did not learn all the curriculum during the *Intifada*. I was obliged to leave school and work with my father in the factory. (HH12, G3, M)

Bassam also supported this view:

The *Intifada* had negative effects on the education process. As the pupils reached the fourth and the sixth grade, they lacked literacy skills. Many students could not write their own names. Children spent their time in the street; no one cared to ask them where they were and what they were doing. Therefore, children's academic achievement during the *Intifada* was very poor. We should focus on education. (HH6, G3, M)

Currently, many teachers in schools have noticed the decreasing level of students' educational skills and increasing level of antisocial behaviour. Hani said:

I am an UNRWA teacher at a preparatory school in Bureij. Many of my pupils are nearly illiterate, for example, many of them cannot even write their names in English. Many pupils are not polite, they have no respect for the teachers or the head-teacher. They used sharp tools in their quarrels. (HH6, G3, M)

War influences the young generation's choice of education; many could not continue their higher education because of poverty or lack of educational opportunities. Munir said:

I finished secondary school and wanted to study in Beirut, Lebanon. However, because of the war in Lebanon, I did not complete my studies in the university. I therefore worked in the textile industry and have remained in this job up to now. (HH6, G3, M)

Economic Conditions

The main economic themes that emerged from the interviews were the repeated generational experiences of poverty, unemployment and loss of private property. The first generation lost their private properties such as houses, land and businesses. Many members of the second generation stayed in the refugee camps and refused to buy land because they considered their living in the camps as temporary until they returned to their place of origin. Many of them still held the keys for their houses and registration papers of their property (e.g., land and houses). Nevertheless, the second generation continued to experience poverty, but started to settle into their refugee camps as UNRWA started to introduce free education for the younger generation. Therefore, many began to focus on education as a way out of poverty. Moreover, this generation witnessed the war in 1967, which created another wave of poverty and destruction; the camps were hit badly by the war and resistance was high among refugees. This war resulted in many people fleeing their homes for the second time and leaving behind their personal belongings.

Rates of poverty and unemployment were high among refugees. Most of the interviewees complained about their poor socioeconomic conditions, the high unemployment rate and their inability to cope with their family needs due to the low salaries and lack of employment. Because of the limited opportunities for jobs in Gaza, many refugees were dependent on the Israeli labour market. Many interviewees mentioned that working in Israel humiliated them, especially when they saw the names of their villages changed to Hebrew. Abu Ahmad expressed his experiences as a refugee and a labourer in Israel as follows:

> My house in the refugee camp is very old and we have only one room. We asked UNRWA for renovation. We waited for their answer for a long time. In addition to my own family, I have two old sisters who are living with us; one is a widow and the other has not married. I was dismissed from my first job in Israel and worked in a clothes factory from 7pm to 6am. I used to sleep from exhaustion on my way from the factory to my home. I used to miss my bus stop due to tiredness and would have to pay more to return back to my home. My sons are working in the clothing industry and there is no work now as the clothes imported from Turkey, China and Syria affect the local clothes industry. (HH6, G2, M)

Teaching in schools was one of the employment options for educated refugees. A few elderly refugees had some form of education and were recruited by UNRWA as teachers. Abu Mohammed said:

> In 1949, I worked as a teacher at a Quaker funded elementary school where there were no classrooms. The students sat and wrote on the ground using coal. Tins and groceries replaced teachers' salaries. The situation was very difficult as teachers came to school wearing *kubkab* [wooden shoes] and dressed in coats and shirts made from blankets. Schools were opened for boys and girls. The graduates were directly assigned as teachers. My first salary was six Egyptian pounds, which was a donation from the United States of America and then my salary became three Egyptian pounds per month. (HH8, G2, M)

Some interviewees connected the difficult economic situation with the political instability. Also many interviewees mentioned that the Israeli labour market affected the standard of living for many Palestinians.

Moreover, many participants thought that the economic situation was worsened due to the wars and political instability in the region. Bassam said:

> The economic and social situation deteriorated due to the wars in 1956, 1967 and 1973. We had great hopes of President Abdel Naser in Egypt. We were disappointed after the 1967 War. Israel increased its power and force. I was afraid that Israel would occupy Cairo. Israel opened the door for the *Shabab* to work in Israel because there was no work in the Gaza Strip. People of Gaza who worked in Israel brought all the rubbish of Jews such as the old TVs, radios, refrigerators, videos and cars. They brought anything and everything. People encouraged their children to marry. Labourers were content to be working. They were working as servants in their land. (HH12, G1, M)

Poverty and limited job opportunities forced many refugees to be dependent on UNRWA assistance (e.g., food supplements and shelter). Salem explained how poverty influenced his family in the early 1970s and how they handled their conditions. He said:

> As refugees we were poor and unskilled; due to poverty we had to be dependents on UNRWA. I remember people queued for one sack of flour when there was hardly anything to feed our families with in the early 1970s. Often I was tired of waiting for hours to get our rations; therefore, my father and I did not queue and returned home without flour. It was very hard for our families to survive with hardly anything to eat but things got better with the opening of the job market where many people started to earn their living. (HH6, G2, M)

Psychological Issues

This section includes the major psychological themes that emerged from the interviewees. The psychological impacts included: trauma, stress and anxiety, tension and aggression.

Stress and anxiety were reflected clearly in the responses of many interviewees. Stress occurred as a result of the uncertainty of facing the unknown. For instance, many people suffered stress and anxiety because of not knowing what the future would hold. Furthermore, living in overcrowded camps increases stress and anxiety. The idea of personal space hardly exists in the context of refugee camps. Lack of personal space might lead to tension between family members or even the whole community, which might lead to aggression. For instance, many young people complained that their fathers were often nervous, irritable, did not listen to their opinions, and were too busy earning a living. Young people also thought that their parents did not talk to them or even love them. The way young people cope with such emotional stress is by avoiding confrontations with parents, especially fathers. Mo'men said:

> I am sure that my father did not love my brothers or me. We feel that he treated us as servants. He is more interested in people knowing how his children were strong and had established themselves without any help. I feel I am not myself; I am the son of my father. I accept and respect my father's authority as the head of the household, but not my mother's. I find it hard to talk with my father and much easier to speak to my mother. This is because my father is often nervous and aggressive; therefore, being around my father is very stressful for the whole family, especially the young generation. I discovered the best way to deal with him is to avoid his anger and do what he asked us to do without discussion. (BFG, G4, M)

Coping with the current stress and destruction for many girls meant sadness and crying. Samyeh provided her personal account:

> Last week, I was watching the painful pictures on television caused by the Israeli military forces. Suddenly, our telephone rang and my mother answered; she became silent and looked sad. We hesitated to ask her what happened. She told us that Ramadan Isamel and three other people were killed while trying to remove a suspected parcel. We were speechless, felt the size of the catastrophe and started crying in silence. Next day I went to school and could not concentrate on my lessons; I sat on the floor and started weeping. One of my teachers noticed my sadness and asked me why am I upset. When I told her the reasons for my sadness, she told me not to be sad and reminded me that Ramadan is not the first martyr. After school, I went home but still feeling miserable; later on I felt a little bit better when I remembered that the martyr is God's favourite. I still remember that painful incident and I will never be able to remove it from my memory. (GFG, G4, F)

Many young interviewees revealed the pain and stress they encountered as a result of watching and/or directly experiencing violent events. For example, many remembered the details of the killing of young children (e.g., Mohammad El Doura and Eman Hejo). Nuha said:

> I saw some painful and sad pictures on TV which made me sad, irritable and weepy. I saw destroyed houses, displaced women and children, burned land and uprooted trees. If I write what I see, the pages of all papers in the whole world will not be enough. For me the most traumatic painful scenes of killings were Mohammad El Doura and Eman Hejo, they were both shot by merciless, heartless soldiers. It is not enough what they did in Sabra and Shatila I feel speechless, because such people lack sympathy and sensitivity; they would not be able to understand the feelings of displaced and humiliated people. (GFG, G4, F)

Repeated generational trauma is presented as one of the features associated with the different generational experiences of forced migration and prolonged conflict. Children heard stories describing the traumatic experiences of their parents and grandparents. Most of them also experienced or witnessed a wide range of traumatic events, especially during the first and the current Palestinian *Intifada*. For example, many people, especially the young generation, witnessed members of their families being killed or injured, and their houses being raided by soldiers and their neighbourhoods being under military curfews. Salem demonstrated his traumatic experiences with the Israeli soldiers as follows:

> I witnessed the Israeli soldiers beating my best friend and they placed him in a dustbin near our house. He was in so much pain and I felt helpless for not being able to protect him. A few weeks ago, I went to buy medicine from a nearby pharmacy; the army caught me in the street; they beat me and threw me into a dustbin in our neighbourhood. When I was with the soldiers, I thought I was going to die, I was terrified and now I avoid the army. (BFG, G4, M)

Many young people observed killings and they felt helpless and frustrated, as they could not do anything to prevent the killings. Islam remembered her experience with her classmate's killing:

> A few weeks ago, the Israeli soldiers conducted raids in my neighbourhood; they beat many boys and threw tear gas bombs into the houses. From our window I observed the soldiers shooting at my classmate, I saw him lying on the ground and covered with blood. I also saw the shooting and killing of our neighbour's son. Witnessing these two killings I was very angry and frustrated and I cried a lot because I could not do anything to prevent the killings. I felt even worse later when the Israeli army entered my home and beat my father and my older brothers in front of me. Believe me, it is very hard to see your own father in tears. (GFG, G4, F)

The experience of killings is not limited to the younger generation; on the contrary, the other generations had many stories that illustrated such experiences. Bassem said:

> During the 1956 war, I saw an aeroplane shooting at a woman, she was injured and I saw the bone of her limb after amputation. We escaped to my uncle's home in the Nuseirat camp. We thought that the Jews would come from the east and that the west would be safer. It was winter and there were a lot of children with no place to sleep. We did not sleep and we were very scared. (HH12, G2, M)

Many interviewees highlighted the acts of aggression and violence within the community, especially among the young generation. While young people agreed that there is an increase of aggression, they also referred to their teachers' aggressive behaviour towards them. Many young interviewees pointed out that their parents do not care about them. Interestingly, there was general agreement between parents that the young generation does not respect adult authority. Many young people turn to their peer groups for advice and support. Hassam said:

> I like my friends and I trust them sometimes more than my family. My friends often talked about their problems with me; because they know that I did not tell my father or anybody about these problems. If anyone beats me, I beat them directly and without waiting. At home I know that my parents think that we don't respect their authority, this is true sometimes because parents are often very strict with their children. I often asked my father's advice on what to do but not my mother. (BFG, G4, M)

The above narrative accounts of the interviewees show that many young people are active participants in the struggle; many were traumatised by a variety of traumatic events, such as the killing of children. Some young people were angry while others were sad and felt helpless, but many have the spirit of resistance. Many, however, showed that they wanted to shape their destiny themselves – many talked about being martyrs.

Summary

This research focused on the impact of prolonged conflict and forced migration on Palestinian children and young people, and how they cope with the difficult situation in the refugee camps located in the Gaza Strip (see Figure 6.1, which summarizes the main themes). The findings of this research revealed that poverty and unemployment were high among Palestinians, especially those who live in the refugee camps in Gaza strip.

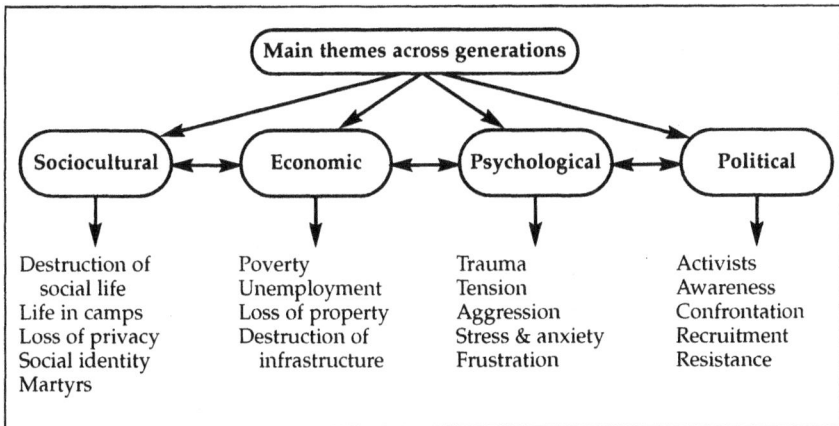

Figure 6.1 The Gaza Strip: Summary of the Main Themes

Several Palestinian generations were and still are active participants in street confrontations. The elderly generation (grandparents) mentioned the selling of their wives' jewellery to buy weapons to defend themselves and Palestine, while many members of the second generation participated actively in the 1967 War. Moreover, the young people were active in the two *Intifadas*. The repeated cycles of prolonged conflict have affected many people, especially the young generation. The high levels of stress and frustration have encouraged many young Palestinians to become activists in the current conflict.

Through political socialisation, children hear stories of their lost homeland from their parents and grandparents. The elderly generation seems to have an active role to play in reactivating and reliving the memories of their lost homeland, Palestine. Such memories are clearly reinforced by seeing the older generation still keeping the keys to their property and refusing to buy pieces of land locally. The media, especially television, and the active recruiting of refugees to political parties reinforce the growth of the Palestinian national identity. Finally, our data show that there is a need for encouraging useful coping strategies in children and young people, to help them cope with daily stressful situations.

Note

1 Acknowledgements and appreciation to the research assistants, including Eitda El Khateib, Salah Hamdan, Jehad Okasha and Samah El Sabhah, for their hard work and continuing support to make this project a success.

References

Barber, B. 2000. 'Politics, Politics, and More Politics: Youth Life Experience in the Gaza Strip'. In D. Bowen and E. Early (eds), *Everyday Life in the Muslim Middle East*. Indiana: Indiana University Press.

Hammami, R. 1992. 'Women in Palestinian society'. In M. Heiber and G. Overnsen (eds), *Palestinian Society in Gaza, the West Bank and East Jerusalem: A Survey of living conditions*. Report No. 151, FAFO.

Manasrah, N. 1989. 'Early Marriage: Temporary Retreat in the March of Palestinian Women'. *Al Kateb Journal*, (Arabic version), August: 24–31.

Mercy, J.A. and O'Carroll, P.W. 1989. 'New Directions in Violence Prediction: The Public Health Arena'. *Violence and Victims*, 3(4): 285–301.

Qouta, S., Punamaki, R.L. and El Sarraj, E. 1997. 'House Demolition and Mental Health: Victims and Witnesses'. *Journal of Social Distress and the Homeless*, 3: 203–11.

7

Policy Implications and Summary of Main Findings

Dawn Chatty and Gillian Lewando Hundt

This multidisciplinary and regional study responds to a number of concerns in contemporary research regarding children in general and Palestinian refugees in particular. It addresses the need to recognise the child and young person as part of a larger social community of extended families, households, neighbourhoods, and local and national communities. It also concerns itself with recognising the importance of regional studies in areas where the case study has reigned supreme. Each of these chapters illustrates how young Palestinian lives are mediated by the specific historical, political and economic realities that bear on them in their most recent place of temporary settlement.

The Local and the Regional

Most studies dealing with Palestinian children have focused on the single community and occasionally on one country. The Gaza Strip and the West Bank have been particularly well represented in such studies and generalisations from these studies have been used to extrapolate information about the conditions, concerns, needs and policy requirements for Palestinian children in the region as a whole. What our study reveals is that though there are commonalities among our five field sites in Lebanon, Syria, Jordan, the West Bank and the Gaza Strip, the particular historical context has varied considerably and thus affected the course of life experiences in each field site.

During our initial start-up workshop in Cyprus in June 1999, we asked each team of Palestinian researchers to create a timeline based on their own life experiences. For many in the team this was the first opportunity they had had to exchange ideas and experiences with Palestinian refugees in other parts of the region. Hence the team based in Syria was for the first time being exposed to Palestinians from the Gaza Strip and vice versa. The lack of shared political and economic experience is clearly expressed in the two timelines drawn by the teams based in Lebanon and in the Gaza Strip (see Figure 7.1). From these visual statements we clearly see the shared experience of *al-Nakba*, but we also recognise the separate histories and the impact which various outbreaks of armed conflict and general violence have had on Palestinian refugees in each field site.

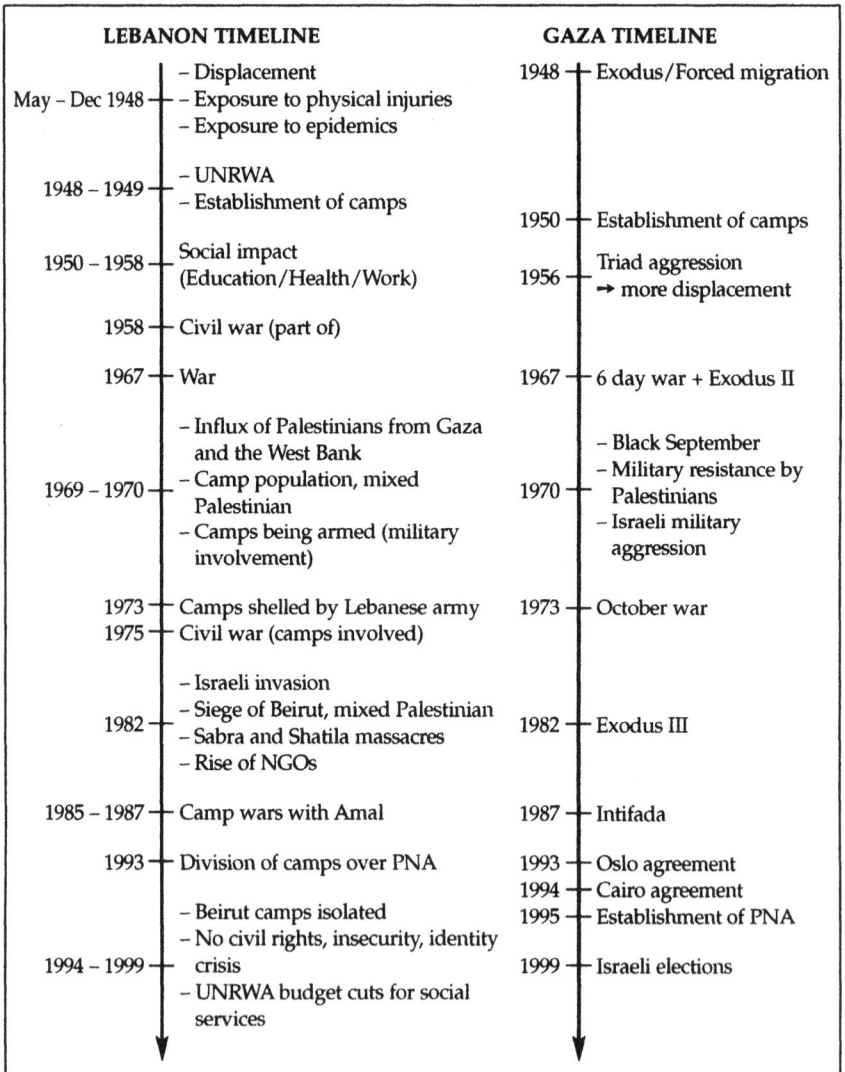

LEBANON TIMELINE		GAZA TIMELINE	
May – Dec 1948	– Displacement – Exposure to physical injuries – Exposure to epidemics	1948	Exodus/Forced migration
1948 – 1949	– UNRWA – Establishment of camps		
		1950	Establishment of camps
1950 – 1958	Social impact (Education/Health/Work)	1956	Triad aggression → more displacement
1958	Civil war (part of)		
1967	War	1967	6 day war + Exodus II
1969 – 1970	– Influx of Palestinians from Gaza and the West Bank – Camp population, mixed Palestinian – Camps being armed (military involvement)	1970	– Black September – Military resistance by Palestinians – Israeli military aggression
1973	Camps shelled by Lebanese army	1973	October war
1975	Civil war (camps involved)		
1982	– Israeli invasion – Siege of Beirut, mixed Palestinian – Sabra and Shatila massacres – Rise of NGOs	1982	Exodus III
1985 – 1987	Camp wars with Amal	1987	Intifada
1993	Division of camps over PNA	1993	Oslo agreement
		1994	Cairo agreement
		1995	Establishment of PNA
1994 – 1999	– Beirut camps isolated – No civil rights, insecurity, identity crisis – UNRWA budget cuts for social services	1999	Israeli elections

Figure 7.1 Timelines for Lebanon and the Gaza Strip

Summary of Findings

In each field site, children and the families to which they belonged were selected purposively to be reasonably representative of the refugee population in terms of socioeconomic measures. The access to families was negotiated through personal contacts of the research teams. The emphasis on transparency and the continuous effort to explain the aims of the research to the children and adults alike, as well as the informality of the participatory research process, contributed to a high degree of repetition of salient themes to emerge from our sample of approximately 100 households. Although voiced in differing expressions and emphasis in the various field sites, the high degree of convergence of topics suggests a reliability of findings.

The themes that emerge in this book revolve around issues of identity, status and kinship ties. Children and young people throughout were concerned about their identity as Palestinians, as refugees, as camp residents and also as Muslims and Christians. While Palestinians shared a common history prior to 1948 and the experience of displacement, marked variation in contemporary civil rights have created rifts among them. In Jordan, for example, the national policy of naturalisation of Palestinian refugees from 1948, but not from the 1967 wave of forced migrants, has created tension and a split among the population. The middle-class Palestinian families tend to be well integrated into Jordanian society, while the lower classes identify with the larger refugee population around them. In Syria, Palestinian civil rights are similar to those enjoyed by Syrian citizens in the country and thus the issue of identity is more subtly contested, as is the social discrimination felt by some Palestinians in Syria. In Lebanon, the sense of discrimination is so pronounced that many Palestinian refugees there feel a sense of despair and look to emigration as an important option for improving their lives. For some, this is seen as an expression of the loss of confidence in a just settlement in the Israeli-Palestinian conflict. Yet in Syria, where discrimination is less pervasive and opportunities of education and employment are present, emigration is not regarded as a realistic option for improving their lives, whereas education is.

Discrimination is reported by Palestinian refugees in Syria, Lebanon and Jordan in their social interaction with citizens in each country. In the West Bank and Gaza discrimination is also reported, as experienced by Palestinian refugees in encounters with other Palestinians who are not refugees.

Structural violence emerges throughout the chapters as a significant explanatory principle. Palestinian refugees and their descendants in each of these countries are structurally placed in such positions that they must deal with lack of civil rights, low status and often insecure livelihoods

(Bourgois 1995, 1998; Farmer 1997). The continuing experience of military and civil violence is vividly described in the testimonies of young people, their parents and grandparents. The external political and military conflict is mirrored by violence that is reported by these young people at all levels of society within Palestinian refugee settings. The young people report that in schools teachers are both physically and verbally abusive, that there are gangs in the neighbourhoods (as there are in most areas of poor urban settlements world-wide) and that there is violence within the home. In addition, satellite television coverage brings vivid and immediate reporting of the continuing and violent Israeli-Palestinian confrontations into the homes of these young people on a daily basis.

Throughout each of the chapters, education emerges as an important theme. It is a complicated territory, as each field site has such specificity in regard to the way in which education is either glorified or demonised. In Lebanon, where access to education after primary school is extremely limited, education is not often raised as a possible strategy for coping with life as forced migrants. Where it does come up it is in the context of improving facilities, giving the young an opportunity to gain further education and improve their job prospects. Thus the young keep asking for computer training, language and vocational training. The energy which these young people are willing to invest in organising learning activity is striking. In Lebanon, international NGOs are working in small steps with young people to give them the further training and education for which they are asking. In Jordan, the West Bank and Gaza, Palestinian young people have made grant requests to help them pay for their own efforts to set up and run a magazine for and by themselves.

The theme of education dominates young peoples' thoughts and is repeated throughout the study as well as being expressed differently in each community. In Jordan, there is a search for space to set up and organise after school clubs and facilities where on-going education can be offered to those who have had to drop out early or who do not benefit as they would like to from the short half-day sessions in the oversubscribed and overcrowded UNRWA-run school. Everywhere the importance of quality education is recognised. In Syria, it is expressed as a 'potential' weapon to make Palestinians more equal opponents in the Israeli–Palestinian conflict. In the West Bank, it is seen as a mechanism leading to more fulfilling and productive lives. Throughout, the lack of an appropriate and meaningful curriculum – except for Lebanon, where Palestinian history is taught – is expressed in distorted and unclear ideas of Palestinian history, culture and society. The requirement by which UNRWA, as the provider of schooling for Palestinian refugees, must teach the history of the country in which the refugees are located is recognised as a weakness. In each field site, nonformal education – in the form of afternoon clubs, youth groups and other religious and social associations

– offers Palestinian youth an opportunity to consolidate their sense of national identity and belonging. In the West Bank this is as much through religious groups as well as through nongovernmental organisations. In Syria, it is through government-sponsored youth clubs that teach the Syrian government's position and views on the Palestinian–Israeli conflict to the young.

In each field site, it is clear that the family is the centre of the individual's life, and kin-based gatherings are frequent. The transmission of Palestinian identity came across most clearly while interviewing the household members of the first generation in the sample about their experience of forced migrations. The field teams discovered that the grandparents were speaking about their experience with the younger members of the family for the first time. Though they had narrated many a story about their Palestinian village of origin, and often kept the keys to the doors of these properties on their person, they had not revealed their personal stories of forced migration before. This opening up and witnessing was important for the entire family in filling in gaps and allowing discussion and a greater sense of solidarity to grow within the family. In Syria, the research teams came across one woman in her eighties who revealed for the first time how she left Tantoura and the conditions under which she left behind her husband and her cousins.

The importance of eliciting, sharing and recording familial oral histories through educational projects is vital in sustaining and understanding the experience of their own families within the general Palestinian narrative. Fortunately there is a growing trend in the region for projects of this type among local Palestinian NGOs. This needs to be encouraged and supported by national and international agencies working with the Palestinian refugee world.

Marriages in Palestinian refugee households tend to be from within the larger family kin group or refugee community. They may be arranged, particularly in the West Bank and Gaza, and often entered into early. Sometimes it is an escape mechanism for girls seeking to get away from an economic or social tyranny they feel in their own homes, and at other times it may be, in some cases, a mechanism to maintain the family on the UNRWA support register – when boys reach the age of 18 their families lose their support status with UNRWA. During times of instability such as the first *Intifada*, in Gaza, there was a tendency for girls to be married at an earlier age as a way of protecting them.

Religious faith and political activism seem to emerge throughout as activities and mechanisms whereby children and young people make sense of their surroundings, as well as being a way to expend their energy and release their sense of political and social frustration. Religious prayer groups and regular attendance at religious places of worship are important, as is political activism. In the West Bank and Gaza this has

been documented in many studies and in many television and film projects. In Jordan, Syria and Lebanon, this activism is also expressed through
membership in various Palestinian youth groups and NGOs, which call
for the Right of Return of Palestinians to their villages of origin.

Within the community and the family various codes of honour and violence operate, making discrimination and physical and emotional violence against girls more pronounced than against boys. Girls' movement
within the family and in the community is circumscribed and in various
field sites their dress is rigidly determined to conform with either
'Islamic' norms or 'traditional' ones. Girls tend to be burdened with
household chores and receive little support in school. The violence which
emerges in the home is also replicated in schools, both between pupils
and between pupils and teachers. Boys, on the other hand, tend to leave
education early in order to support their families, believing it is the right
thing to do to be considered honourable. Boys as young as 9 were taking
on employment after school and in some cases, it was instead of school,
so needy was the family.

Marked gender differentiation appeared throughout all the chapters.
Girls articulated and explained their relative lack of social freedom compared to boys, as well as the way in which early marriage could be a
mechanism offering them security but preventing them from completing
their education. There are many examples of fathers and grandfathers
who encourage the achievements of women in the family, as well as
examples of families and the wider society constraining opportunities for
girls. Men and boys are more directly involved than women in political
activity, in terms of membership in groups, taking part in confrontations
and being imprisoned. Women's accounts, however, attest to how their
lives have been and continue to be shaped by the experiences of prolonged conflict.

Everywhere in the five field sites, people's unhappiness with the physical environment was palpable. The overcrowding, the lack of privacy, the
nonexistence of any 'green space' or playing fields, the lack of public services, libraries, clubs, and poor sanitation were overwhelming. Life is
framed by these basic elements of life as refugees. It is a poverty from
which there is no escape because it is politically engineered. But it is a
poverty which the children and young people in Palestinian refugee
camps do not accept as unchangeable. Although they recognise that no
more space is available, they actively seek, through a variety of mechanisms and coping strategies, to make the very best out of a very raw deal.

What is the relevance of these findings for policy makers and practitioners? Palestinian children and young people are active, politically
aware individuals. Policy making on their behalf should start with their
input and involvement. This requires a significant shift in the NGO world
from top-down to bottom-up. Political street activism needs to be under-

stood. The current lack of alternative spaces which Palestinian youth may occupy also needs to be carefully considered: play areas, computer centres, libraries, and sport fields are the right of every child. Those growing up in refugee camps should not be so deprived and dehumanised. There is also a need to raise awareness of the multiple discrimination which female Palestinian children and young people face at home and in school. This includes increased workloads and reduced educational opportunities. There is a need to encourage self-expression and peer group solidarity by provision of youth clubs for girls. Finally, there is an urgent need to recognise that, although Palestinian refugee children and young people face a special set of disadvantages, in which poverty and deprivation of civil rights are common, they do belong to a society which has succeeded in maintaining its coherence despite more than a half-century of displacement. This reality needs to be reinforced through projects which record the memories of the first generation, which will shortly be gone. Such activity can be through projects that record narratives of family and national history through formal and informal education systems. Our study endeavours to contribute to this effort through documenting and sharing the experiences of Palestinian young people and their families who continue to demonstrate resilience in situations of prolonged conflict and forced migration. This book gives voice to their views and aspirations, mediated by the Palestinian researchers who led each country team. Through their testimonies, they speak for themselves.

References

Bourgois, P. 1995. *In Search of Respect: Selling crack in El Barrio*. Cambridge, U.K.: Cambridge University Press.

———— 1998. 'Families and children in the U.S. inner City'. In N. Schepar Hughes and C. Sargent (eds), *Small Wars: The Cultural Politics of Childhood*. pp. 331–351. Berkeley: University of California Press.

Farmer, P. 1997. 'On suffering and structural violence: A view from below'. In A. Kleinman, V. Das, and M. Lock (eds), *Social Suffering*. pp 261–83. Berkeley: University of California Press.

Appendix I: Methodology

The project was sponsored by the Andrew W. Mellon Foundation and was undertaken by the Refugees Studies Centre at Queen Elizabeth House, University of Oxford under the direction of Dawn Chatty, who was the Principal Investigator. She had carried out research and consultancy over many years in Lebanon, Syria and Jordan and she managed the research teams in these countries. Gillian Lewando Hundt, then at the London School of Hygiene and Tropical Medicine but later at the University of Warwick, served as the Co-Investigator. She had carried out previous European Community (EC) funded research in Gaza and coordinated a network on maternal health in the region. She identified and managed the team leaders in Gaza and the West Bank.

The process of selecting the five team leaders was long and consultative, requiring several trips to the region and numerous meetings at universities, research centres and NGO offices, particularly in Jordan, Syria and Lebanon. It was decided that each field team would be led by a Palestinian researcher, and that their respective research teams would, as much as possible, be composed of Palestinian research assistants and fieldworkers. The primarily Palestinian make-up of the research teams, as well as the principal role they were to take in the data collection and analysis, would make for a uniquely collaborative project whereby local research capacity building would also be achieved. In Lebanon and Jordan, colleagues in universities and research were approached for suggestions and advice. In Lebanon, a small panel at the American University of Beirut identified Dr Bassem Serhan, a sociologist with extensive teaching and research experience in Lebanon, Kuwait and Libya, as the team leader for the Lebanon-based study. In Jordan, the Director of the Centre for Research on the Modern Middle East (CERMOC), Dr Riccardo Bocco, was very helpful in identifying Dr Randa Farah, an anthropologist with a Ph.D. from the University of Toronto, as the team leader for the Jordan field site.

In Syria the situation was more difficult. The Dean of one of the Graduate Facilities at the University of Damascus called a meeting to discuss possible researchers. However, it was agreed that formal government permission for such a project would have to be requested if the researcher was going to come from a university department. Such a request could take more than two years to be acknowledged, thus we were urged to look for researchers more informally from within the government-recognised NGOs that worked with Palestinian refugees in the country. We duly approached the Palestinian Women's Union, who then identified Dr Adnan Abdul-Rahim, an education specialist with extensive experience of working with UNRWA and UNICEF in Syria.

In the West Bank and the Gaza Strip, Hundt asked researchers with whom she had previously worked on two EC-funded projects in the area of maternal, reproductive and child health to take on this project. In the Gaza Strip, the team was based at the Gaza Health Services Research Centre and led by a psychiatrist, Dr Thabet, who had experience in community psychiatry and post-traumatic stress disorder. In the West Bank, the team was led by a postdoctoral fellow, Dr Alzaroo, who had returned to the region after completing his doctorate in Comparative Continuing Education and who during his studies had worked on these other projects. This meant that the five teams each had a Palestinian team leader and that the coordination of these country teams was split between the two U.K.-based investigators according to their previous research experience within these countries. The team leaders then recruited their own research assistants independently.

In Lebanon, Dr Serhan worked closely with a project assistant, Samia Tabari, who had significant experience of working with local NGOs to collect the oral history of Palestinian refugees in the country. Their field assistants were drawn from Palestinian refugees living in the camps which were selected for the study. Some of these had earlier experience working as survey enumerators for the Norwegian Institute for Applied Social Science (FAFO). Dr Abdul-Rahim, in Syria, approached a number of researchers with academic experience from their association with the Centre for Social Research established by Dr Sofouh Akhras at the University of Damascus, as well as work experience among Palestinian refugees with UNRWA. All but one of these field assistants and helpers were Palestinian refugees. In Jordan, the team leader used her contacts from a previous study on the history of UNRWA for the Centre d'Etude et de Recherches du Moyen-Orient Contemporain (CERMOC) to identify her core field team. The final identification of her field assistants came from the camps in which she conducted her in-depth interviewing. In the West Bank, Dr Alzaroo worked closely with two research assistants from the refugee camps, who both had extensive interviewing experience. In Gaza there were three assistants, one of whom was a social worker and well known in Khan Yunis refugee camp; the others had previous experience in psychological methods.

The research methodology was developed and outlined by the U.K.-based investigators and derived from their background and interests in anthropology and participatory and action-oriented research. A participatory approach to elaborating and augmenting the research methodology was adopted which consciously mirrored the methods and approaches that would be used in fieldwork. This was done both as a training device and also to enable the study to incorporate the academic and local expertise and knowledge of the team leaders across the region.

The project was divided into two phases: the first, a participatory appraisal exercise to reach a broad cross-section of the study sites; and the second, in-depth interviews with multi-generational households. There was an awareness that the team leaders came from different academic and professional backgrounds and represented the diverse experiences of Palestinians living in these countries in the region; therefore generating methods within a participatory framework was particularly important.

Throughout the study, regional meetings were held at critical junctures to plan, train and share interim findings. The first full five-team training workshop was held in Cyprus in June 1999, because it proved to be impossible to find any location in the Middle East where all the Palestinian research team leaders would be permitted entry. Hence Cyprus, the U.K. and the U.S. became the focus of project-wide meetings. During the following year, Chatty made frequent trips to Lebanon, Syria and Jordan to meet with the research teams, to conduct local participatory training workshops with the team field researchers, and to generally support the team efforts. Several on-site training workshops were held with the teams in Lebanon and Syria, and a three-team workshop was held near the end of the data collection phase to review materials and to begin the drafting of the final team reports as well as papers for international conferences. In spite of restrictions on travel in Palestine, Hundt was also able to hold one joint West Bank and Gaza team workshop.

The second full five-team meeting was held in Oxford in September 2000 to begin preliminary analysis of data collected. Third and fourth full project team meetings were held in Cyprus in October 2000 and September 2001 to support the writing-up process, to review and critique team drafts of papers and book chapters and to continue the process of disseminating findings to policy makers and practitioners. An English/Arabic *Lessons Learned Report* was outlined and the highly contentious issue of translating English terminology into Arabic was raised and discussed at length. Preparations for booklets, flyers and other dissemination materials were also agreed, each team selecting the approach and format which most suited their situation. Further dissemination workshops were held in Washington in November 2001 at the American Anthropological Association (AAA) annual meeting and at the Migration Policy Institute (MPI) (Table 1).

Table 1 – Regional Team Meetings

Date	Location	Concern
June 1999	Cyprus	Initial training workshop. Setting of method-ological framework.
September 2000	Oxford	Preliminary analysis. Only research teams.
October 2000	Cyprus	1st dissemination workshop. Wide NGO audience.
March 2001	Lebanon	Regional workshop. Analysis of data.
September 2001	Cyprus	2nd dissemination workshop. Finalisation of findings.
November 2001	Washington	3rd dissemination meeting. AAA and MPI.

In addition, the U.K. investigators had the support of several research assistants: during the initial planning stage, Rulla Khadouri helped organise the first regional meeting in Cyprus and Mezna Qato assisted in the closing workshops. Maha Damaj, the research assistant during the critical fieldwork stage, helped to coordinate the meetings and workshops during active fieldwork and edited a six-edition project newsletter that kept members in touch with one another and shared findings and approaches. These facilitated the development of a regional approach and were critical to the internal dissemination strategy.[1]

Management of the Project

The management of collaborative international research is a source of some debate. The recent Nuffield Council on Bioethics report (2002) on the ethics of research related to healthcare in developing countries points to the tendency for externally funded research to utilise developing countries as field sites for data collection and testing of possible treatment, which is then exploited elsewhere. This one-sided relationship of dubious ethical nature was something the U.K. investigators sought to avoid. As much as possible this project looked to develop local skills and build local capacity. The management decision to employ only Palestinian researchers and field assistants was one step in the direction of reducing the potentially exploitative nature of such studies.

In addition, the team leaders received training in participatory techniques, data collection and analysis. They also contributed elements to the research design at the regional workshops. One example of such team learning emerged during our initial training session on participatory timeline charting. We had hoped to use this technique with Palestinian families participating in the study. In doing their own timelines in the regional meeting, the team leaders were able to share very different and often hitherto unknown experiences with each other. At that time, between 1999 and 2001, it was very difficult for Palestinians in Syria and Lebanon to travel to Palestine and vice versa. When the team leaders first met at the Initial Training Workshop in Cyprus in June 1999 they shared their experiences with each other as Palestinians for the first time. One Gazan participant insisted on taking a photograph with a Palestinian participant from Syria to show to others in Gaza. It would record the first time he had ever met a Palestinian from Syria. The timelines were later disseminated within the team newsletter.

In summary, the U.K. investigators led the study, but the country team leaders were participants who influenced the study design and were active in disseminating findings and recommendations to practitioners and policy makers locally and internationally. This was done in a partnership model with an exchange of skills between the researchers on the regional team.

Choice of Methods

In order to obtain a holistic, contextual account of the experiences of Palestinian young people in coping with prolonged conflict and forced migration, it was felt that the methodology should include their social environment and households. There were two ways in which this was addressed – through participatory appraisal of the refugee camps and neighbourhoods in which the study population lived and subsequently through in-depth interviews with different members of twenty households composed of three generations and including children between the ages of 8 and 18. The preliminary participatory approach was deemed important in order to draw the community into the study as participants and active actors, and to help the team identify the key concepts, concerns and individuals for the next phase of the project. Achieving a relationship of trust and confidence with the community was vital and the participatory approach was important in achieving these ends. In the transition to the second phase of the study, it was also important that the community understood the aims of the project and freely gave their informed consent to take part.

Participatory Research Approaches

This is an approach which has been developed over the past two decades, growing so rapidly in popularity as to become nearly a 'fashion'. It has its detractors and critics (Cooke and Kothari 2001; Pottier 1997) as well as its supporters (Chambers 1992; Pretty et al. 1995). Its philosophical origins can be traced back decades to the pioneering work of Paulo Freire (1987), which highlighted the importance of bringing the poor and underprivileged into the development process. Contemporary participatory approaches in the social sciences trace their roots back to a set of workshops in Thailand in the late 1970s which sought rapid methods to data gathering for development studies. It emerged from a synthesis of tools and techniques in fields as diverse as agricultural systems, geography and anthropology, and quickly came to be accepted in rural sociology (Chambers 1997) and subsequently within international health and applied social research. As an approach it moves away from the extractive nature of most research designs to one where the field respondents become participants instead of informants and share in the learning and collection of data. It relies on the recognition of the importance of all members of the community or research site – men, women, young and old. It recognises the specialist but also sees the contributory power of all members of the community. It also strives to bring people together, sometimes in small groups, to share their understandings and knowledge with each other, and to address their concerns in an active manner. The field researchers take on the roles of facilitators rather than information extractors.

Core and Variations

This was a multi-site research project encompassing five field sites in the Middle East. Originally designed as a four-site venture, it soon became obvious that the difficulties of moving around Palestine would necessitate splitting the site into two: a West Bank site and a Gaza site. Each site used a similar core methodology that was developed in detail during an initial training workshop for all the team leaders. The five teams followed the methodological framework and the core participatory methods and added local variations which were particular to their expertise, research interests or field skills as well as the peculiar characteristics of each local setting.

In Phase I, participatory tools drew the community into the research and basic sociodemographic data was collected in an open, participatory manner that established trust and confidence. Community social mapping, matrix and ranking to establish community ideas of well-being, mental and physical health, wealth and cohesion, along with other techniques such as community and village timelines, were also employed.

In Phase II, a sample of ninety-five households (twenty from four field sites and fifteen from one) with children from age 8 to 18 was drawn. The sample was stratified by socioeconomic status, direct experience of forced migration and by age spread of household members.

The specific research tools for gathering data during this phase included:

- collection of narratives and life histories with a focus on critical incidents from children and adults of different generations within the same households;
- semi-structured interviews with key informants;
- group interviews with groups of men, women and children in homes and schools;
- participant observation.

Variations to the Core Methodology

Lebanon

The study team[2] worked in three areas: Borj El-Barajneh camp (Beirut), Borj El-Shemali camp (Tyre, South Lebanon) and with displaced families in the four buildings of an ex-hospital in Sabra (near Shatila camp, Beirut). A survey was conducted in the two refugee camps early on during the study in order to gather socio-economic indicators of the population and get a general idea of their concerns and interests in the project. Some group interviews were carried out with youth at this stage and this activity was continued throughout the study among youth, teachers and other interest groups. Twenty households which met the criterion of three-generational units with children between the ages of 8 and 18, and with some experience of forced migration, were eventually selected for in-depth interviewing and the collection of migration history narratives.

In addition to the core research design of mapping, focus groups and in-depth household-based interviews, the Lebanese team conducted a survey in the camps in order to collect socioeconomic indicators of the inhabitants. The social mapping of the three sites identified services available to the residents. The team then held focus group interviews with key adults in contact with youth in the camps such as parents, teachers and NGO activists. They also conducted group interviews with three age groups of young people (9–11, 12–14 and 15–18-year-olds, in which boys and girls were interviewed separately). They conducted sixty-nine in-depth interviews in nineteen households: with six households from Borj El-Barajneh camp, seven from Borj El-Shemali camp, three from the Gaza Hospital Complex and three in Beirut City. The sample included three households headed by widows.

In each household, parents were interviewed separately, as were two of their children (a son and a daughter). Parents of various ages were interviewed and nine grandparents were included to examine the effect of the first generation on the second and third generations within the context of the extended families. The researchers conducted pilot interviews. Informed consent was requested from each individual concerning participation in the study and for the interview to be tape-recorded. Only two families preferred note-taking. The use of timelines referring to historical periods was encouraged in all interviews.

The majority of mothers worked domestically within in the home. A few were working as agricultural labourers or seamstresses at home. The majority of fathers were manual or agricultural workers, as well as low-level skilled labourers, plumbers, electricians, and tile setters. Young males 16–21 years old were mostly working as manual labourers, semi-skilled labourers or simply unemployed. Young females of the same age group were either staying at home or worked at low-level jobs.

Syria

A multi-method approach was taken by the team.[3] The first step was a Participatory Rapid Appraisal (PRA) exercise in Yarmouk camp, and some focus group interviews with UNRWA schoolteachers and youth leaders.

The team conducted participatory social mapping to study the infra-structure of the Palestinian camps in Syria, working with the local residents to identify the main social services. The research team liaised with key individuals from the camps and with UNRWA social workers, who assisted them in the selection of the sample. Twenty households were selected from three different socioeconomic groups (rich, average, poor). The team interviewed sixty individuals in these twenty households. Ten households lived in refugee camps, eight were located within Damascus and two were in Homs and, although the majority of households were Muslim, two were Christian.

Each household created social maps of their environment. A timeline of the main events in Palestinian history since 1948 was used as an aid when interviewing, although many interviewees created their own timeline based on their own experiences. A family tree was created by the household during the interviews. Each household was interviewed several times in order to hear the voices of all three generations. Generally the three generations were all present during the interviews, which were written up in brief notes during the interview and expanded through recall, a few hours after the interview.

Jordan

Two camps were chosen: Hitteen refugee camp, which was heterogeneous in terms of village of origin, routes of flight and displacement and legal status, and Hayy al-Mahasreh urban area, which was homogeneous in terms of village of origin, flight, displacement and legal status. The Jordanian team decided to incorporate the participatory psychological approach developed by MacMullin and Oudeh (1999) during this preliminary phase of research – a child-focused psychological intervention was carried out in a school setting. In Phase II, twenty households were interviewed, with the focus on collecting life history narratives of forced migration. There were both group and individual interviews. Participant observation was carried out in the neighbourhoods of the camps and focus groups were conducted with youth.

Focus groups for children and adolescents of differing age groups were held both in the camp and in the Hayy. In addition, community workshops involving women and children were held in the camp. The purpose of workshops was to engage the community as a whole in the study, and also to continuously update them on the research and results. Last but not least, a review of the various publications, statistical reports and studies on refugees was conducted.

Today there are around 40,000 people living on 917,000 square metres in Hitteen camp, which is 10 kilometers northeast of the Jordanian capital, Amman – the same land area allocated for the camp in 1968. Most of the inhabitants originate from destroyed and depopulated villages in central and southern Palestine, of the districts of *Hebron, Gaza, Bir al-Sabe', Jaffa, al-Ramleh* and others. Upon its establishment, people attempted to reestablish family and village networks, thus the people of *Deir Nakhass* lived in one area, *al-Dawaymeh* lived near the market area, people from the Jericho area in another, those from *Ajjour* also sought to cluster together and those from *Bir al-Sabe'* in an area called *al-Barr*. Over time, however, the areas have become heterogeneous, although clusters of extended families may still be found in the same area.

Most of the streets in the camp need repair, as do the water and sewer networks – the pipes often burst, creating puddles of dirty water. Overpopulation means that there is no space to erect parks or establish new playgrounds for children, or even to build new houses, except perpendicularly. Hence, camp streets and alleyways have become the play areas for the younger generations and are outlets for adults, especially for males. There are two markets in the camp, where many of the local entrepreneurs transformed their housing units into retail stores, storage areas or mechanical repair shops. The main market is close to the entrance of the camp, while another, cheaper, market has evolved at the other end, sometimes referred to as the 'Gaza area'.

In Hitteen camp there are several organisations, some of which emerged spontaneously and locally; others are branches of national, regional and international organisations. UNRWA has several installations: two schools (one for males and the other for females) running on a double shift, a 'Mother and Child Centre,' a Community Rehabilitation

Centre (CRC) and a Women's Programme Centre (WPC). During the period of research there were very few programmes for children and adolescents and none for adolescent girls.

West Bank

A PRA exercise was conducted in al-Fawwar camp to start the data collection stage of the project. In addition a workshop was held with employees of NGOs and governmental organisations working with youth to review current provision and challenges and to assess needs and interests. The team conducted fifteen semi-structured interviews in two camps: al-Fawwar and al-Aroub in the Hebron area and in the city of Hebron. The households were all three-generational households and were located in different neighbourhoods within these camps. The households were visited two or three times and each generation was interviewed separately. The young people were interviewed when possible outside the home in a community centre. In addition, in the spring of 2001, two group interviews were held to explore the effects of *al-Aqsa Intifada*, which started in September 2000, on children and young people in al-Fawwar and al-Aroub refugee camps.

Most of the older refugees in these two camps left their place of origin over fifty years ago. All children and young people in these were born in the camps. The majority of these young persons had witnessed political violence in the camp and most of them were familiar with the first and second Palestinian *Intifada* (Uprisings).

Data were collected using semi-structured interviews and verbal consent was obtained. A pilot interview was conducted with the four interviewees of the different generations sitting together at the same time. This revealed several obstacles. Interviewing several generations at the same time and place influenced the answers, especially from the third generation, who were conscious of the presence of their elders and the interruption of family members during the interview. Additionally the social interactions of the participants and the interruptions created difficulties in documenting the interviews. The team decided to interview each family member separately and interviewed the third generation (children and young people) outside their homes in a community centre. Each interview lasted an average of two hours.

We intended to select twenty households but during the fieldwork the second *Intifada* (*al-Aqsa Intifada*) commenced and violence spread widely; therefore, we reduced the number of households to thirteen, of whom seven were from al-Fawwar refugee camp, and six from al-Aroub refugee camp. We interviewed a total of forty people using the three-generation model. Later we interviewed an additional two families from the City of Hebron.

For each household a family tree was drawn to obtain a clear idea of the relationship between the interviewees. Each interview involved two interviewers; one conducted the interview and the other took notes that were written up in extended form shortly afterwards. We did not use tape-recorders because taping was not acceptable at that time.

Moreover, two group interviews (one in al-Fawwar and the other in al-Aroub) were held to explore the effects of the current *Intifada* (started on 28 September 2000) on children and young people. We asked those previously interviewed to attend a meeting and invited additional children as well. There were ten participants from the al-Fawwar refugee camp (five boys and five girls) and eight from the al-Aroub camp (five boys and three girls). In each of the group interviews, both sexes were initially interviewed together and then separately. All the interviews were conducted and written up in Arabic and then translated into English. Each interview was subsequently analysed using content analysis to identify themes.

Gaza Strip

The sample was stratified by socioeconomic status, direct experience of forced migration and by the age of the household members. The study took place in three out of the eight camps in the Gaza Strip and two areas outside the camps (El Bureij, Khan Younis, Beach Camps and El-Zaytoon and Sheikh Radwan area). Five families were selected from each camp and five from the two urban areas. In all twenty three-generational households were selected, with grandfathers who were at least 11 years old in 1948 and grandchildren who were between 8 and 18 years of age. Grandparents were interviewed with parents and sometimes grandchildren present. Women and girls were interviewed separately. A copy of the interviews, with a family picture, was given to them on the completion of the study, along with gifts of stationery. In addition, focus group interviews were held separately with the teenage boys and girls from these households. Also, a questionnaire using a structured validated instrument to measure coping – the A Cope Questionnaire – was administered to 154 young people in these twenty households. Subsequently, after the first nine months of *al-Aqsa Intifada*, in the summer of 2001, additional focus group interviews were held with young people at summer camps.

Two social workers and a female nurse who took notes conducted the household interviews held with members of different generations within the household during three visits. The women and girls in the household were interviewed separately from male family members. Detailed notes were written within the next 24 hours. In addition, six focus group interviews took place with the children and young people aged 9–18 from these households.

Table 2 – Demographic Characteristics of 154 Children and Young People in the Gaza Strip Sample

Demographic characteristics	Main features	Frequency (Number of people)	Percentage (percent)
Gender	Male	81	53
	Female	73	47
Age	Less than 15 years	110	71
	Above 15 years	44	29
Location	Gaza	55	36
	Middle area	50	32
	South area	49	32
Family size (Number of people in family)	1–4 people	39	26
	5–7 people	62	41
	8+ people	52	34
Monthly household income (US$)	Less than 350	90	59
	351–750	40	26
	More than 750	24	15
Father's educational level	Illiterate	6	4
	Primary	47	30
	Secondary	27	18
	Higher degree	74	48
Mother's educational level	Illiterate	8	5
	Primary	46	30
	Secondary	63	41
	High degree	37	24
Father's occupation	Unemployed	19	12
	Unskilled labour	65	42
	Employee	53	35
	Others	17	11
Mother's occupation	House wife	123	80
	Unskilled labour	3	2
	Employee	24	15
	Others	4	3

Table 2 shows the demographic characteristics of the 154 young people who completed the questionnaire. The mean age of children was 14.5 years. Seventy-one percent were 15 years or less and 29 percent were above 15 years. Seventy-five percent of households had more than four children. Household income was low – more than half of the sample reported that their monthly income was less than US$ 350; however, they might have had additional sources of income from other family members that they did not report.

Literacy levels were similar between mothers and fathers and in terms of primary schooling. However, in secondary and higher education fathers had a slightly higher educational level than mothers. The vast majority of women (80 percent) worked as housewives, compared to 42 percent of men who worked as labourers and one-third who worked in white-collar employment.

Summary

All the teams adopted participatory tools in Phase I of their data collection and engaged in in-depth interviewing with a purposive sample of twenty households selected on the basis of socioeconomic variation, three-generational household composition and the presence of children between the ages of 8 and 18. Furthermore, each team conducted focus group discussions with girls separately from boys. The main methodological differences between the five research teams were that in Jordan, a psychological survey was carried out in schools; in Lebanon, a survey was carried out as part of the PRA exercise in the two camps; in Gaza a questionnaire designed to measure psychological coping, using a validated instrument, was administered to the young people of the households. In Syria, entire households were present during much of the in-depth interviewing, while in the West Bank, different generations within households were interviewed separately. In Gaza, women and girls were interviewed separately from the men in the household in order to facilitate maximum freedom and to hear clearly the difference between his-stories and her-stories. Table 3 summarises these variations.

The multidisciplinarity of the research teams is reflected in the chapters. Each has a distinctive approach and flavour that reflects not only the particular circumstances of Palestinians in that country but also the academic and professional training of the team leader. In Lebanon, Dr Serhan was a sociologist by training with a long career teaching in Lebanon, Kuwait and Libya. These career moves mirrored the fortunes of Palestinians in Lebanon during the tumultuous 1980s and early 1990s. At the time of the study, he was associated with The Welfare Association, an important Palestinian NGO in Lebanon. His substantive interests and written work focused mainly on the political sociology of Palestinian life in Lebanon. Dr Abdul-Rahim was trained in pedagogy at the University of Budapest, and continued to work in the field of education on his return to Syria. Nominated as the liaison officer between UNICEF and the kindergarten schools of UNRWA, he maintained an ongoing interest in the significance of early schooling and nonformal education in the shaping of the identity of Palestinian youth. Dr Farah, a Palestinian originally from Haifa, was particularly interested in narratives and oral histories and was well versed in the holistic approach to the study of a community. She had only recently completed her doctoral studies in anthropology based on fieldwork conducted in the refugee camps of Jordan. She had also just finished a project with CERMOC studying its history and impact on Palestinians in Jordan. Her focus of interest throughout the study remained the role of oral history in the creation of a Palestinian identity.

The experiences of children and young people in Palestine as represented by the Gaza and West Bank chapters in this book are shaped by the two *Intifadas* and the military occupation and presence of the Israeli army. Continuing violence is not a memory but a backdrop or foreground to everyday living. The chapter on the West Bank by Dr Alzaroo reflects his perspective as an academic in the field of comparative continuing education and focuses on education as a means of coping in situations of conflict and instability. Education, both formal and informal, is valued and utilised as a means of understanding the world and surviving in it when individual and family security in terms of place, livelihood and freedom are at risk. Theoretically the chapter owes its focus to the work of Freire (1987) in the way that it views education as a means to understanding and coping with the world and as a means of liberating the individual and the group.

The Gaza chapter by Dr Thabet and Dr Abuateya reflects their respective psychiatric and psychological training. Thabet has published extensively on post-traumatic stress disorder amongst Gazan children but this chapter focuses on the intergenerational experiences and trauma of displacement and forced migration as well as the views and feelings of the young people today.

Table 3 – Variations on Core Methods

Country	Field sites	Variation on Methods
Lebanon	Borj El-Barajneh (Beirut), Borj El-Shemali (Tyre), Sabra (Beirut)	Socioeconomic survey in Phase I
Syria	Eight camps near Damascus (focus on Yarmouk) and two near Homs	Focus interviews with teachers in Phase I; interviews with all household members present
Jordan	Hitteen (Amman), Hayy al-Mahasreh (Amman)	Psychological survey in schools in Phase I
West Bank	Al-Fawwar (Hebron), Al-Aroub (Hebron) City of Hebron	Workshops with NGOs and government organisations; each generation in each household interviewed separately
Gaza	El Bureij, El Zayton, KhanYounis, Sheikh Radwan, Beach Camp	'A Coping Questionnaire' administered to 154 young people in the sample; interviews conducted with other household members present

Notes

1 Excerpts from these newsletters are included in Appendix III to give a flavour of how they were an enabling device. They not only informed the participants of each other's progress and difficulties but also were a means of reinforcing and supporting learning. They were distributed electronically and were an essential part of the team management of this regional study involving six teams in five countries (including the U.K.).

2 The research assistants in Lebanon included Su'ad Hammad, Sana Hussein, Fayza Khalaf, Samia Jammal, Hiba Izahmad and Mohammad Hamza.

3 The Syrian team research assistants included Maria Salem, Fuad Suradi, Mai Barkawi and Manar Rabbai.

4 The research assistants for the Jordanian field site included Suzanne Al Salhi and Yousef Sa'adeh.

5 Some of UNRWA's figures show a total of 65,000 people, 50,000 of whom are registered. However, this figure includes people who live around and near the camp rather than inside, but they utilise UNRWA's services in the camp.

6 Ajjur or Ajjour, al-Dawayimah and Deir al-Nakhass are villages that were destroyed and depopulated as a result of the 1948 war and they belonged to the Hebron district. Beer al-Sabe' is the Arabic word for Beersheba in al-Naqab or Negev.

7 The research assistants on the team in the West Bank team included Maesa Irfaeya and Hisham Sharibati.

8 The team research assistants were Eitdal El Khateib, Salah Hamdan, Jehad Okasha and Samah El Sabhah.

References

Chambers, R. 1992. *Rural Appraisal: Rapid, Relaxed and Participatory*. Discussion Paper No. 311, Institute of Development Studies, University of Sussex.
——— 1997. *Whose Reality Counts?* London: Intermediate Technologies.
Cooke, B. and Kothari, U. (eds) 2001. *Participation: The New Tyranny?* London: Zed Books.
Freire, P. 1987. *Literacy: Reading the Word and the World*. South Hadley, Mass., U.S.A.: Bergin and Garvey.
MacMullin, C. and Oudeh, J. 1999. 'What is Worrying Children in the Gaza Strip?' *Child Psychiatry and Human Development*, 30(1): 55–72.
Nuffield Council on Bioethics. 2002. *The Ethics of Research Related to Healthcare in Developing Countries*. Plymouth Latimer Trend Group.
Pottier, J. 1997. 'Towards an Ethnography of Participatory Appraisal and Research'. In R.D. Grillo and R.L. Stirrat (eds), *Discourses of Development: Anthropological perspectives*. Oxford: Berg Press.
Pretty, J., Guijt, I., Thompson, J. and Scoones, I. 1995. *Participatory Learning and Action: A Trainer's Guide*. London: International Institute for Environment and Development.

Appendix II: Literature Review

This is not an exhaustive review of the literature available on Palestinian refugees in the Middle East. It is a reference compiled by the local research teams from materials available in each of their field sites. Some of these materials are in the category of 'grey literature' and are difficult to access outside of the region.

Lebanon

Palestinians in Lebanon are a popular subject for Western journalism and a wide range of short reports and studies are available locally. Subjects that are broadly covered by foreign and local researchers include studies on services for Palestinian refugees and their needs; the political situation of Palestinian refugees in Lebanon (e.g., political affiliations among Palestinian refugees, the peace process, the refugees' right of return and political aspirations); the issue of civil rights such as the right to work, travel, own businesses; economic conditions, for example unemployment, income and wages; and the demographic characteristics of the Palestinian camps' population.

The major institutes or bodies that carried out research or statistical data compilation included UNRWA, UNICEF, the Norwegian Institute for Applied Social Science (FAFO), the Institute of Palestine Studies (IPS), the Palestinian Red Crescent Society (PRCS), NGOs, and some local and international researchers. UNRWA compiles its own annual statistics on health, education and special hardship case families. UNICEF commissions individual researchers and/or the Palestinian Central Bureau of Statistics and Natural Resources to conduct social surveys and studies focusing on the conditions of children and youth and the biannual demographic survey of Palestinian camps. For instance, UNICEF has carried out studies on child labour among Palestinians in Lebanon and the needs of youth in Palestinian camps (2000). The Palestinian Social Research

Committee[1] conducted a comprehensive study (over two years, 1996–7) of educational problems facing Palestinian children and youth in the camps, of whom 95 percent study at UNRWA schools. In 1999, FAFO (2000) carried out a comprehensive survey of 3,500 families on the living conditions among Palestinians in the camps and gatherings in Lebanon. The study measured demographic characteristics, migration, household composition, health, income, education, unemployment, labour force composition, households' economy and housing.

The IPS published several articles and research papers on the conditions of Palestinian refugees in Lebanon that were published in various issues of the *Journal of Palestine Studies*. More recently, IPS has commissioned a researcher (B. Serhan) to conduct a study on Palestinian families in exile: a comparative study of the experience of Palestinians in Lebanon and Syria (in press). The PRCS carried out studies on the health conditions of the camps' populations (1994). The Palestinian Human Rights Committee in Lebanon conducted one study on attitudes of the camps' population towards return and/or compensation. In 1996, the Lebanese Studies Centre at the University of Oxford organised a conference on the Palestinians of Lebanon, during which several papers on various aspects and issues were presented (the papers appeared in a special issue of the *Journal of Refugee Studies*). The Norwegian People's Aid (NPA) and the Technical and Vocational Training Committee carried out tracer surveys in 1999 on the condition of their graduates in the field of employment and unemployment.

In addition, a number of studies were conducted by Palestinian and foreign researchers, some of which were for academic theses and dissertations. Among Palestinian researchers in Lebanon, Rosemary Sayigh (1993), Mohammed Ali Khalidi (1997), Bassem Serhan (1999), Jaber Suleiman (1998), Samia Tabari and Leila Zakharia (1997), and Suhail Natour (1997) are particularly noteworthy.

Syria

The main resources for demographic data dealing with the Palestinians in Syria are the Syrian Central Bureau of Statistics (SCBS), the UNRWA records, the statistical yearbooks of the Palestinian Central Bureau of Statistics (PCBS) (1997) and the statistical reports issued by the General Association for the Palestinian Arab Refugees (GAPAR). Several studies conducted by PCBS included the examination of Palestinian children's labour, the educational reality of Palestinian children, and children's health and environment in the Palestinian camps in Syria. The Palestinian Red Crescent Society produced a report (PRCS 1999) on living conditions of Palestinian refugees in Syria. Al-Mawed (1999) conducted a study on the Palestinian refugees in Syria. Some international organisations have conducted studies on the situation of Palestinian refugees in Syria, such as the Canadian Mission (1999) on the general conditions of the Palestinian refugee camps in Syria, the annual reports of the UNRWA general commissioner (UNRWA 1999) and UNICEF's (1999) assessment of the situation of Palestinian children in Syria.

Jordan

In the past decade, a growing body of literature on refugees and refugee camps began to emerge, propelled mainly by the peace process in the early 1990s. Consequently, this literature is generally policy driven and focuses on socioeconomic data and issues of 'integration.' An important research institute active in producing such literature is the Norwegian Institute for Applied Social Science (FAFO).[2]

In addition, there are a growing number of reports produced by non-governmental and intergovernmental agencies such as UNICEF and Save the Children Fund (SCF) with the purpose of implementing projects in poor neighbourhoods in Jordan. One example is the 'Family Planning' programme, (it acquired different titles over time and in different countries), which often conflicts with many local cultures and histories. For Palestinians, having many children is not only culturally and socially significant, but it has a political dimension, whereby having many children is viewed as a response to the 'demographic battle' waged by the Israeli state. In addition, the consequences of international policies and programmes that do not respond to local needs compel many local NGOs to change their programmes to meet international requirements so that they will be eligible for funding.

There is a third body of academic literature on refugees and refugee camps, produced by individual researchers, scholars or research institutions.[3] Again, most of this literature adopts a psychological, sociological or demographic approach at the expense of anthropological and participatory methods. The exception in this body of literature are individual studies and those produced by researchers, such as work done by the Centre d'Etude et de Recherches du Moyen-Orient (CERMOC) in Amman and Beirut.[4]

A review of the literature found in the library at the University of Jordan showed that most of the existing literature on children and adolescents is in the discipline of politics (especially the relationship with Islamist organisations), sociology (with a focus on violence), psychology, economics (unemployment and labour) or biology (behaviour and developmental stages). What is disturbing in these studies is the two extreme views which seem to dominate: adolescents and youth are either responsible for existing social problems or, alternatively, they are regarded as passive victims of corrupting and immoral trends and political movements. The studies usually place blame directly on globalisation, the West and political Islam.

It is clear that the writings on children and youth seem also to fall within the aforementioned disciplines. A brief reading of some of the titles of articles and studies will clarify the point: *'Reflections on Religious Revivalism and Violence,' 'Arab Youth and the Problems They Face,' 'Youth and How to Utilize Free Time in the United Arab Emirates,'* and *'Behavioral Problems and Alienation Among Youth in Kuwait.'* A list of titles was gathered by Ahmed Ebeid Abdel-Hamid Adawi and published in a journal titled *Majallat al-Shu'oun Al-Ijtima'iyyah* (Journal of Social Issues) in 1995. It includes the following headings: 'Islam and Youth,' 'The Media and Youth,' 'Alienation and Youth,' 'Youth and Psychology,' and 'Youth in Political International Relations.'[5]

West Bank and the Gaza Strip

In Palestine, several studies have been carried out to unravel the effects of the Israeli occupation on different aspects of Palestinian lives. A study was conducted on 954 teenagers in West Bank villages, cities and camps, showing the extent of direct contact with violence. Of these teenagers, 59 percent reported having had family members shot at, with 44 percent having been shot at themselves and 64 percent having been harassed and humiliated by soldiers (Awad 1990). Baker (1991) pointed out that the psychological environment of the West Bank and Gaza Strip has a variety of characteristics that cause psychological strain within the population and its children. Stress accompanies the loss of personal and political freedom resulting from military occupation. Thus there is evidence that a large proportion of the refugee population displays psychological and physical symptoms of stress.

A draft report by UNICEF (1992), examining the physical and psychological effects of violence on Palestinian children, showed that, since 1987, the West Bank and Gaza Strip have witnessed a period of intensive and violent conflict between the Israeli army and Palestinian population. Clashes have led to more than 1,000 deaths and tens of thousands of Palestinians have been arrested. Abu Hein and Van Tienhoven (1994) investigated the effects of the deportation of 415 Palestinian men to south Lebanon in 1992 on the mental health of their close female relatives. The study demonstrated that all the women investigated showed elevated levels of depression, anxiety, obsessive thinking and psychosomatic disorders. This study revealed that occupation was the main form of conflict and deportation and had a major effect on an important aspect of life, namely the psychological status of people.

The survey on the mental health conditions of 1,500 Palestinian women in the West Bank and Gaza Strip (Sansour 1995) significantly emphasised the role of political occupation on women's mental health. In that survey, 62.4 percent of women reported the arrest of close relatives and 49.7 percent of women experienced harassment by settlers or the military. Life events that were distressing to these women were ranked as follows: deportation of a close relative, 54 percent; arrest of a close relative, 46 percent; and Israeli military – (or settlers) related trauma, 13 percent. A report on the Israeli violations of Palestinian children's rights, prepared by Defence for Children International for the year 1997–8, focused on the different and increasing types of violence among young people (DCI/PS 1998).

The local literature on the refugees is sparse, the bulk of it focusing on the historical development of the refugee issue and the meaning of 'refugee', as well as the services and access provided for them (Hathaway 1991). For instance, the UNRWA definition of the Palestinian refugee is specific and states:

> [T]hose persons whose normal residence was Palestine during the period of 1 June 1946 to 15 May 1948 and who lost both their homes and means of livelihood as a result of the conflict. (Instructions 1984)

There has been an oral history study carried out by the refugees themselves (Yahya 1999), in which 209 refugees were interviewed. The study revealed that most refugees were taken by surprise when the Arab–Israeli war of 1948 erupted. The refugees took little, if any, of their belongings with them. Some tried to hold on to, or hide, their more valuable belongings, especially their land-ownership papers and the keys to their houses. However, the majority left empty-handed. Out of the sixty-eight respondents, 62 percent affirmed that they had no clue as to where they would end up. They simply desired to flee as far as possible from the fighting, while remaining as close as possible to their original villages and towns in the event that the war ended and they were able to return to their homes.

All refugees, especially those of village origin, faced overwhelming difficulties as a result of their flight. The refugees from rural areas were hit hard because they lacked the skills to earn a living in an urban setting. Their livelihood was lost when they lost their land. In addition, most refugees were not previously mobile. They had rarely travelled or changed their place of residence.

Very limited literature is available on the effects of conflict on children and young people in the West Bank. This therefore justifies the need to carry out research into the effect of being a refugee and the effect of conflict on children and young people in the West Bank.

Notes

1 The Committee dissolved itself in 1998.
2 See, for example, FAFO 1993, 1994a, 1994b and 1994c.
3 See Farah in the references cited in the chapter on Palestinian refugees in Jordan.
4 For example, *The Palestinian Refugees and UNRWA in Jordan, the West Bank, and Gaza, 1949–1999*, ed. R. Bocco, Beirut, CERMOC, Paris, Karthala, 2002.
5 The titles were translated by the author. The annotated bibliography mentioned by Ahmed Abdel-Hamid Adawi is found in *Majallat al-Shu'oun al-Ijtima'iyyah*, 46 (1995): 207.

References

Abu Hein, F. and Van Tienhoven, H. 1994: Deportation and its Effects on the Mental Health of Palestinian Women in Gaza, Unpublished report.

Al-Mawed, H. 1999. 'The Palestinian Refugees in Syria: Their Past, Present and Future'. Unpublished research.

Awad, E. 1990. *Extent of Direct Contact with Violence*. Paper presented at the World Conference of the World Federation of Mental Health, Mexico City.

Baker, A. 1991. 'Psychological Response of Palestinian Children to Environmental Stress Associated with Military Occupation'. *Journal of Refugee Studies*, 4(3): 237–47.

Canadian Mission. 1999. Canadian Report on Palestinian Refugees in Syria. Unpublished manuscript, Damascus.

DCI/PS (Defence for Children International/Palestinian Section) 1998. *Rights of Palestinian Children in Times of Peace: A report on Israeli violations of Palestinian children's rights (1997–1998)*. Jerusalem: DCI/PS.

FAFO (Norwegian Institute for Applied Social Science) 1993. *Palestinian Society in Gaza, West Bank and Arab Jerusalem: A Survey of Living Conditions*. (prepared by Marianne Heiberg and Geir Øvensen).

———— 1994a. *Responding to Change: Trends in Palestinian Household Economy*. (prepared by Geir Øvensen).

———— 1994b. *The Potential of UNRWA Data for Research on Palestinian Refugees: A Study on UNRWA Administrative Data*. (prepared by Lena C. Endresen and Geir Øvensen).

———— 1994c. *Finding Ways: Palestinian Coping Strategies in Changing Environments*. (prepared by Signe Gilen, Are Hovdenak, Rania Maktabi, Jon Pedersen and Dag Tuastad).

———— 2000. *Living Conditions of Palestinian Refugees in Camps and Gatherings in Lebanon*, Lipril Study initial findings, Lebanon and Norway, February.

Hathaway, J.C. 1991. *The Law of Refugee Status*. Toronto and Vancouver: Butterworths.

Instructions. 1984. Document Rev. 7183, January 1984, UN document, Consolidated Eligibility.

Khalidi, M.A. 1997. 'Formulating the Right of National Self-determination'. In T. Kapitan (ed.), *Philosophical Perspectives on the Israeli-Palestinian Conflict*. New York: Sharpe.

Natour, S. 1997. 'The Legal Status of Palestinians in Lebanon'. *Journal of Refugee Studies*, 10(3): 360–77.

———— 1998. *Education Statistics in the West Bank and Gaza Strip: Current Status.* Report Series, No. 5, Ramallah, Palestine.

PRCS (Palestinian Red Crescent Society) 1999. *The General Report.* PRCS.

PRCS and PCH (Palestinian Red Crescent Society and Palestinian Council of Health) 1994. *An Overview on the Situation of the Palestinian Refugees in Diaspora: Demographic, Socio-economic Characteristics and Health Status.* Paper presented by the Palestinian delegation in Rome, 25–27 January.

Sansour, M. 1995. *Palestinian Women and Mental Health: A Survey of Mental Health Conditions of Palestinian Women in the West Bank and Gaza Strip.* Jerusalem: Child and Family Consultation Centre.

Sayigh, R. 1993. *Too Many Enemies.* London: Zed Books.

Serhan, B. 1999. *Education of Palestinian Camp Residents in Lebanon: Reality and Problems.* Beirut: Palestinian Social Research Committee Publications.

Suleiman, J. 1998. 'Refugees Unsheltered: The Case of Lebanon'. *Journal of Arab Thought,* 94.

Tabari, S. and Zakharia, L. 1997. 'Palestinian Women in Lebanon: Health, Work Opportunities and Attitudes'. *Journal of Refugee Studies,* 10(3): 411–29.

UNICEF. 1992. *The Situation of Palestinian Children in the West Bank and Gaza Strip.* Draft, Jerusalem.

———— 1999. *A Report on the Situation of the Palestinian Children in Syria.* August, Damascus.

———— 2000. *The Situation of Palestinian Children in the West Bank and Gaza Strip, Jordan, Syria, and Lebanon: An Assessment Based on the UN Convention of the Rights of the Child.* Jordan.

UNRWA. 1999. *UNRWA and Palestinian Refugees – 50 years.* Gaza: UNRWA.

Yahya, A.H. 1999. *The Palestinian Refugees, 1948–1998 (An Oral History).* Ramallah: Palestinian Association for Cultural Exchange (PACE).

Appendix III: Sample Newsletters

PROJECT NEWSLETTER

Children & Adolescents in Palestinian Households: Living with the Effects of Prolonged Conflict & Forced Migration

ZERO ISSUE – NOVEMBER 99   An Internal Team Newsletter for the Mellon Project.

CONTENTS:

Compiled by Maha Damaj, Research Assistant, Mellon Project, Refugee Studies Programme

LAUNCHING PAD – Introduction

There are many things that indicate that this is the first issue of our internal newsletter.
1. It is actually listed as the "Zero Issue".
2. It remains without a name, and has been labelled "Project Newsletter" temporarily.
3. It contains flashbacks of the proceedings of the June workshop and very little information from the fieldwork that has taken place since then.
4. It is not in its final format, which would clearly include at least two additional items: (a) updates from the teams, and (b) corners that are of relevance to all the teams as they go about their fieldwork.

Project Timeline

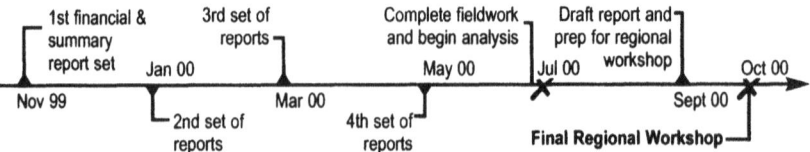

As such, it acts more as a launching pad for future newsletters, which would become one of the platforms for our collective communication. Consequently, it requires much of your feedback and contributions. At present, this could at least come in the form of:

- Suggestions for a name.
- Suggestions for fixed items you would always like to find in the newsletter.
- Feedback on the accuracy of its contents.
- Feedback and comments of any type.

It is projected that a new issue of the newsletter will be compiled every two months, in the month that follows receipt of the separate field reports. ■

PROJECT TIMELINE

The drawing below is a very crude illustration of the milestones ahead of us towards the completion of this project. You will note that it does not include field work milestones as it is not possible to estimate these without your feedback. However, this timeline does highlight a suggestion to have reporting procedures every two months. The reports would be expected within the month indicated, with the financial report covering expected expenditure up to the end of that month. This remains, at present, a suggestion, so please let us know if you find this pattern unsuitable.

The project timeline shall appear in each issue of the newsletter, and any suggested modifications will be duly included. ■

Project Timeline

1st financial & summary report set	3rd set of reports	Complete fieldwork and begin analysis	Draft report and prep for regional workshop	
Nov 99	Jan 00	Mar 00	May 00	Jul 00 Sept 00 Oct 00
	2nd set of reports	4th set of reports	**Final Regional Workshop**	

Mellon Project Newsletter – Zero Issue

FLASHBACK JUNE 99 WORKSHOP:

The following pages contain transcribed flipcharts from the workshop, all of which shall be added as annexes to the original workshop report.

- ## TIMELINES

*"The workshop participants were divided into two teams to carry out some techniques. The first technique to be performed was a **historical timeline** of Gaza and Beirut, by each of the two teams respectively."*

BEIRUT TIMELINE

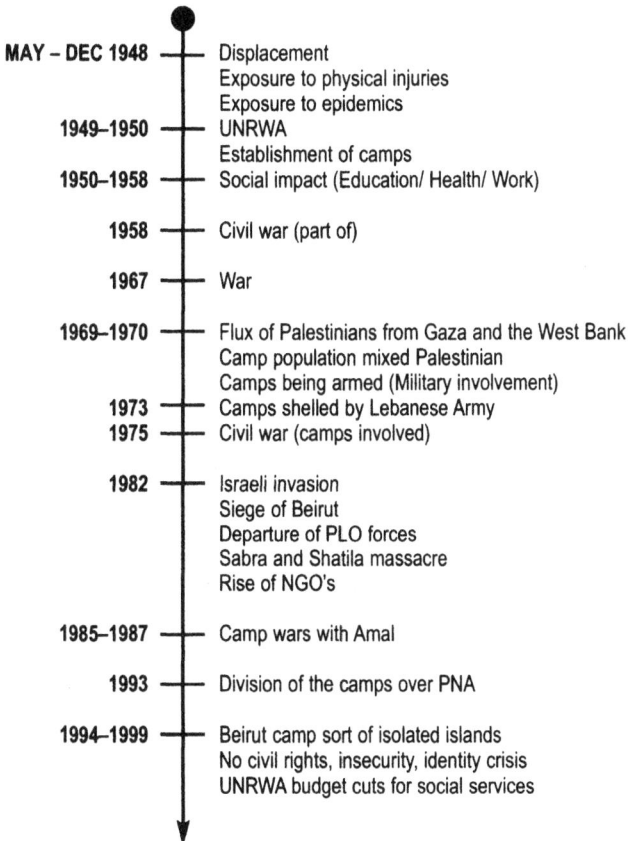

MAY – DEC 1948 — Displacement
Exposure to physical injuries
Exposure to epidemics
1949–1950 — UNRWA
Establishment of camps
1950–1958 — Social impact (Education/ Health/ Work)

1958 — Civil war (part of)

1967 — War

1969–1970 — Flux of Palestinians from Gaza and the West Bank
Camp population mixed Palestinian
Camps being armed (Military involvement)
1973 — Camps shelled by Lebanese Army
1975 — Civil war (camps involved)

1982 — Israeli invasion
Siege of Beirut
Departure of PLO forces
Sabra and Shatila massacre
Rise of NGO's

1985–1987 — Camp wars with Amal

1993 — Division of the camps over PNA

1994–1999 — Beirut camp sort of isolated islands
No civil rights, insecurity, identity crisis
UNRWA budget cuts for social services

GAZA TIMELINE

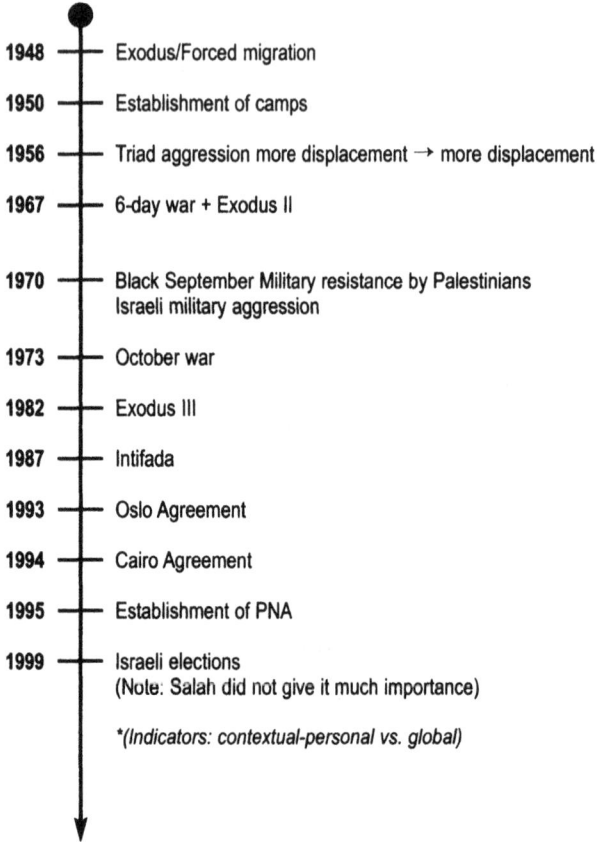

1948	Exodus/Forced migration
1950	Establishment of camps
1956	Triad aggression more displacement → more displacement
1967	6-day war + Exodus II
1970	Black September Military resistance by Palestinians Israeli military aggression
1973	October war
1982	Exodus III
1987	Intifada
1993	Oslo Agreement
1994	Cairo Agreement
1995	Establishment of PNA
1999	Israeli elections (Note: Salah did not give it much importance)

(Indicators: contextual-personal vs. global)

- **SOCIAL MAPS:** *"The second PRA methodology to be attempted by the workshop participants was **social mapping**, where one team had to map a refugee camp of their choice in Gaza, and the other team had to map a refugee camp of their choice in Beirut."*

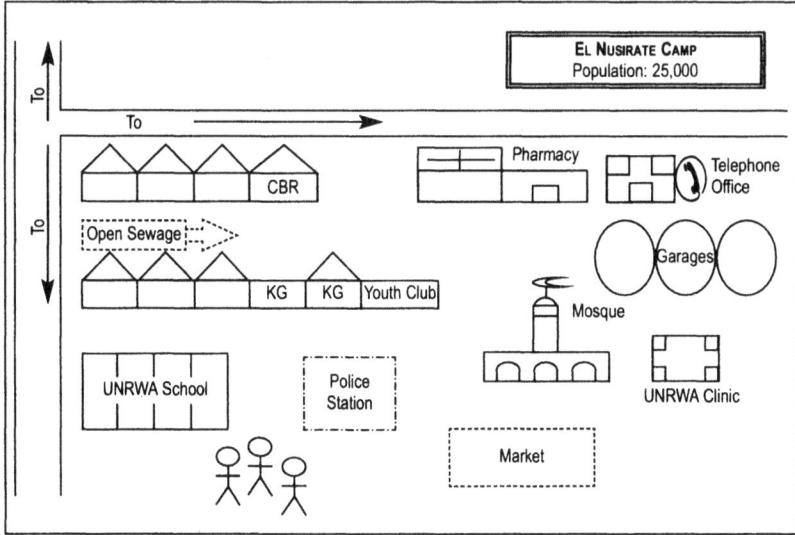

EL NUSIRATE CAMP
Population: 25,000

To
To
To

CBR
Open Sewage
KG KG Youth Club
UNRWA School
Police Station
Market
Pharmacy
Telephone Office
Garages
Mosque
UNRWA Clinic

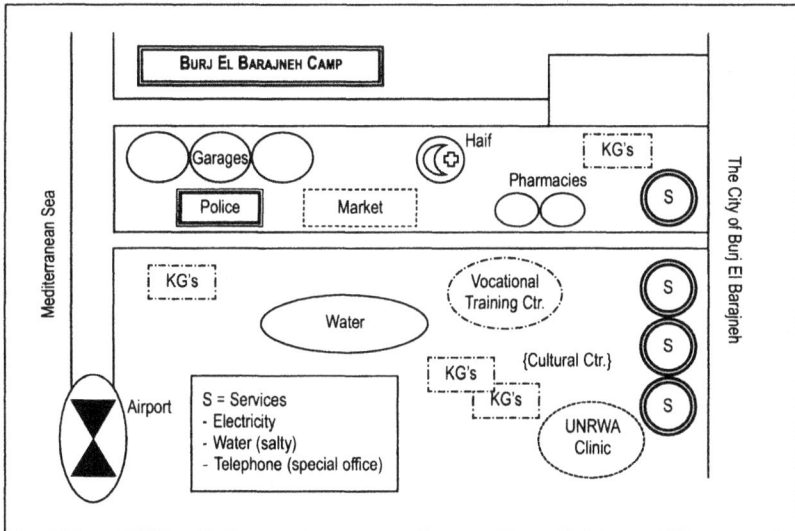

BURJ EL BARAJNEH CAMP

Mediterranean Sea
The City of Burj El Barajneh

Garages
Haif
KG's
Police
Market
Pharmacies
S
KG's
Vocational Training Ctr.
Water
S
S
{Cultural Ctr.}
KG's
KG's
Airport
S = Services
- Electricity
- Water (salty)
- Telephone (special office)
UNRWA Clinic
S

AKHBARUNA

Children & Adolescents in Palestinian Households: Living with the Effects of Prolonged Conflict & Forced Migration

ISSUE #2 – JANUARY 2000   An Internal Team Newsletter for the Mellon Project

CONTENTS:

Compiled by Maha Damaj, Research Assistant, Mellon Project, Refugee Studies Programme

STEPPING STONES – Introduction

This may be the second newsletter, but it has really only just emerged into its first issue, as this is the first one to contain information collated from your reports from the field. The first stepping stone in our field research has also meant that the newsletter grew considerably in size!

PROJECT TIMELINE

The project timeline shall appear in each issue of the newsletter, and any suggested modifications will be duly included. ■

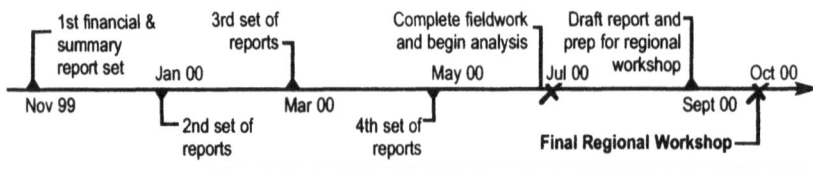

The newsletter has been divided into sections corresponding to the categories of the summary report framework (which is reprinted on page 9). Relevant excerpts from the field summary reports are then collated into these sections to share findings of the different teams in these categories. Some notes about the following pages:

- As it was not possible to print the reports in their entirety, specific excerpts were selected and presented. *Where text appears in italics, it is to indicate that it is a quoted part of a larger, more detailed section of the report.* Full reports can be made available to you upon request.
- As such, **all the excerpts of the reports listed here have been quoted in their exact original format, with little to no editing**.

To tie things together from another dimension, an overview of all of the reports and their contents can be found in page 2. This will perhaps illustrate that the reports were very uneven in character, scope and detail. It is necessary for these reports to go into greater detail, analysis and explanation. This is important for each team to assess its progress and the progress of the rest of the project teams. It is also a very useful tool which will make later reporting and writing up more efficient and coherent. If nothing else, perhaps this newsletter will act as a platform for viewing our texts as a reader would, and discerning the ideas and facts that we wish to highlight as important.

1st financial & summary report set	3rd set of reports		Complete fieldwork and begin analysis	Draft report and prep for regional workshop	
	Jan 00		May 00	Jul 00	Oct 00
Nov 99		Mar 00			Sept 00
	2nd set of reports	4th set of reports		Final Regional Workshop	

The following pages also illustrate the sections that remain missing from the different teams. We hope that these gaps in knowledge will be filled in in the upcoming reports due at the end of this month.

Lastly, since no suggestions were received regarding a title for this newsletter, it has been called "Akhbaruna" for now, but alternative recommendations are still welcome. ∎

OVERVIEW OF THE REPORTS ...

JORDAN

The Jordan team grew from one to three as Jihad (Muna) Ghosheh and Yousef Saadeh came on board as the research assistants.

The team has since been very active, selecting the field sites, visiting the local community, and meeting with NGO's and INGO's that work in the area. (Details of all of these can be found in the following pages.)

Furthermore, the team administered Colin McMullin's (CM) psychological test with grades 7 and 10 of the UNRWA boys' and girls' schools in Hitteen camp. They were then able to capitalise on CM's presence in the region (he was visiting the West Bank) to bring him in and discuss with him questions and issues they had faced while administering the tests in the schools.

The Jordan team has determined its activities for the next quarter as: (1) implementing steps 2 and 3 of CM's approach, (2) Organising PRA training sessions with individuals and NGO workers from the local community, (3) Collating the compiled socio-economic and demographic data, and (4) Evaluating phase one and reformulating the short term plan. ■

LEBANON

Two detailed reports were received from the Lebanon team. One described the events of the training workshop that was held in coordination with the Syria team (please see pg.6–7). The second contained information on progress on the following fronts:

1. Secondary literature search (please see pg.3)
2. Contact with Palestinian NGO's (please see pg.4)
3. Selecting the research team (please see pg.5)
4. Workshops and training: in addition to the three day workshop, teams from Beirut and the South are meeting regularly to share implementation and research tips.

5. Gaining access to the two camps: the Lebanon team has determined the communities that will be covered in the research and gained access to the camps after several visits. Furthermore, the "popular committee", or "political authority" in both camps has been contacted and their approval secured.

As of the date of this report, social mapping in one of the camps was just starting and the first stage of the data collection was about to take off. ■

SYRIA

The report from Syria contained an outline of the activities and changes that the team had faced. Namely, it informs of the recruitment of Ms. Maria Salem as the secretary, team reporter and researcher for the field work in Syria. Two other researchers were recruited and in house training on the project and social research methods have commenced.

Literature relevant to the research has also been collected, and, in addition to meetings with youth organisations and the like (please see pg.5), the team also "started analyzing the content of the national guidance textbooks that are assigned to the pupils in the preparatory and secondary schools, especially those texts devoted to presenting the Palestinian questions to the children in the 8 – 18 age group."

The Syria team also participated in a joint workshop for the Lebanon and Syria teams, details of which is listed on pages 6–7. ■

WEST BANK

The West Bank team, which had previously only consisted of S. Zaroo, now boasts a research assistant, interviewer and stand-by computer specialist.

The team has proceeded to make contacts with local organisations (please see pg.5) and compile a literature search (which will most likely appear in the next newsletter). And aside from the joint training days with the Gaza team (please see below and pg.7) the team has also coordinated a workshop in Hebron (on 18/11/99) to introduce the project to the local community. This workshop was attended by 25 people from interested NGO's and the social work field. ■

GAZA

The team in Gaza went through preparatory groundwork through regular meetings, by co-ordinating with the West Bank team, and with G.Hundt (GH) during her field visit in August.

The team also collected extensive data and literature (from the Gaza Community Mental Health Program, UNRWA library, Education college library, School of Public Health library, Ministry of Health library and others) that is relevant to the project. Unfortunately, details of this work have not yet been received. Perhaps during GH's upcoming field visit.

The team also recruited two social workers as part of the field research team.

The Gaza and West Bank teams had arranged to have regular joint training meetings. Details of the first such training can be found on page 7. Unfortunately, these could not be continued due to permits and travel restrictions, and so the teams have proceeded to work separately. ■

1. LITERATURE SEARCH

LEBANON

One must say at the outset that the search results of secondary literature on Palestinian children and youth in Lebanon are not impressive at all.

First, most available literature on Palestinians in Lebanon dealt with adults i.e. women, elderly, handicapped etc.

Second, most available literature dealt with needs, and available services (health, education and housing), and with various aspects of camp-life in Lebanon, i.e. civil rights including: legal rights (the right to work, travel etc.) civil rights including: economic condition (unemployment, wages); and political situation, i.e. (political affiliations and aspirations, right of return, the peace process); and demographic characteristics of camp-population.

Third, there is no solid body of social-science research on Palestinians in Lebanon.

Reasons for this are:
a) There are not many qualified Palestinian social scientists/researchers still residing in Lebanon.
b) Funds are not available locally or internationally to carry out such research.
c) The Lebanese State is not interested in, nor concerned with conducting research on its Palestinian population.

Anyhow, the following material was found in relation to children and youth:
1. Research on Child Labour
2. Research on Vocational Education Trainees
3. Research on Demographic and Socio-economic Characteristics
4. Research on Educational Problems Facing Palestinian Youth in the Camps
5. Research on Cultural Life of Children

"The Culture of Palestinian Children in the Camps in Lebanon". This is the title of a study commissioned by the Arab UNESCO and carried out by Dr. Najla Nusair in 1996. The study was conducted on a random sample of 1064 children less than 15 years old in

three camps: Ain El Hilweh (South Lebanon); Bourj El-Barajneh (Beirut) and Nahr El-Bared (North Lebanon). Major findings were:

a) *77% of families in the sample could not afford to buy books other than school texts for their children; 11% used to borrow general reading books from NGOs libraries. Only 7% of families were able to buy 1–5 books per year for their children.*

b) *Only 12% of families were able to buy magazines for their children, while 80% could not buy any. 7% of families secured such magazines from NGOs. By magazines, the researcher specifically referred to children's magazines published in Lebanon such as "Samer", "Majed", "Ahmad". UNICEF distributes a children magazine "SAWA" free of charge to NGOs.*

c) *Toys and Games. 40% of families were unable to purchase any toys or games for their children. Only 2.5% were able to buy 7 or more toys per year, while 11% were able to buy 3-5 toys, 16% bought 1-2 toys only, and 31% bought toys during feasts and on special occasions only. NGOs do not offer any toys or games to children.*

d) *Television. The researcher found out that 69% of children watch T.V. programs indiscriminately. Only 26% of families reported that their children watch children's programs only. The rest (5%) said their children never watch television. The researcher concluded that the T.V. remains the most powerful cultural tool in the camps. She recommended that this has to be circumscribed by making books, magazines and games available to children in the camps.*

6. Research on Post-Traumatic Effects of Prolonged Conflict

This study was carried out by the school of Public Health at the American University of Beirut in 1999. It covered both Lebanese and Palestinians in the greater Beirut area. However, unfortunately it studied the post-traumatic effects and coping mechanisms of adults only.

7. Research on Living Conditions Among Palestinians in Camps and Gatherings in Lebanon

8. Research on Palestinian Culture and Identity.

The Arab Resource Centre for Popular Arts is the only NGO that works mainly on preserving Palestinian culture and identity. They did a lot in the area of oral history, especially recording folk tales and songs from the elderly generation.

They also recorded the "collective memory" of that generation on life in Palestine before 1948. They involved Palestinian children in various activities such as "A Trip to Palestine", "Interviewing their parents and grandparents" through active learning. However, they did not carry any specific research on the children themselves, nor did they collect any material on Palestinian children's living conditions, world-view, aspirations, perceptions etc. ■

Literature searches...

Please inform us of any references or material that you need or that you consider relevant to the project.

EXCERPTS FROM SUMMARY REPORTS – CONTACTS & MEETINGS IN THE COMMUNITY

2. CONTACTS AND MEETINGS IN THE COMMUNITY

JORDAN

Contacting and meeting UNICEF, CARE, SCF, NTFC & UNRWA

- Meeting with **CARE**: Met with Johan and Anis and shared the information with them regarding our project. They were very interested and Johan's interest revolved around the question of how the younger generations identify with Jordan/Palestine. I wanted to know about their programs and they gave me a brief review, some of it was focused on train-the-trainer courses, and geared to local water management/ rehabilitation- irrigation and small scale agricultural projects in uplands, water saving techniques and irrigation from springs. They had just completed a training session with the Canada Fund. They cooperate with other local and international NGO and IGO's such as UNICEF and CIDA.

- Meeting with **SCF**: Met with Golda El-Khoury, the Field Office Director and Jumana Theordore. I also explained the major themes and approaches to the study and was introduced to the person I will be working with and who will be interested to participate. We exchanged phone numbers and I asked if we (research assistants and other involved members in the research project) to attend some of their meetings regarding activities in the areas of Jabal and Mukhayyam al-Nasser. I asked if they had any activities in Schneller camp and she said they had just started.

- **UNRWA**: Between October 1 to October 20, 1999 I had several meetings with UNRWA officials and employees. The purpose was to get clearance and support to conduct research in UNRWA run schools, without going through the bureaucracy of the DPA which would have hampered the whole study for a long time. This took some time; however, I found most of UNRWA's employees and officials I spoke to very supportive and interested in the project. To get official approval, I wrote a letter to Mr. Gunnar Lofberg, the Field Director in Jordan and he was very cooperative. Mr. Lofberg wanted to follow up on the study and to be informed as to the results of the research project, especially those relating to UNRWA schools. Ms. Maha Abdel-Hamid , Assistant deputy of Relief and Social Services for the Jordan Field, personally accompanied us to the schools and participated in some of the tests, she was very eager to join some of our research activities and was key to facilitating our work. Matar Saqer and Fuad al-Shawwa, all were extremely and specially supportive.

- **UNICEF**: I tried contacting Misreak from UNICEF several times, beginning in August, but she was either out of the country or busy. Therefore, I went to the offices and met with several people and handed Misreak the material provided by Dawn on the project. I met with several UNICEF employees who are active in the area of children and adolescents. They are planning to run a project on youth and were interested in cooperating with us. I provided them with information on our project and we planned further meetings in the coming month.

- I contacted the **National Task Force for Children** and collected available studies on children and most importantly the list of the various NGO's and organizations concerned with children in Jordan

With Research Assistants: Several meetings took place to decide on the dates and the schools where we would conduct Colin's psychological approach to study what worries children and adolescents as part of our overall study. We conducted the test at the beginning of November.

(In addition, the Jordan team paid field visits to the organisation operating in their chosen field sites. Details of these are listed on pg.8)

LEBANON

The team leader and the co-researcher contacted several NGOs that work in Palestinian camps and informed them about the research project on Palestinian children and youth, about its objectives, scope and discussed their role in facilitating the fieldwork and in disseminating the research findings. Their response was extremely positive. They expressed their willingness to cooperate fully. The NGOs contacted so far are: Association Najdeh and the National Institution for Social Care and Vocational Training (NISCVT). Both NGOs operate and have centres in all camps. Other NGOs contacted are: The Palestinian Arab Centre (in Bourj El-Barajneh camp); The Children and Youth Centre – Shatila camp; Save the Children – U.K. (operates in camps of South and North Lebanon); the Arab Resource Centre for Popular Arts, and El-Huleh social club (Burj El-Shemali camp).

Main facilities and activities offered by these NGOs are: Kindergartens, youth clubs, folk dancing, summer camps, vocational training, dental clinics, computer courses. NISCVT takes care of 1400 orphans who reside with relatives in the camps. It offers them psychological counselling, financial assistance, health care and various social activities. Najdeh is the only NGO that runs a "small loans" program, especially for women in the camps.

A major NGO that would be contacted next is the "Popular Aid for Relief and Development". This NGO operates mainly among war displaced families, mostly from destroyed or devastated refugee camps. Its main domain is preventive health and mother and childcare. Last year, it started a youth program in its centre in Sabra (Beirut) for 250 displaced families residing in vacated hospital buildings.

It is worth mentioning that Palestinian NGO's programs over the past two decades were geared towards very young children and adults. They did not develop any social or cultural programs that serve the needs of youth i.e. those of the age group 12–18. However, in the past two years some NGOs become aware of the necessity of addressing the situation and the needs of youth in that age bracket.

WEST BANK

Contacts with some local organisations and NGOs were established, such as:
UNRWA
UNRWA Director of Alaroub Refugees Camp
UNRWA Director of Alfuar Refugees Camp
Save the Children
Directorate of Education in Hebron
Directorate of Education in Southern Hebron
Defence for Children International/Hebron Office
Palestine Diaspora and Refugee Centre – SHAML
UNICEF – Jerusalem (Rose Shoumali)
The Palestinian Statistics Department – Hebron Branch.

SYRIA

We started doing some kind of social mapping and we organized a few informal meeting with youth organization cadres, evaluating their past experiences and the prospects for the future. We also organized informal meetings with the Palestinian woman's union, Syrian branch, trying to understand and analyze the role of the mothers in keeping the image of the lost homeland alive in the immigration of their children.

We organized informal meetings with groups of Palestinians teachers working in the UNRWA preparatory schools in order to explore their attitudes and their activities in politicizing their children. This will help us to complete our draft and the content of the interviews and understand the role of UNRWA schooling in the identification of the Palestinian children of their national identity. ■

3. RESEARCH TEAM

– CRITERIA FOR SELECTING TEAM MEMBERS

JORDAN:
Jihad (Muna) Ghosheh. I based my selection on the following criteria:

- Her extensive experience working with various grassroots and international organizations, such as UNICEF.
- Her familiarity and knowledge of Palestinian-Jordanian history and society.
- Her ability to communicate at various levels in society, she is trusted, welcomed and liked as an active member of the community in poor areas and refugee camps.
- Her ability to write and communicate in Arabic and English. In addition, she grasps the concepts used in research regarding various social, political and cultural issues.
- Her extensive network of contacts and familiarity with various organizations, communities and individuals.

I met with Muna several times and discussed with her the project, objectives and general approach.

Yousef Saadeh. The basis for the selection:
- Yousef lives in one of the areas chosen as a field site, namely Hay al-Mahasreh and is accepted as an active local community leader.

- He is a student and knowledgeable and interested in various social and methodological concepts and theories.
- Has experience in community work and research.

Both assistants worked on contract basis with UNICEF.

LEBANON:
The two camps the Lebanon team is going to work in are Burj El-Barajneh camp near Beirut and Burj El-Shmali camp near Tyre-South Lebanon. We thought it is best to use interviewers from the camp community.

Suad Hammad
She is a 45-year old woman. She resides in the camp. She has an M.A. in linguistics. Until recently, she ran an NGO in the camp, namely the Palestinian Arab centre. She was its director for three years. The centre offered several programs to children and youth. Suad has a long history of activism in student unions, women's union, youth organizations and girls' scout's organizations. Last summer she was the camp leader of a national camp organized by Welfare Association for Palestinian children 9–13 year old.

Sidebar (rotated text): EXCERPTS FROM SUMMARY REPORTS – CONTACTS & MEETINGS IN THE COMMUNITY & RESEARCH TEAM

Fayza Khalaf
She was born in Burj El-Shemali camp in 1966. She is married and lives outside the camp now. She is very well acquainted with the camp-population. Her main experience is being an interviewer in several surveys conducted by the Palestinian Central Bureau of Statistics. ■

4. TRAINING THE RESEARCH STAFF

LEBANON & SYRIA:
(excerpts from the training workshop report)

The Lebanon and Syria research teams conducted a joint workshop over a 3-day period (Nov. 5–7). The workshop's main objectives included:

- a comprehensive introduction of the research project to both the resource persons and team field research assistants;
- informal training sessions on the research tools;
- a participatory exchange of experiences and visions in relation to the research content and reality context.

The total number of participants was fourteen.

Day 1: Friday 5/11/'99
Opening Session: The research contents and objectives

Session 1: The Social Context of Palestinians in Syria and Lebanon (focus on children)
Presentations were given by Ms. Samira Gibril (Syria team), Ms. Sabah Baalbacki (Assoc. Najdeh - Lebanon) and Ms. Alia Chana'a (SCF-U.K., Lebanon).

There are clear differences in the situation of Palestinian refugees in the discussed countries. In Syria, Palestinians totalling around 358,000, constitute 2% of the country's population, with 30% residing in refugee camps. Palestinians in Lebanon, around 361,000, make up 10.5% of the country's population with 54.5% in camps and an additional approximate of 23% living in the so-called 'unofficial' camps (i.e. not UNRWA camps). Camp infrastructure in Lebanon suffers more than that in Syria in regards to availability of water, sanitation, etc.

The Lebanese government denies Palestinians their civil rights imposing severe restrictions on Palestinian employment and the accesses to public services (e.g. health). Unlike in Syria, education in

Lebanon witnessed long periods of cessation due to internal and external conflicts.

Although the vital need for UNRWA schools was highlighted, there were several reservations regarding UNRWA's educational services (overcrowded classes, unmotivated teachers, increasing student drop-out rates). It is to be noted that discussants from Lebanon portrayed a more critical situation.

Social deviance amongst children and adolescents is seen as more prominent in Lebanon than in Syria (e.g. theft, drug use). Cases of child prostitution and child abuse in Lebanon are beginning to surface.

Services provided to children/ adolescents are seen as lacking in both countries, while those providing professional psychological consultation are almost nonexistent.

Session 2: The research approach: methods & tools
Ms. Tabari (Lebanon team) presented the research methods and tools. The research, essentially a qualitative one, follows a multidisciplinary approach, including anthropology, sociology, psychology, economics, and educational studies. Phase one of the project will be implemented at a community level relying on PRA (Participatory Research Approach), while phase two focuses on a household sub-sample as case studies. A sample of 20 households, in each country, with children aged 9-18 will be drawn.

Participatory research tools for phase 1, include: community social mapping, matrix and ranking, and timelines. Such close interaction with the community facilitates the collection of basic socio-demographic data, also taking place in the first phase. Techniques for the second phase include: oral history with different members of the family (focus on generation differences and key incidents/events); semi-structured interviews with key informants; group interviews; and participant observation. Brief explanation on the related tools was given (elaboration was scheduled for day 2).

Session 3: PRA approach and Discussion
Dr. Abdul Rahim (Syria team) spoke of PRA. The approach had the support of the attendants, specifically the practitioners as they are already using this method in their work with the community.

Day 2: Sat. 6/11/'99

Session 1: Social mapping techniques

Session 2: Interviewing techniques and approach to case studies

Session 3: Oral history and popular memory

Mr. Moataz El Dajani (ARCPA, Lebanon) presented his organization's work in the collection of oral history and popular memory. The discussion also entailed a slide-presentation. Mr. El Dajani spoke of ARCPA's popular memory project, which entailed the collection of oral histories, over a two-year period, of Palestinians who lived in Palestine prior 1948. The information now serves as an educational resource for the Palestinian refugee community, especially the post-exodus and the young generations.

The related project was followed up by a similar one, this time also involving children, ages 8 to 12, in the collection of oral histories. Project implementation took six months, after which ARCPA launched its "Young Journalists" program. Children set out the main issues for investigation, focusing on those most relevant to their own realities and interests. They grouped their research issues into three categories: (1) Memories of the older generations (e.g. parents, grandparents), (2) Poverty, and (3) Children's wishes and aspirations.

Dissemination of collected information targeted other children in a number of refugee camps. Children set up small exhibits, at youth clubs and centers, in which they displayed essay-photo books, wall posters (newspaper format) and a number of photographs.

A discussion followed the presentation. Participants spoke of the weakness of UNRWA's national program (history & geography of Palestine). They all realized the need of getting organizations working with children more involved in cultural awareness. Many saw the prevalent danger of Islamic fundamentalism which is affecting the children's perception of their own identity. Children are increasingly molding their identities along religious lines.

Questions were raised about the techniques and difficulties faced in the collection of oral histories. Mr. El Dajani (ARCPA, Lebanon) mentioned mock interviews as a method of training. ARCPA is also currently formulating a training for trainers guide (on collection of oral histories). He highlighted recurrent difficulties such as the interviewees' mood, digressing from the intended subject matter, and mistrust.

Session 4: Group activity (timelines and group interviewing)

Day 3: Sun. 7/11/'99

Session 1: Reporting and recording and research ethics
Dr. Serhan (Lebanon team) spoke of participant observation as well as recording and reporting techniques. Examples of possible traps/mistakes were given. Cross-checking the given information was highlighted. The presence of a tape recorder may affect the spontaneity and/or accuracy of given answers. It might also cause suspicion on the part of the interviewee.

EXCERPTS FROM SUMMARY REPORTS – TRAINING OF THE RESEARCH STAFF

Dr. Adnan Abdul Rahim (Syria team) and Ms. Tabari (Lebanon team) introduced issues related to research ethics. This was followed by a general discussion around the presented topic. Issues of focus included: gaining the trust of the interviewees (e.g. social visits before the interviewing begins, explaining the purpose of the research); respecting their privacy; sharing information with them (e.g. give them copies of tapes); not being persistent (esp. in informal interviews); being sensitive to their feelings; etc.

Closing session: General discussion and evaluation

Final note:
The workshop's objectives were met as all participants left with a clear idea of the project and a basic knowledge of the research methods and tools. The exchange amongst all was very beneficial for elaborating components relevant to the project objectives as well as enforcing it at a community level. Follow-up training will be conducted for the teams' field research assistants. Future joint activities/cooperation between the Syria and Lebanon teams will be planned in their meeting in early December. Both teams realize the need for exchanging experience and skills.

WEST BANK & GAZA
(excerpts from details of a training workshop for the teams in West Bank and Gaza Strip)

Objectives:
1. To enable participants of knowing the method of communication with people.
2. To enable them of knowing methods of interviewing children and adolescents.

Lecturers:
1. Dr. Abdel Aziz Thabet:
   child interview / coping strategies / resilience in children.
2. Dr. Ayoub El Alam:
   communication skills in interviewing people for qualitative data collection.

(The workshop was held on 23/10/99 and was attended by 11 participants.)

The first session was run by Dr. Ayoub El Alem in which he defined the communication types and methods which can be used in our project.

The afternoon session was conducted by Dr. Abdel Aziz Thabet, in which he defined the interview techniques used with children and adolescents, types of interviews ... and methods of research such as qualitative data collection in children using interviews.

He also introduced the types of coping and resilience in children and adolescents during conflict situation and showed that we can use Coping Scale by Lazarus as structure interview with sample of the study. ■

5. SELECTING THE FIELD SITES

JORDAN:

A. Hay al-Mahasreh: An area where the majority of inhabitants come from one Palestinian village destroyed and depopulated during the 1948 war – Bayt Mahsir.

B. Jabal al-Nasr and **al-Emir Hassan** refugee camp: This is an area part of which is an 'unofficial' refugee camp, while the other is considered a poor urban area. 'Unofficial' is a term given the three camps in Jordan which are not administered by UNRWA.

C. Hitteen or **Schneller Camp**: A refugee camp administered by UNRWA, its inhabitants come from various areas in Palestine. These include refugees, displaced and refugees who hold the Gaza identity card.

The above areas were chosen, because they cover a heterogeneous segment of refugees:
Hay al-Mahasreh is an area whose inhabitants are a homogeneous community by original village and not withstanding other dimensions which are heterogeneous. **Jabal al-Nasr** includes a community which does not inhabitant a 'camp' and an 'unofficial' camp and finally **Hitteen** is an UNRWA administered camp and its population is heterogeneous in terms of original village and town as well as period of displacement. g

FIELD VISITS

Jabal al-Nasr with Muna: There we went to Sayyidat al-Nasr Committee center (Ladies of al-Nasr). We met Imm Adel, who runs the center and noted the center was not very active. Imm Adel manages the center. Also, we visited the Islamic clinic, the Jordanian Women's Union and Save the Children nurseries and The Jordan River Office and the Camp Services Committee.

October 3, 1999: Attended a meeting of the Coordinating committee, which includes members from various local committees.

The meeting regarding the work of the various local committees and the annual plan was important to attend, not only to identify local and international actors (a member of UNICEF was present) but also to introduce myself to the various members and share with them information about the project. I will be meeting and working with the local committees as well as the members of international organizations active in the areas under study.

Hay al-Mahasreh: Al-Mahasreh quarter is an area inhabited by Palestinian refugees who originate in Bayt Mahsir, a village that was destroyed and depopulated in 1948. It is almost a 'homogeneous' area at that level, although recently, a few families from various places moved in. Yousef – the male research assistant – is from **Hay al-Mahasreh**. We first visited the 'Society of Work and Development,' Yousef is the president of this society. He gave us a detailed history of the Society and its planned projects. In addition, he gave us an elaborate history and tour around the area, which he knows well, having lived in it all his life. Further questioning revealed basic information on adolescents, such as the places they meet and that they are organized in various groups who have particular interests: e.g. those interested in sports, usually huddle together in the evening, in particular areas and streets. We met older men, who also meet in special streets. The contact with these individuals was important to follow up on interviewing and knowledge about the community within which children and adolescents live.

An important juncture in the history of the area is **the Urban Development Project,** initiated by the government. The area - because it is not a refugee camp does not fall under the mandates of either UNRWA or the Department of Palestinian Affairs. However, most of the inhabitants hold UNRWA registration cards. According to Yousef, the impact of the Urban

EXCERPTS FROM SUMMARY REPORTS – SELECTING THE FIELD SITES

Development Project is mainly the **infra struc- ture**, such as the asphalting of roads and sewage networks.

Organizations in the area:
(a) The Society for Work and Development
(b) The Zakat (alms)
(c) Women's Rehabilitation Cooperative (Ta'heel al-mar'a al-ta'awuniyyeh).

Hay al-Mahasreh is very congested, the paths are very narrow and although asphalted, they are rather dangerous and not very clean. As we walked we saw boys and girls who went either to the government or UNRWA schools. Some women were standing in front of their houses, but not too many. While we were there, a conflict had erupted between neighbors causing physical injuries.

Hitteen Camp: The visit was mainly to the UNRWA schools to administer the psychological test provided during the Cyprus meeting and presented by Dr. Colin McMullin. We met with the heads of both the boys' and girls' schools and some of the teachers explaining to them the purpose of our visit and following visits. They were supportive and provided us with their opinions regarding the problems faced by children and adolescents as well as information about the camp and its inhabitants ... Further visits are planned for the coming months and they will include visits to families and neighborhoods in the camp. ∎

SUMMARY REPORT FRAMEWORK

TASK	DESCRIPTION	DATE
1. Literature search		
(a) Search results – what is available	• It would be enriching to know of the results of the local literature searches: what type of studies have been done in the area before, with this target group, etc.	
(b) Analysis of the search	• A brief analysis of this literature as is relevant to the project.	
(c) Photocopies	• Everybody is encouraged to make photocopies of studies/publications that they consider relevant or important, and to either mail them to Oxford, or leave them for Dawn or Gillian to carry back with them from their field visits.	
2. Contacts & meetings in the community	• Briefings on meetings with concerned local IGO's and NGO's. • A suggested emphasis on meeting with UNRWA and Save the Children Fund (if they operate in the area) as the more important foci to the research project, in addition to other organisations working in relevant domains.	
3. Research staff (assistants and interviewers)	• A brief description on the how and why the research assistants and interviewers were selected.	
4. The training of the research staff.	• A summary of the type of training offered to the research staff as preparation for the fieldwork.	
5. Selecting the field sites	• A brief description of the selected field sites. • Reasons for selecting these field sites.	Report 1 & 2 **January 2000**
6. Implementation of PRA/social mapping/timelines/ other social research tools	• A summary of the process of implementing these social research tools in the fieldwork. • A summary of the results of this fieldwork.	Initial phase of research/report 3 **March 2000**
7. Interviewing and narrative phase of the project	• A summary of the process of implementing these social research tools in the fieldwork. • A summary of the results of this fieldwork. • A narrative report of the research from the teams.	Next phase of research/report 4 **May 2000**

NOTICES & REMINDERS

As of the dawn of the new millennium **the Refugee Studies Programme (RSP)** became **the Refugee Studies Centre (RSC)**. This does not change any of the centre's activities or, more importantly, its contacts and addresses.

Financial reporting: please be sure that you are, whenever possible, obtaining and main-taining receipts for the transactions reported in your financial reports. Otherwise, please be sure to keep a record of these transactions. This will greatly facilitate reporting back to the fun-ders at a later stage.

REMEMBER: The second set of reports is due at the end of January 2000!

Field Visits

Lebanon:	Syria:	Jordan:	West Bank & Gaza:
22–23/12/1999 – M.Damaj	25–26/1/2000 –	Late March/ Early April	Last week of March
24/1/2000 – Dawn Chatty	Dawn Chatty	2000 – Dawn Chatty	– first week of April
			2000 – Gillian Hundt

NO COMMENT

Found on the wall of a NGO centre in Burj El Chemali Camp, Sour, Lebanon.
In a weekend session with youth (roughly 8 – 19 years old) in the sponsorship programme,
they were asked to express what "Palestine" meant to them in one word.
This is part of what they wrote.
(Originally in Arabic, the translation is my own.)

treason   division   camps   labour   siege   homelessness
martyrdom   soldier (fidai)   seizure   displacement   denial
grandfathers/ forefathers   escape   loyalty   patriotism   enmity
carelessness   tradition   refugees   promise   hope   service
arab   land   relinquishment
settlement   sacrifice   invasion   people   intifada   homeland
wars   future   solidarity   holy land   memory
olives   events   news   world powers   culture
cooperation   jews and zionists   injustice   independence
destruction   sea ports   naturalisation   conspiracy   forgetfulness
poverty   battles and wars   orange groves living alongside in peace
challenge   rights   surrender   weapons
massacres   symbol   return   al nakba   insult   depression
misery   loss   political parties   rebellion   politics

AKHBARUNA

Children & Adolescents in Palestinian Households: Living with the Effects of Prolonged Conflict & Forced Migration

ISSUE #3 – MARCH 2000 An Internal Team Newsletter for the Mellon Project.

CONTENTS:

Compiled by Maha Damaj, Research Assistant, Mellon Project, Refugee Studies Programme

MID-POINT – Introduction

This third newsletter marks the middle of the 'newsletter' cycle, as two more will most likely appear before the fieldwork is completely wrapped up.

In the last few months, putting this newsletter together has become my own benchmark to make sure that I have organised the information received from you in proper order ... and a reminder for me to see if I have received your information at all. It is, perhaps, not surprising that this newsletter comes out almost a month after it was scheduled. After all, this is also the middle of the fieldwork cycle, when the research activities are no doubt developing a momentum of their own. All the more reason why we need to keep our collective calendar synchronised as we work our way towards the completion date. It is essential that you inform of us any unexpected twists or turns that would delay you from meeting this date.

Other than that, I hope the newsletter is equally acting as a benchmark for you. With a two-month based metre with which to stop and check how you are progressing.

That's the short of it for this introduction. I think the rest of the newsletter says it all! ■

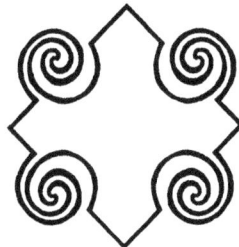

OVERVIEW OF THE REPORTS...

Information received as of the date of issue of this newsletter is tabulated below*:

	Jordan	Gaza	Lebanon	Syria	West Bank
Literature Search – results					
– analysis					
– photocopies					
Contacts & Meetings in the Community					
Research Staff Recruitment					
Training Research Staff					
– training workshop report					
Selecting the Field Sites					
– sociodemographics of population under study					
– description of infrastructure					
Social Mapping					
PRA etc.					
Interviews & narratives					

Financial Report, Nov 99					
Financial Report, Jan 00					

* PLEASE NOTE: The checklist format of the above table does not reflect the type of information and amount of detail in which these parameters were described.

Implies that there has been an indication of the work taking place, but information about the outcome of the activity has not yet been received.

If you feel that the above does not reflect the work that your team has undertaken to date, then please let me know. This discrepancy may be due our different readings of the reports, implying that we need to clarify where our reporting expectations lie.

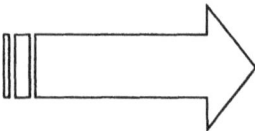

PROJECT TIMELINE

Nov 99

1st financial & summary report set

- Literature Search
- Contacts & meetings in the community
- Research staff recruited
- Training of research staff
- Selecting field sites

JAN 00

2nd set of reports

3rd set of reports

- Implementation of PRA/ social mapping/timelines/ group interviews/other social research tools

MAR 00

4th set of reports

- Interviewing and narrative phase of the project

MAY 00

Mid-project financial statement

The project timeline has grown in size and detail, which has warranted dedicating this whole page to it.

Please make note of the additions and/or modifications.

Please note the dates that have been set as endpoints for the particular activities. If you feel that they are not in line with the stage that you are at presently, then we need to know as soon as possible.

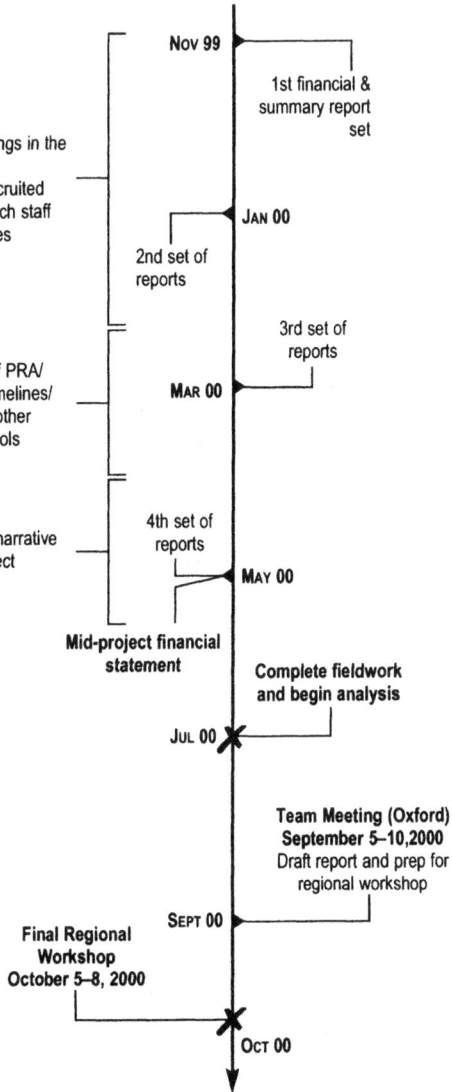

Complete fieldwork and begin analysis

JUL 00

Team Meeting (Oxford) September 5–10,2000 Draft report and prep for regional workshop

SEPT 00

Final Regional Workshop October 5–8, 2000

OCT 00

1. LITERATURE SEARCH

SYRIA

During the last six months we have been reviewing the available literature on the Palestinians in Syria.

In fact, and compared to studies on other Palestinian communities in the West Bank, Gaza and Lebanon, we can say that it was notable that previous serious area studies were conducted on the Palestinian community in Syria.

We noticed a recent interest in supporting and financing new researches about the Palestinians in Syria. FAFO, the Norwegian Documentation Center, is supporting and financing a comprehensive survey on the Palestinians in Syria in collaboration with UNICEF and the Palestinian Central Bureau of Statistics and Natural Resources.

A Canadian mission to Palestinian refugee camps and gatherings in the Syrian Arab Republic had published a report about its findings as a result of the mission visits to the Palestinian camps during October and November 1988. The report presented valuable data about Palestinians in Syria and mainly about UNRWA services presented to the refugees in the camps and their social and economic needs. The study was officially supervised by GOPAR, the Syrian General Organization for the Palestinian Arab Refugees.

The annual report of UNRWA General Commissioner also presented precise data about social, health and economic needs of the Palestinians and UNRWA services presented to them.

Other data were collected from the publications of the Palestinian Central Bureau of Statistics and Natural Resources, especially the three studies about Palestinian children's education in Syria, Palestinian children's labour in Syria and the school drop-out of Palestinian pupils in UNRWA schools.

Hamad Maw'ed was supported by the International Development and Research Center in Canada to publish the "Palestinian Refugees in Syria".

In addition to the above-mentioned literature, we managed to review certain samples of Palestinian journals assigned to pioneers and adolescents (Al Ghadd and Al Kifah journals). The aim was to analyze the politicization process of the Palestinian children during the 80s and the 90s of the last century.

We also reviewed secondary sources about the Palestinians in Syria, especially the books issued by the Palestinian Studies' Center: mainly Ellias Zurayq "The Palestinian Refugees Question and the Peaceful Settlement" that deals with the dominant international attitudes towards the solutions of the refugees' question. Salim Tamari's study about the future of the Palestinian refugees, "The Works of the Refugee Committee", discusses the same problem.

We are not going to mention here all the available literature about the Palestinians in Syria but we have pointed out here the fact that almost all available literatures are theoretical in general. They deal mainly with abstracts and they lack the fieldwork aspect.

We hope our project will enrich the Palestinian studies in Syria and will present an image of their collective memories, their children's politicization, their coping strategies and the way they managed to resist the military, social and political pressures that distinguish their daily life in their households.

It is worth mentioning that the above-mentioned literature will help us a lot to learn more about the Palestinian young generations in Syria, and to understand the way they are or were politicized and how did they manage to cope with unbearable inhuman circumstances. Thus, it is very important to conduct a realistic detailed research that studies the true situations of Palestinians in Syria.

GAZA

Collection of data between the team was continued out by searching all available resources in the Gaza strip such as Gaza Community Mental Health program, UNRWA Library, Education College library, School of Public Health Library, Ministry of Health Library, Upsalla University, and Denmark University and local Al Quds and Al Hayat Journals. A file for data collection was opened and all materials are in place. An abstract for 15 papers was prepared as a part of the literature review. A copy of the material will be handed to Dr. Gillian Hundt in her site visit. A continuous contact was done with Dr. Salah El Zarou to standardize the type of data collection in both sites.

WEST BANK

The collected literature was classified, and the bits related to the West Bank are identified and currently under review. This process will be completed by the end of February. ■

2. CONTACTS & MEETINGS IN THE COMMUNITY

SYRIA

Last month we managed to achieve several formal and informal group meetings with the general secretariats of the Palestinian Youth Organizations. We were able to discuss the role of their organizations in the politicization of the Palestinian pioneers and adolescents and after-school activities, including summer clubs. At the same time we organized meetings with more than 12 UNRWA teachers working in various schools in different Palestinian camps (elementary and preparatory cycles). Those interviews helped us to analyze and evaluate the role of the Palestinian teachers in keeping the image of the lost homeland alive in the minds of the Palestinian children, also to know to what extent they managed to offer their children the real national culture and a Palestinian identity.

Meetings with the directors of the Palestinian Red Crescent Society were held to analyze the health services presented to their Palestinian clients. We also met intellectuals who offered us precious information about the Palestinians in the camps in Syria.

Data and conclusions included in these meetings will help us to analyze the Palestinian children's politicization process, along with thirty pages of content analysis of Syria's civics textbooks, especially those dealing with the Palestinian question and the Arab-Israeli conflict. ■

3. RESEARCH TEAM

– CRITERIA FOR SELECTING TEAM MEMBERS

SYRIA

Three researchers were selected in November.

The first is **Maria Salem** who is already working as a Project Secretary of the Palestinian Programme at UNICEF office in Damascus. She is now working actively with the project in reporting, typing and keeping contact with the project administration. She will later be engaged in translation and research activities. She masters English and French. She is a sociology department Diploma graduate from Damascus University.

The second researcher is **Mai Berkawi**, she is a sociology department graduate from Damascus University. Working in the UNRWA social affairs section, she will be active in interviews and social mapping.

The third researcher is **Manar Rabbani**, she is also a sociology department graduate from Damascus University. Participated in Lebanese researches dealing with UNRWA services, she will help Mai in organizing interviews.

GAZA

We chose the field researchers:
Eitdal El Kahtieb, a sociologist with much experience in PRA, focus groups and narrative data collection,
Salah Hamdan, a social worker with great experience.
We also appointed an assistant researcher, **Jehad Okasha**, to write the reports and follow other issues.

LEBANON

The Beirut research staff witnessed the withdrawal of Ms. Fahd (for health reasons), who was replaced by **Ms. Sana Hussein** soonafter. Sana has a BA in sociology and an extensive experience in field surveys. She resides in Shatila camp and has frequent contacts with the Gaza center community (targeted in this research). The

Tyre research staff was completed with the addition of **Ms. Samia Jammal**. She is a sociology student and has experience as an animator in summer camps for children. She resides in Borj El Shemali camp and is very familiar with the camp community as she also works at her brother's pharmacy. **Mr. Mahmoud Juma'a** was commissioned to assist the Tyre staff. He is a key figure in the community with extensive involvement in youth programs. Mahmoud is the director of Beit Atfal Al-Sumoud center, encompassing a kindergarten, a dental clinic, vocational training for adolescents, and a club holding regular weekly activities for the youth. ■

4. TRAINING THE RESEARCH STAFF

SYRIA

In addition to the workshop that took place in Lebanon last November, the staff were subject to five training sessions in Damascus during the months of December and January. The training included the following subjects:

1. The goals and dimensions of the project.
2. The PRA technique, its social, political and philosophical background, its techniques and the importance of the learners' participation in the process of learning, the disadvantages of the questionnaires techniques and similar approaches....etc
3. The content and techniques of interviews and group interviews.
4. Oral history, collective memories and testimonies.
5. Reporting.

The three researchers participated actively in the training. However, we all still need further instructions about oral history and its techniques. We intend to organize a workshop at the beginning of next month with cadres of the Arab Resource Center for Popular Arts in Lebanon, which enjoys rich experience in this field.

WEST BANK

In order to complete the training which started in Gaza in 1999, the team contracted Ms. Siham Burghouti – the Director General of Rural Development/ Ministry of Local Government – to provide 3 training sessions (9 hours) in Participatory Rapid Approach. The training was held on 15, 16 and 18 February 2000 at the Centre of Islamic Culture, Hebron.

GAZA

The team members discussed the different types of methodology to be used. At the end all agreed to use narrative, story telling, semi-structured interview as the main methods of interviewing the families.

Etidal proposed that we conduct a pilot study of two families, one in Rafah and the other on Al Bourij camp. The team agreed to take the following timelines: 1948, 1956, 1967, 1973, 1982, 1987, 1991, 1994. In starting on 1948 the following will be asked:

1. Mapping of the area of living before the forced migration.
2. Time of forced migration (Alone or with others).
3. Reason of leaving the original cities.
4. Traumatic experiences during this stage and coping strategies.
5. Number of people started the journey and number left at the next station.
6. Resources available on leaving their cities such as money, food, and furniture.
7. Did some of them go back to their original place to bring foods or valuable things?.
8. Some items from Lazarus coping scale will be chosen as questions to sort out the type of coping during migration.
9. The next station on camps including the mapping of the camp at that time, type of resources, coping strategies at that station, number of people left after the journey.

The other station will be discussed after the pilot sample to have feedback from families. In the meeting all of us raised the issues of sensitivity or using tape recorders in meetings with families so three people will conduct each interview (one observer, one interviewer, and one recorder) and no tape recorder will be used. For mapping a sheet of white paper with colored pencil will be used.

LEBANON

Preparation for the fieldwork started in December. The team researchers carried out a number of field visits and formulated a questionnaire for surveying the basic socio-economic indicators of the targeted communities. Following the training sessions on community social mapping techniques, the team researchers trained the research staff on interviewing techniques. Two training sessions were given to the Beirut group (Dec. 12 & 26) and one for the Tyre group (Dec. 17). Procedures and principles, both theoretical and applied, were introduced. Structured and semi-structured interviews (questionnaires) were explained with examples of closed and open-ended questions.

The team researchers held a training session on group interviews for the Tyre & Beirut research staff, in Borj El Shemali camp (Jan. 14). This was followed by an exercise on the related method, at Beit Atfal Al-Sumoud youth club. A group of thirteen children, ages 13–18, was interviewed. The research staff was exposed to the roles of facilitator (interviewer) and recorder/observer. All agreed that it was a large group to handle and that the ideal group should not exceed 7–8 children. Report writing was seen as advisable immediately after the interview.

...additional staff training on interviewing techniques, specifically group interviews, is planned for February. A number of group interviews will be conducted in each site. ■

5. ABOUT THE FIELD SITES

LEBANON

Three field sites were chosen for the study. These include Gaza center and Borj El Barajneh camp (Beirut) and Borj El Shemali camp (Tyre). The first basis for the selection was regional: Beirut, the capital, and Tyre, a predominantly agricultural area in South Lebanon, still enduring Israeli air raids at times. At another level, the Gaza center for the displaced provides the opportunity for observing refugee children in a non-camp setting.

A description of the selected field sites is provided below (*excerpts only*). It is to be noted that since the two camps are densely populated (approx. 17,000 prs. in each), a fairly representative sub-community (neighborhood/block) was chosen.

The research staff ... collected data regarding the basic socio-economic indicators of 386 families from the targeted communities: Gaza center (104 families), Borj El Barajneh camp (119) and Borj El Shemali camps (163). Data analysis was conducted by the team researchers in January. Full details are provided in a separate report.

(The following are selected excerpts. The detailed report may be provided upon request.)
A. Borj El Barajneh camp, Beirut
Camp's population is estimated at 17,000 persons.
● *EDUCATION*
There are nine kindergartens in the camp... Most are run by NGOs and two belong to Islamic groups (Al-Huda & Bara'em Al-'Aksa).
There are three vocational training centers (VTC). One for Association Najdeh, targeting mainly women (ages 16 & above) and has a scholastic tutorial program for intermediate school children as well, another for UNRWA (women's program only) and a third for the Development Association, targeting the youth.

All UNRWA schools are located outside the camp.
● *EDUCATIONAL CENTERS & CLUBS...*
● *LEISURE OUTLETS FOR THE YOUTH*
The camp is very overcrowded, allowing little space for any outdoor activity. There are no playgrounds in the camp. There are a few squares where children and adolescent play or 'hang out', each square does not exceed 25m.sq. There are a couple of pool places, four play-station amusement centers, and one small café. It is to be noted that girls do not go to these places (traditional community).
● *HEALTH*
There is only one hospital in the camp, Haifa hospital run by the Palestine Red Crescent Society (PLO institution). It has been witnessing grave funding cutbacks since the early nineties, thus affecting its service delivery. The same situation applies to the UNRWA clinic. The PRCS offers most of its services for free and charges nominal amounts for some services, while all those of UNRWA are free.
● *INFRASTRUCTURE*
Electricity: there are no government meters regulating the camp's supply of electricity, thus resulting in weak power output and frequent electricity cuts. The Camp's Popular Committee manages the electricity networks by collecting fees from the community and dealing with the electricity company.
Water: the government utility water supply reaches only the eastern part of the camp. The rest of the camp gets water from wells, managed by the Camp's Popular Committee. The water, very salty, is pumped to the community 2-3 times per week (for an hour or two).
Drinking water is supplied through public tanks and/or bought by the gallon (from shops).
Sewage system: is regulated by UNRWA. UNRWA also tends to garbage collection on daily basis (except Sundays).
● *OTHER*
The Security Committee looks after the camp's security. The SC has an office in the camp and deals with all issues except criminal law, as it is the government's task.

There is one mosque. There are no cemeteries, but there is one close to the camp.

• **CHOSEN SITE**

The area (Tarshiha), selected for this research, encompasses an estimated total of 225 families, of whom 119 are included in the targeted sample. Of these, 81 have children between the ages of 9 and 18. They all have access to the already listed services. In the Tarshiha neighborhood itself, there are five grocery shops, two vegetable stores, a poultry shop, a sweets shop, a bakery, two barber shops, two stores for home-appliances, a clothes shop, a store for medical shoes, a dental laboratory, a pharmacy, an amusement center, and two kindergartens.

B. Gaza Center for the Displaced, Beirut

Gaza center, formerly a hospital, is an agglomeration of four buildings housing displaced Palestinian refugees. The hospital was destroyed during the early eighties and is unfit for habitation. There are 244 families residing in the four buildings, the majority, 75–80% , are Palestinian refugees and the rest are Lebanese and Syrian. Most of the Palestinians are originally from Tal Zaatar camp (destroyed in 1976) and some were displaced from Shatila camp (their houses were destroyed after the attacks of 1982 & 1985). Gaza center is adjacent to Shatila camp and is off the main road of Sabra market. It is a very crowded area, with heavily flooded and muddy streets all throughout winter.

• **INFRASTRUCTURE**

Buildings One and Three are the most populated parts of Gaza center. There are around seventeen families living on each floor. Most of them live in one room, lacking both ventilation and proper lighting as well as access to sunlight. In building One, the families share bathrooms. There are six bathrooms on each floor (until recently there were four bathrooms only). These bathrooms have no light or ventilation and lack water extensions. In some of them, a number of families extended light bulbs from their own rooms. At night, many families use tin containers instead of going to the bathroom. It is to be noted that these bathrooms

are unisex, imposing more difficulties on the residents.

Electricity: is meagerly supplied which forces most of the families to illegally hook onto external lines.

Water: is pumped to the four buildings from a nearby well on a daily basis (for 6 hours). The Popular committee manages this operation. Bldg. One has twelve water tanks on the roof, bldg. Two has six, while buildings Three and Four share one big tank. Lacking water extensions, on each floor of the related buildings, there are four faucets attached to their respective tanks by a water hose. Drinking water is generally bought or filled up from adjacent buildings.

Sewage system: all four buildings have inadequate sewage pipes and suffer from leakage.

Residents of building One collect their garbage and dispose it in a nearby dump. Residents of the remaining three buildings contract a private company for their garbage disposal (this is arranged by the Popular Committee). Still, the basements of the four buildings are hampered by seepage and garbage accumulation, spreading the growth of insects and diseases.

The related buildings do not fall under UNRWA's mandate; thus, the agency does not intervene in alleviating the prevalent living conditions there. The nearest access to UNRWA's as well as other NGOs' **health** and **educational** services is Shatila camp in addition to UNRWA's school in Al-Dana area (both are within walking distance), while access to UNRWA's secondary school, in Beir Hassan, requires transport.

The Popular Aid for Relief and Development (PARD) is the only organization providing services in Gaza center. These include reproductive health awareness for women, as well as scholastic tutorials, computer skills, and recreational activities for children, ages 7–18. There is also a small library in the center. PARD's center is in building One. It opens only on Fridays during the scholastic year but everyday during the summer break.

• **Chosen sample**
This research covers a total of 104 families from the four buildings. Of these 72 have children between the ages 9 and 18.

C. Borj El Shemali Camp, Tyre, south Lebanon
Camp population estimated at 17,000 persons. Camp's size is approx. 134,000m.sq
The majority of the camp's working population works in agriculture. It is a day-wage labor, so providing an irregular income. Men make 10,000 LL/day (7US$), amounting to less than 200US$/month, in other words, less than the official minimum wage. Women make half of that. Construction, another possible venue for work, has been hampered by the government's ban on allowing construction material into the camp. This oppressive ban extends even to include simple material such as nails, door & window fixtures, adding to the community's countless frustrations.

The camp is overcrowded with little space for outdoor activity. Since 1949, its population rose from 7,000 prs. to 17,000, but the camp's space was not expanded. Borj El Shemali endures electricity shortages, water pollution, rudimentary sewage systems and garbage accumulation despite UNRWA's presence. Drinking water is usually bought. The camp's main road suffers from sewage overflowing.

There is only one **hospital** and two **clinics** in the camp. Al-Jaleel hospital, run by the Palestine Red Crescent Society (PLO institution), has clinics and an obstetrics section, but lacks a section for general surgery. It has been witnessing grave funding cutbacks since the early nineties, thus affecting its service delivery. The same situation applies to the UNRWA clinic ... Prevalent chronic illnesses in the camp include thalassaemia, anemia, sickle-cell, high blood pressure, heart condition, and diabetes.

There are three UNRWA **schools**, two elementary and one for both the elementary and intermediate levels.

UNRWA also has **two** offices in the camp - one for social affairs and the other for distribution of food rations.

• **Present institutions (listed in detail)**
... There is no cemetery. There is one mosque but without a loud speaker.
• **Chosen site**:
Al-Wasat neighborhood, housing approx. 500 families. Selected sample includes 163 families, of whom 123 have children aged 9 to 18. All have access to the above mentioned services.

SYRIA
The Criteria: We searched for different geographical sites that cover the majority of the camps in and around Damascus. We selected Yarmouk camp in Damascus (Yarmouk street, which is the biggest and most populated Palestinian camp in Syria). Jaramana camp was also selected, which is populated by Palestinian who were forced to leave Palestine in 1984, then later left the Golan heights after the war of 1967, and finally forced to leave to another camp in 1978. We selected some families living in Khan Dannoun camp on the road to Amman and Al Hussainiyeh camp near Damascus.

The second criteria were the economic and social conditions of the families (poor or middle class families).

The third criteria were selecting the families who were directly influenced by wars and violence who suffered from the loss of a father, a mother or a brother as a result of conflicts.
A family living in Damascus will be interviewed in order to examine differences in political awareness and political Palestinian identification between the Palestinians living in Syrian urban cities, their rearing of children and the Palestinian families' socialization of children living in the refugees' camps. Informal visits to the families in these camps took place this month and we hope that we'll start formal interviews by the end of this month.

WEST BANK

As there are two refugee camps in the Hebron district, and the refugees live outside the camps as well (in Hebron city and the surrounding villages), the team decided to distribute and pull the sample as follows:

7 households from Alaroub refugee camp
7 households from Alfwar refugee camp
3 households from the city of Hebron
3 households from the surrounding villages.

GAZA

We started choosing the sites of the data collection by randomization. We will take the sample from three camps: Jabalia, Rafah and El Burjj. ■

6. Social Mapping (preparation...)

SYRIA

A preparatory social mapping for the selected areas of the camps is already completed. This social mapping includes the sub-structure, health, social and educational services and institutions that belong to UNRWA or to the Syrian Government. The dominant social and moral values, families, social relations and characteristics, social system of populations' references, rituals and habits, the socialization of children ... were also included.

We also agreed to adopt a timeline that include the following:
1. 1948: memories.
2. 1950: establishment of UNRWA.
3. 1956: the aggression against Egypt.
4. 1958: the establishment of the Egyptian-Syrian Unified Arab Republic.
5. 1961: the disintegration of the unity.
6. 1961: the beginning of the Palestinian armed struggle.
7. 1967: the war of 67.
8. 1968: March, Al Karami battle in Jordan.

9. 1970: Black September in Jordan.
10. 1973: clashes between the Feda'eyeen and the Lebanese army.
11. 1973: the October war.
12. 1975: the Lebanese civil war.
13. 1982: Israeli invasion of Lebanon.
14. 1982: PLO departure to Tunisia.
15. 1983–1984: attacks against camps.
16. 1987: Al Intifada
17. 1993: Oslo Agreement.

It won't be a fixed timeline, the researcher can always add and omit whatever he thinks is relevant or irrelevant. ■

EXCERPTS FROM SUMMARY REPORTS – SELECTING THE FIELD SITES & SOCIAL MAPPING (PREPARATION...)

SUMMARY REPORT FRAMEWORK *PLUS*

TASK	DESCRIPTION	
8. Literature search (d) Search results – what is available	• It would be enriching to know of the results of the local literature searches: what type of studies have been done in the area before, with this target group, etc.	
(e) Analysis of the search	• A brief analysis of this literature as it is relevant to the project.	
(f) Photocopies	• Everybody is encouraged to make photocopies of studies / publications that they consider relevant or important, and to either mail them to Oxford, or leave them for Dawn or Gillian to carry back with them from their field visits.	
9. Contacts & meetings in the community	• Briefings on meetings with concerned local IGO's and NGO's. • A suggested emphasis on meeting with UNRWA and Save the Children Fund (if they operate in the area) as the more important foci to the research project, in addition to other organisations working in relevant domains. ⊃ *Descriptions of the meetings with / in the community (members of the community, active individuals and organisations, meetings with IGO's working in the area such as UNICEF, UNRWA, etc.)*	
10. Research staff (assistants and interviewers)	• A brief description on how and why the research assistants and interviewers were selected.	
11. The training of the research staff.	• A summary of the type of training offered to the research staff as preparation for the fieldwork.	
12. Selecting the field sites	• A brief description of the selected field sites. • Reasons for selecting these field sites. ⊃ *Socio-demographic data of the population under study* ⊃ *Description of the socio-economic variety of the population under study (as well as ensuring some form of socio-economic variety)* ⊃ *Illustration of the gender balance in the study population (as well as ensuring some form of gender balance!)* ⊃ *Comparative information about the population in terms of those living in camps and outside of camps.*	Report 1 & 2 **January 2000**
13. Implementation of PRA/ social mapping/ timelines/ other social research tools	• A summary of the process of implementing these social research tools in the fieldwork. • A summary of the results of this fieldwork. ⊃ *Description of the social mapping and PRA (results, analysis, inherent meanings...)* ⊃ *Comparative information about the population in terms of those living in camps and outside of camps.*	Initial phase of research/ report 3 **March 2000**
14. Interviewing and narrative phase of the project	• A summary of the process of implementing these social research tools in the fieldwork. • A summary of the results of this fieldwork. • A narrative report of the research from the teams. ⊃ *Details of the narratives being collected (parents, grandparents, caregivers and other adults or relatives).* ⊃ *Comparative information about the population in terms of those living in camps and outside of camps.*	Next phase of research/ report 4 **May 2000**

DRAFT BIBLIOGRAPHY-IN-THE-MAKING...

Author	Name of Resource	Publisher / Date	Language
Abu Hein, F. et al	Trauma and mental health of children in Gaza	*British Medical Journal*, 306: 1130–1131 / 1993	English
Arafat. C et al.	The political economy of Palestinian children: an examination of the linkages between economic policy and child welfare	Submitted at the Secretariat for the National Plan of Action for Palestinian Children / 1999	English
Barber, B.	Political violence, social integration and youth functioning: Palestinian youth from the intifada	Forthcoming in the *Journal of Community Psychology*	English
Barber, B.	Political violence, family relations, and Palestinian youth functioning	*Journal of Adolescent Research*, 14:2 pp 206–230 / 1999	English
Barber, B.	What has become of the "Children of the Stone"?	In press, *Palestine-Israel Journal* 2000	English
Barber, B.	Palestinian children and adolescents during and after the Intifada	*Palestine-Israel Journal*, 4:1, pp23–33 / 1997	English
Barber, B.	Youth experience in the Palestinian Intifada: a case study in intensity, complexity, paradox and competence	In *"Roots of Civic Identity"*, Cambridge Univ. Press / 1999	English
Barber, B.	Politics, politics and more politics: Youth life experience in the Gaza strip	Forthcoming in Bowen & Early, (Eds.) *"Everyday Life in the Muslim Middle East"*	English
Bryce, J. et al.	Life experiences, response styles and mental health among mothers and children in Beirut, Lebanon	*Social Science & Medicine*, 28: 7, pp 685–695 / 1989	English
Canadian Dept of Foreign Affairs	Activities of the Canadian mission to Palestinian refugee camps and gatherings in the Syrian Arab Republic	www.dfait-maeci.gc.ca / 1998	English
Eisenbruch, M.	From post-traumatic stress disorder to cultural bereavement: diagnosis of Southeast Asian refugees	*Social Science & Medicine*, 33: 6, pp 673–680 / 1991	English
Farhood, L. et al.	The impact of war on the physical and mental health of the family: the Lebanese experience	*Social Science & Medicine*, 36: 12, pp 1555–1567 / 1993	English
Gibreel, S.	Palestine in the teaching curriculum at the intermediate and secondary level in the Syrian Arab Republic	–	Arabic
Hourani, L et al.	A population-based survey of loss and psychological distress during war	*Social Science & Medicine*,23: 3, pp 269–275 / 1986	English
Madi, Y.	The socio-demographic parameters of Palestinian refugees in Lebanon: Comparative study of the camps in Lebanon	PCBS & UNICEF / 1996	Arabic
PCBS & UNICEF	Analytical study on children labour force in Palestinian camps in Syria	UNICEF Damascus / 1998	English
PCBS & UNICEF	Analytical study on education of Palestinian refugees in camps in Syria 1997/1998	UNICEF Damascus / 1998	English
PCBS & UNICEF	A survey assessment to identify risk factors and priority needs for Palestinian youth in Lebanon with focus on adolescent girls	PCBS & UNICEF / 1999	English
Tamari, S.	The future of the Palestinian refugees: activities of the refugees working group in the multilateral negotiations and the quadri-partite committee	Institute for Palestinian Studies/ 1996	Arabic
Zureik, E.	Palestinian refugees and the peace process	Institute for Palestinian Studies/ 1997	Arabic

These were obtained either during the literature search here in the U.K. or during our field visits abroad. This list shall be updated as more literature is uncovered. Please send us copies of any literature you find that is relevant to the project.

NOTICES & REMINDERS

Financial reporting:
- A detailed and cumulative mid-project financial statement is requested in May.
- please be sure that you are, whenever possible, obtaining and maintaining receipts for the transactions reported in your financial reports. Otherwise, please be sure to keep a record of these transactions. This will greatly facilitate reporting back to the funders at a later stage.

REMEMBER: The third set of reports is due at the end of March 2000!

Field Visits

Jordan:
Late March/Early April 2000 – Dawn Chatty

West Bank & Gaza:
Last week of March–first week of April 2000 – Gillian Hundt

NO COMMENT

An excerpt from Brian Barber's "Politics, Politics and More Politics: Youth Life Experience in the Gaza Strip", forthcoming in Bowen & Early (Eds.), Everyday Life in the Muslim Middle East.

Perhaps the central defining characteristic of being Palestinian is the inescapable role of the political in personal and collective identity. This is so regardless of where a Palestinian might currently live because of enduring controversies about the basic elements of what makes up a person: home, heritage, nationality, culture. What is a Palestinian?

Palestinian children and youth in the West Bank and particularly in the Gaza Strip live a life that contrasts starkly from this apolitical Western experience. For them, it seems that every facet of their lives is informed and shaped by political history and current political dynamics and realities of which they are very aware. This pervasive influence of the political in the lives of young people is at the least fascinating, given the dramatic contrast with experience of children in many other parts of the world, but it is also potentially quite informative when it comes to attempting to understand the capacities of children and the course of their development.

My very first exposure to Palestinian youth taught me the power of politics in their lives. In 1994, when preparing with colleagues to begin a research project on Palestinian family life, I interviewed four Palestinian teenage males from East (Arab) Jerusalem. My questions during the interview were broad and general, designed to reveal insight into the thinking processes of Palestinian adolescents. I was alerted to the role of politics in their life early in the interview when I asked them to think about a Palestinian man they admired, to talk about him, and to tell why they admired him. All of them identified a political figure; two mentioned Yasser Arafat and the other two mentioned members of the Palestinian negotiating team from the 1991 Madrid conference. They did not refer to sports figures or TV or movie actors as their Western counterparts tend to do. However, another question revealed much more profoundly and poignantly how politics can penetrate the everyday experience of youth.

This later question asked each youth to give an example of a time when he is most happy. All of them immediately responded politically, as in "I am happy when the peace negotiations are going well", or "I will be happy when we achieve a Palestinian state". I had to probe several times before they grasped that I was after a personal answer ... Finally, Tareq understood what I was after and replied, "I am happy when I run. I love to run." But with the same breath he added, "But whenever I run the soldiers (Israelis) want to arrest me." Thus, even the momentary diversion to considering a personal issue was regulated immediately by a political reality.

AKHBARUNA

Children & Adolescents in Palestinian Households: Living with the Effects of Prolonged Conflict & Forced Migration

ISSUE #4 – JUNE 2000   An Internal Team Newsletter for the Mellon Project.

CONTENTS:

Compiled by Maha Damaj, Research Assistant, Mellon Project, Refugee Studies Programme

Introduction

This little introduction is usually written after the newsletter is fully completed. Whereas I would normally exploit this space to mention pending issues that came up while I was compiling the newsletter, this time, I find myself overwhelmed with the amount of information that I (finally) received. This is not surprisingly reflected in the continually growing length of the newsletter.

Indeed, the larger part of this issue is formed completely of direct quotes from your reports. The hardest decision I had to face was in determining which parts of the reports to include here, as most of them were brimming over with information that is too detailed for the scope of this newsletter – but are ideal for the research project.

And now, I shall return to exploiting this space to list a few important highlights and reminders:

- The table on page 2 (**overview of reports**) is meant to help us keep track of the information that we have received. If there are items that you feel you have covered – as in, there are no additions to be made to them – then please let me know such that I may make note of it.
- As we approach our own **preset deadlines** (last set of reports by May, complete fieldwork by July), we urge you to keep us informed of your progress and of your projected completion dates.
- Through your correspondence, and during Dawn and Gillian's field visits, it was felt that additional care should be taken in collecting and transcribing interviews and testimonies. This is the data that becomes our **primary data** for this project and for other future projects, therefore its accuracy and reliability is essential. Consequently, a **'Fieldwork Tip'** corner has been included. If there are other issues that you would like covered in this corner, please let me know and I shall research the relevant literature.

OVERVIEW OF THE REPORTS ...

- Preparation for our meetings in September and October are coming up. Please be sure to inform us of the names of the September participants soon. And please remember that the local NGO participants for the regional workshop need to be able to **contribute to the workshop**, as well as **take an active role in the local dissemination** that will follow.

And as we approach completing the field-work, and embarking upon analysing the data, excitement levels run high and hope-fully, the rewards will also be plentiful. With that in mind, have a great summer. ■

OVERVIEW OF THE REPORTS ...

Information received as of the date of issue of this newsletter is tabulated below*

	Jordan	Gaza	Lebanon	Syria	West Bank
Literature Search – results					
– analysis					
– photocopies					
Contacts & Meetings in the Community					
Research Staff Recruitment					
Training Research Staff					
– training workshop report					
Selecting the Field Sites					
– sociodemographics of population under study					
– description of infrastructure					
Social Mapping					
PRA etc.					
Interviews & narratives					

	Jordan	Gaza	Lebanon	Syria	West Bank
Financial Report, Nov 99					
Financial Report, Jan 00					
Financial Report, Mar 00					

* PLEASE NOTE: The checklist format of the above table does not reflect the type of information and amount of detail in which these parameters were described.

Implies that
a) there has been an indication of the work taking place, but information about the outcome of the activity has not yet been received, or,
b) work in progress – part of the documentation has been received.

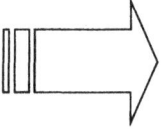

If you feel that the above does not reflect the work that your team has undertaken to date, then please let me know. This discrepancy may be due to our different readings of the reports, implying that we need to clarify where our reporting expectations lie.

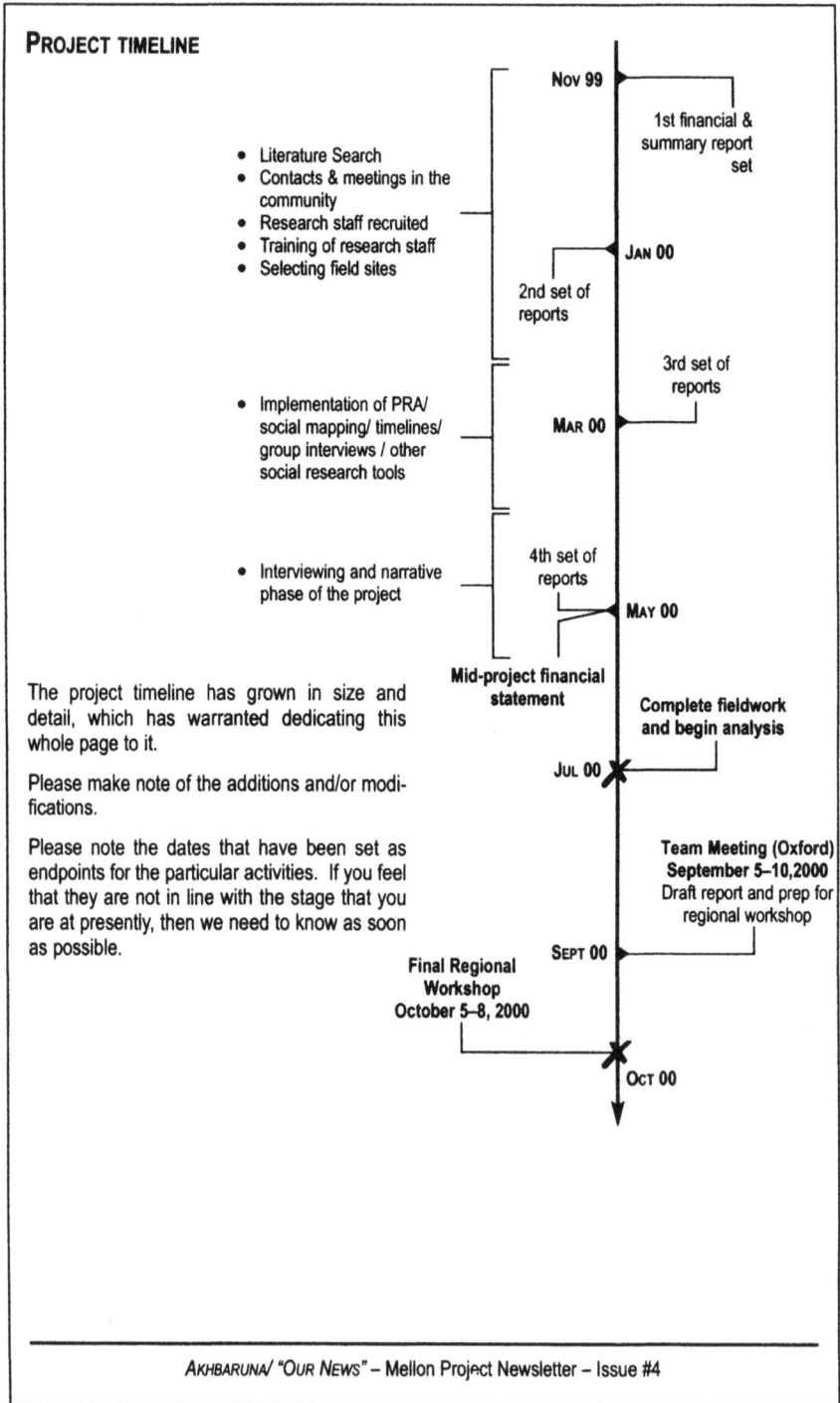

PROJECT TIMELINE

Nov 99

1st financial &
summary report
set

- Literature Search
- Contacts & meetings in the community
- Research staff recruited
- Training of research staff
- Selecting field sites

JAN 00

2nd set of reports

3rd set of reports

- Implementation of PRA/ social mapping/ timelines/ group interviews / other social research tools

MAR 00

4th set of reports

- Interviewing and narrative phase of the project

MAY 00

Mid-project financial statement

The project timeline has grown in size and detail, which has warranted dedicating this whole page to it.

Please make note of the additions and/or modifications.

Please note the dates that have been set as endpoints for the particular activities. If you feel that they are not in line with the stage that you are at presently, then we need to know as soon as possible.

Complete fieldwork and begin analysis

JUL 00

Team Meeting (Oxford)
September 5–10, 2000
Draft report and prep for regional workshop

Final Regional Workshop
October 5–8, 2000

SEPT 00

OCT 00

◆ **LITERATURE SEARCH**

SYRIA

We have been busy in the last two months in collecting materials on the targeted group (8–18) age group including their percentage to Palestinian population in Syria, their access to health services, educational institutions, recreation institutions and activities, youth organization, after-class educational and recreational activities, peer groups, and children's journals and books.

In addition to that, we examined pre-school educational programmes and the process of politicizing children in the kindergartens and UNRWA and preparatory schools.

Besides literature and abstracts, we organized several formal and informal discussions with UNRWA schoolteachers to evaluate their role in socialising and politicizing their children in the classroom and outside it. Reports of these discussions are already edited and they will be used in organizing our final report and in leading us to formulate the agenda for our fieldwork.

Discussions and formal meetings with Palestinian Youth Organization leaders also revealed an important source of the system of references of politicizing Palestinian children. These discussions and meetings covered the leadership of the existing Palestinian youth organization in Syria ... (the draft of the chapter concerning our findings and conclusion will be sent to you soon, and it will also include the conclusion of dealing with the Palestinian question in addition to the conclusions of the above-mentioned vivid sources).

The fieldwork will help us to understand the role of the family in the process of socialization and politicization of the Palestinian children and adolescents in the age group 8-18, including coping strategies and their attitudes towards the other Syrian peers, self-identification and their Palestinianism.

The above-mentioned readings and discussions allow us to conclude the following:

1. Schooling and school textbooks in UNRWA and Syrian schools provided the Palestinian children and adolescent with the basic information about Palestinian households, Palestinian people and the Palestinian tragedy in 1948, it also offered a proper political guidance concerning his role in fighting for his homeland (it is similar to the solutions and guidelines presented by different Palestinian political movements).

2. The teachers especially in UNRWA schools were not able to participate actively and to a satisfactory level in the process of politicizing the Palestinian children and in after-school activities. They complained of the number of working hours and their hard obligations during working hours in schools but that didn't stop them from organizing exhibition trips and celebrating national festivals.

3. Youth organization leaders complained of the low percentage of children and adolescents in their ranks and admitted that the majority of the Palestinian children and adolescents were not among the members of cadres in the summer clubs, trained to deal with children and on the psychological and political levels.

4. The relative absence of children's club and adolescents' cultural centers forced the majority of young people to spend most of their free time in the narrow streets of the camps.

5. These preliminary findings and conclusions will help us as an introduction to our fieldwork and to understand the children and adolescents' family socializing process.

EXCERPTS FROM SUMMARY REPORTS – LITERATURE SEARCH

JORDAN

There is an increasing number of studies on children and adolescents in Jordan, primarily by IGO's such as UNICEF, studies by the National Task Force for Children and a few by independent researchers. Generally, the literature produced by the IGO's and NGO's is donor directed and motivated by available funding and the recent international focus on adolescents and youth. A large number of these studies are hurriedly put together, many utilising the language of participatory methods and instruments of research, that limit the scope of the study, rendering these extremely specific, but not analytical enough to make them useful for other research or even to implement other programs. Some funding hinges on proposals that include a general study of the area. One such proposal for children in Hay al-Mahasreh is titled 'Participatory Rapid Appraisal, PRA To Assess Problems and Needs of Mothers and Children'. A look at the project shows that it has all the 'right' items, ranging from graphs and statistics to pictures drawn by children, and a few other studies on different areas include case histories. Another is a project titled 'Safe Childhood Project,' and it defines children as between 1 and 15 years of age, a category further divided between 1 and 12, referred to as 'early and middle childhood,' while 12–15 year-olds are a category that fall under 'late childhood!'

A fifty-page study, for example, on an urban area utilised PRA and was completed 'within days', in this case eleven days. It involved many of the instruments that we are using, such as mapping, drawings, household surveys and even a short historical synopsis of the area. Notwithstanding the uses of such 'rapid' studies, in that they provide the reader with a general picture – literally and metaphorically – of the area being studied, yet these kinds of studies are lacking in depth, mainly in analysis and historical perspective. They are closer to 'reports' to show, for example, that there is poverty, gender inequality, early marriage

and so on to solicit funding for projects. In other words, no 'lessons learned' can be deduced from these studies, neither do they tell us much about coping mechanisms, or social and cultural relations and the wider social and political context, besides the classical themes.

Similarly, there is no specific study on Marka camp, although there are a few studies on camps in general, or other specific camps, such as al-Hussein, al-Wehdat and al-Baq'a. Yet, UNRWA publications and interviews provided a lot of information on the camp, mainly, population, their origin, the various organizations and programs working in the camp, general distribution of employment across the various economic sector and so on, which offers a good basis for this study. In addition to the work of the research team, the UNRWA school staff got involved in the study and also provided assistance on this aspect.

A worthwhile study on children in Jordan titled: 'National Study on Child Labour,' by Janet Abboud for the National Task Force on Children, provides a general background on the economic imperatives that compel children to go to work. It includes employment-related variables, such as kind of work, hours at work, sectors of employment and evaluates the prevalence of child-labour. The selected study sites included urban poverty pockets, refugee camps and industrial sites in Amman and the neighbouring cities of Zarqa and Jerash. Nonetheless, Abboud points out that her study did not include "children engaged in agriculture, in family enterprises or in domestic labour, occupations in which female children are engaged. " (Abboud, 1997: 85) Some of the articles or studies include adolescents under the category of youth. Others are focused on children and these mainly examine child-care methods and approaches and many are the result of workshops in Early Childhood Education.

A quick glance at the existing literature will show that most of the studies are based on classical psychological, behavioral, economic or sociological approaches.

There is a tendency in these studies to render both children and adolescents as in constant need of molding and remolding so that they become 'mature' and 'responsible adults' who follow social norms, defined again by adults. Most of these studies perceive children as going through a universal scale of development and hence focus on the natural 'biological needs' and the role of parents in socialising them 'into' society.

As for the adolescents, the word in Arabic 'murahiqeen' (male) and 'murahiqat' (female) has a sexual connotation and one that connotes irresponsible behavior. In fact, the word is often used to refer to 'wild' or 'irresponsible' adult behavior. Consequently, it is probably better to use the word 'fitya' (both male and female), or, 'fityan' (male) and 'fatayat' (female). Again, the youth is conceived as a 'dangerous' and 'uncontrolled' segment of society. A short study I conducted in the West Bank and Gaza shows that youth are increasingly losing their role as 'heroes' to 'hooligans.' As is the case in many Arab societies, the perceptions of youth reflect a functionalist view of society, which considers a particular social order and values as the 'norm.' Those who threaten the social 'order' are viewed as 'outside' the mainstream of society – youth being such an 'anomaly' in need of socialization into the 'social order.' The Intifada was a unique period, when the struggle against occupation was accompanied with new social spaces for the youth and women to emerge and play new roles, challenging social norms, however, with the end of the Intifada, the spaces closed and women as well as youth complain of social norms and structures which are oppressive.

Studies on adolescents may be found in the fields of psychology and sociology. There is hardly any study in Jordan on adolescents, adopting an anthropological approach, or, for that matter, a qualitative research involving participant observation and is long-term.

Finally, the studies extract a segment of society, in this case 'adolescents', out of the family and community context and study this group in isolation of wider relationships. Thus, there are many studies in the Arab world, on 'youth' (a term which often includes adolescents) in the context of the university, school, and/or the new Islamic movements. Many refer to 'youth and 'fundamentalism/extremism,' implying they are a passive group easily influenced by extremism, drugs, or more relevant to recent discussions on youth and adolescents, the 'satellite dish' and 'western corruption'. In these types of studies, the quick survey/questionnaire instruments are used, handed out to the target population and analysis is based on the results of these questionnaires.

WEST BANK

The following are excerpts from the literature review compiled by the West Bank team. A full report may be provided upon request.

Definition of a Refugee

There have been several definitions for a refugee and from several perspectives. In addition to this, regional organizations defined a refugee by different definitions.

The definition of a refugee applies to any person who was obliged to leave his homeland and search for a shelter in another place outside the original homeland as a result of outside hostility, occupation, foreign invasion or dangerous situations that threaten general safety in a part or all his homeland.

The definition of the European charter for the refugees are those who "are unable to or unwilling to - for several reasons - to come back to origin homeland".

As for the definition of the Palestinian Refugee in specific; the UNRWA definition of refugee states ("those persons whose nor-

LITERATURE SEARCH

mal residence was Palestine during the period of 1 June 1946 to 15 May 1948 and who lost both their homes and means of livelihood as a result of the conflict"). But this definition was contested by Bristol Report for two reasons. The definition excludes those refugees who did not register with UNRWA as refugees, those who lost their registration as a result of their changed status and thousands of rural refugees in Gaza and West Bank who lost their land and sources of livelihood but who did not lost their residence. This last category also includes people who lost access to coastal markets and work sites in pre-1948 Palestine.

It was also stressed that the definition of UNRWA did not include those emigrants who are out of the responsibility of UNRWA and its definition. They include:
1. Palestinian refugees as a result of 1948 war who were located in places outside the responsibility of UNRWA like in Egypt, North Africa, Iraq and the Gulf.
2. Internal forced-to-leave Palestinians who stayed in the area that is called now Israel. These were under UNRWA responsibility but were excluded on the assumption that Israel will treat their status.
3. People from West Bank and Gaza (including East Jerusalem) and descendants who were forced to leave for the first time in 1967.

4. People who were transferred by Israeli occupation from West Bank and Gaza Strip after 1967.
5. Those who were called 'late comers', those who left occupied territories for study, relative visits, work, marriage, ... etc, and then whose residence permits expired and then were prevented from coming back to Palestine.
6. Rich Palestinians who took refuge in 1948 but their pride prevented them from registering themselves with UNRWA.

From a perspective of refugees themselves there has been a study of oral history by a group of researchers who interviewed (209) refugees. One of the questions was the meaning of the word refugee in their perspective. One refugee (interview with Mr Abdul Aziz Sajdia, 28 years old, from Dheisheh camp and originally from Sar'ah) defined "a refugee is someone who is lost, he does not know where he is. He is unsettled and unable to stay in one location." In that study, most refugees interviewed (94.1%) defined their refugee status in terms of loss of "homeland", and/or loss of "land". 58.6% highlighted the loss of their "homeland" while 35.5% defined refugees as people who lost their land. Only 3.9% responded that refugees are poor people who live in refugee camps, 1.3% defined refugee as someone who lost his house or job. One interviewee gave no clear answer.

Table 1. Distribution of Refugees in the five areas.

Area	Registered refugees	In Camps	# of camps	Outside camps	% outside camps	% of total population
Jordan	1,288,197	252,089	10	1,036,108	80.43%	31.5%
Gaza Strip	63,560	379,778	8	302,782	4.44%	76.8%
West Bank*	517,412	132,508	19	384,904	74.3%	37.1%
Lebanon	346,164	185,581	12	160,583	46.3%	10.2%
Syria	337,308	94,866	10	242,442	71.88%	2.4%
Total	3,172,641	1,044,822	59	2,127,819	67.07%	–

Source: *Palestinian Refugees and UNRWA, 1996. * West Bank: does not include those parts of Jerusalem which were annexed by Israel in 1967.*

In addition to the definition of refugee from a political perspective, the definition expanded to include the economical refugees whose reason to leave was the economical system, natural or environmental disasters, and psychological persecution.

Richmond (1994) pp. 67–70 defined not less than twenty-five groups of refugees whose reason for emigration to outside or inside was as one "factor or more from the following five factors: political, economical, environmental, social and psychological".

Historical Overview
- The Impact of 1948 War

Statistical Overview
The mass of the approximately 750,000 Palestinians expelled and dispossessed in 1948 and their descendants came under the Jurisdiction of UNRWA. These refugees were distributed on five areas, which are Palestine including West Bank and Gaza Strip, Syria, Lebanon and Jordan. Table 1 shows more details about the situation on these five areas as was published by UNRWA.

The Status of Refugee Camps
- Education, health, and social status

UNRWA Program
1. Educational Program
2. Health Program
3. Program of Social Welfare

Coping mechanisms/strategies
There have been few studies about the coping strategies of refugees.

To see the effect of conflict on children, a study carried out by Quta and Sarraj in 1993, on 547 children between ages 6 and 12 years on the effect of curfew on children, the study revealed that children suffered from various behavioural and neurotic symptoms during curfews. 66.2% began to fight with other, 54% were afraid of new things, 53% became angry.

Curfews in upper middle class areas of town and suburbs tend to be less stressful than in densely populated poor and heavily patrolled refugee camps. Curfews create frustration, which means unpleasant emotional state resulting from a blocked goal, rather than the event itself.

The sector of children has been neglected. The overall development of these hundreds of thousands of children and youth has been dramatically affected by the violent environment prevailing since beginning of the *Intifada*. This group has been hard-hit by the military response to the uprising. Recent indicators show increasingly negative discharge of energy, i.e. higher stress levels, aggressive behaviour, widening drug use, and robberies.

A research conducted in the Occupied Territories pinpoints the following problems amongst young children and youths, high anxiety, frustration, aggression, lack of motivation, poor attention skills, depression, poor academic achievement, high school drop out of rates, increased child labour and psychosomatic disorders.

Children are well aware of the differences between living conditions in their dirty camps and the newly built Israeli settlements. These differences tell them that Jewish children living in the settlements deserve big, clean play grounds and swimming pools, while their refugee camps have open sewage system and garbage piled high at every street corner.

The results of study on the relations between the level of traumatic experiences, degree of active participation in the *Intifada* and cognitive and emotional responses were studied among 108 Palestinian children of 11–12 years in Gaza Strip. The results showed that the more traumatic experience the children had or the more they participated in the *Intifada*, the more the

EXCERPTS FROM SUMMARY REPORTS – LITERATURE SEARCH

EXCERPTS FROM SUMMARY REPORTS – LITERATURE SEARCH & CONTACTS AND MEETINGS IN THE COMMUNITY

concentration, attention, and memory problems they had.

It is worthwhile to mention that there is very limited literature on the effect of conflict on children in the West Bank; most of the studies on this topic and the effects of the *Intifada* on children were carried out in Gaza Strip by the Gaza Community Mental Health Program. It could be true that children both in the West Bank and Gaza Strip were under the same conditions and stress, but there were no studies that focused on the effect of this stress on children, specifically the refugee children, in the West Bank. So, this justifies the need to carry out a study in the West Bank to study the effect of being a refugee and the effect of conflict on children.

GAZA
The following are excerpts from the report received. A full report may be provided upon request.

• Education
The school system in the Gaza Strip is based on three cycles:
  – Kindergartens for children 4 years old
  – Ten years of basic school
  – Two years of secondary school
At the end of 12 years of schooling, students take the General Secondary Education Certificate Examination (Tawjihi Exam). Admission into institutions of advanced education is determined largely by Tawjihi Exam

results. Education in the Gaza Strip is provided by three principal sectors: government schools, private schools, and UNRWA schools.
- Kindergartens
- Kindergarten Teachers
- Basic Education
The total number of schools for 1996/1997 school year about 1532, of which 98 per cent held classes at the basic stage. The number of schools in the West Bank was 1193, while 339 were in Gaza Strip. The schools are distributed by supervision authority as follows: 1113 (72.7 per cent) are government, while 261 (17.0 per cent) are UNRWA, and 10.3 per cent are private.
  – Students at the Basic Stage
  – Repetition and Dropout
  – Classes
  – Three education authorities
  – Education laws
  – Literacy rate
  – Approach to Classroom Teaching
  – Corporal punishment

• Labour
• Child Health
  – Accidents and injuries among children
  – Illness among children
  – Health indicators in the Gaza Strip 1993–1998
• Child Mental Health
• Social program
  – UNRWA social services program
  – Governmental social services program ■

◆ **CONTACTS AND MEETINGS IN THE COMMUNITY** ⸺⸺⸺⸺⸺⸺⸺⸺ ▼

JORDAN
The main contacts that have been made in the community are the children and adolescents themselves, UNRWA employees and personnel and community based organizations.

In Hayy al-Mahasrah and al-Amir Hassan camp (unofficial camp):
a- Several visits to the areas, basically to

informally meet some of the people who live there and to get a general sense of the locality in regards of place, the streets, the market, its proximity to the city, the buildings and the infrastructure in general. Following visits were meant to observe children's mobility in the area, where they meet, the times they are in the streets and neighbourhoods and what they do.

b- Meetings with the children and four of the day-care teachers in Hay-al-Mahasreh. (There is only one day-care). Meetings also included observing children being taught. Discussion with the teachers as to their observations, their level of training and their needs.

c- A meeting with ten boys between the ages of 10 and 13, which was held in a local center and away from the homes, to allow them the freedom to express themselves. This was a taped session and the boys expressed their views as to the different aspect of their lives, including the problems they face and how they perceive their neighbourhood.

d- A meeting with a girls' focus group in the house of one of the girls, because many of the girls are not allowed in public places. The age group was the same as that for the boys and the session was also taped.

e- Field visits to al-Amir Hassan camp and recently. A focus group with girls (17 years old) was held there, which utilized Yousef's (the assistant) ideas that he developed, which will be sent for the next report or Newsletter.

f- A meeting with some of the staff working with the Jordan River Society who are working in al-Amir Hassan area.

g- A meeting with a local organization (Abi dhu al-Ghafari) which is very active in the camp and another with the Popular Committee.

h- A meeting with the Jordanian Women's Union/al-Amir Hassan Branch.

i- Several meetings with UNRWA teachers and workers.

j- A timeline was developed; however, it was done through the eyes of the older adults only and by the assistants. Therefore, another one is planned for the near future.

The meetings were focused on updating them on the study, soliciting their active participation, sharing information and discussing issues pertaining to the study.

In Marka (Hitteen) Camp:

a- Several visits to UNRWA schools, both boys and girls, mainly to conduct research based on Colin's approach, but only as a first step to the study. This part of the study in Hitteen camp is almost completed, in both the girl's and boy's schools and results of this study will be sent in the near future. However, these are only initial and partial results. Some of the tapes of the focus groups need to be transcribed and further visits to the homes of the students will take place this month. Colin's method was very useful in getting at the main issues, which children and adolescents find important and regard as sources of anxiety. It also provides a general trend as to their prevalence among students of the age range: 12/13 and 15–18.

b- Several meetings with UNRWA employees, teachers and members of the local Women's Programme Centers took place. Here, it is important to observe that UNRWA staff has been extremely helpful and interested in the project. ■

◆ **TRAINING THE RESEARCH STAFF**

SYRIA

During the months of February and March we arranged five meetings for the research team in addition to a workshop in Beirut. During these meetings we reviewed our activities as a team and exchanged our point of views concerning the progress of our work. At the same time we used to examine our techniques and the obstacles we face in our fieldwork, we also restudied the processes of social mapping and the terminology. We tried to unify our expressions and approaches used in formal interviews and to determine the content and the frontiers of our fieldwork. There was a common feeling that we still need more practice and experience to achieve successful interviews with children. We noticed that the researchers' agenda lacks information on UNRWA and UNICEF services to the Palestinian children and adolescents and to what extent does these services help in their survival and education and what are their future expectations.

We are also trying to improve the researchers' skills of reporting since they don't have rich experiences in this field and they have to work hard in order to learn how to get the basic information needed for the research, but we noticed a slow progress in this field.

Workshop on "Oral History", March 11, 2000 / Arab Resource Centre for Popular Arts, Beirut.
The following are excerpts from the report received. A full report may be provided upon request.

WORKSHOP'S OBJECTIVES:

1. To train the Syrian research team and to exchange experiences with the Lebanese research team of the Arab Center in Beirut.
2. To provide the researchers with information on the techniques of oral history.

3. To discuss with the Lebanese team the obstacles they faced during their activities in the Lebanese camps and how did they managed to overcome these obstacles.

Dr. Munzir Jaber ... began his lecture by explaining the importance of their research (oral testimonies) since most of those people who witnessed the catastrophe of 1948 are dying because of old age and something must be done in order to register the memories of those people. Dr. Munzir thinks that their testimonies are more honest and reflects the realities they faced during 1948. ... This will enable young generations born in exile to understand what happened in 1948 and help them to defend their Palestinian identity.

Ordinary people are the source of oral history and collective memory doesn't only reflect material realities and details but also people's suffering, emotions, attitudes and aspirations.

The problems of oral history researches:
(See report from Lebanon below – the Syria and Lebanon teams attended separate workshops organised by the same centre.)

Khaled Maw'ed mentioned that many of the people who were interviewed by him were very eager and enthusiastic to tell their own story of their forced migration in 1949 and they mentioned that nobody before Khaled asked them to do so. Sometimes the interviews were interrupted by emotional stresses as a result of recalling tragic memories.

The other researchers spoke about the problems of recording interviews. It was evident that many of the problems they faced are similar to the problems of the Syrian team during their informal and formal interviews with the Palestinians in Syria.

JORDAN

- Both Yousef and Muna, the research assistants, received training in PLA, mainly based on the outline provided by Dawn and from presentation notes and general readings.
- Training in Colin's method, which was later utilized in Marka camp.
- How to interview children in focus groups.
- How to record and collect life-histories and their significance.

LEBANON

The following are excerpts from the report received. A full report may be provided upon request.

A one-day workshop on oral history was held on the 25th of February with the collaboration of the Arab Resource Centre for Popular Arts (ARCPA). ARCPA invited some of the team members who worked on its oral history project to share their experiences with the Lebanon team. After round-the-table introductions of the workshop participants, the team researchers introduced the project's objectives and research tools to the ARCPA team.

Dr. Monther Jaber then began explaining the importance of oral history to the preservation of Palestinian heritage and history, especially as most of the population is in the Diaspora. He proceeded to elaborate on pointers and difficulties entailed in the collection of oral testimonies:

- the course of the interview can be "politicized," for instance the interviewers and interviewees have their own ideological/political background affecting the way questions are asked and the way they are answered
- it is preferable to have the interviewer from the same region and/or camp of the interviewee
- the authority's control, whether the government (external) or political factions (internal) may affect the interviewee's feedback (he/she may be suspicious)

- it is often hard to focus on one epoch of their life, that is their history, especially as their present is hard to endure and their future is unknown; the interviewee is bound to share these different epochs with the interviewees as they are a compilation of his/her concerns and continuity; at times present-future concerns may affect the ability to remember the past or to concentrate on it
- interviewers must appear as neutral and not give away his/her own views, otherwise interviewees might "give" them what they want to hear
- to back an interview get information on the composition of the community (social map)
- the room is almost never empty during the interview (interruptions)
- when interviewing the youth, it is essential to gather information on them from their parents and teachers as well – at times the security committee can be another source of information (deviance behavior)
- role of the woman is highly important as she keeps history alive more than men do – women remember more details, relate events, are more daring in revealing facts (care less for social consequences than men), they are more emotional and transparent (interviewer can detect inaccurate answers more easily)
- the interviewer's knowledge of the subject enriches the interview (more questions, more accuracy)
- there is a need for familiarity – visit the interviewee a couple of times before the interviewing process begins
- a tape recorder can hinder the interview's intimacy, but it is useful – each situation is to be assessed differently – can switch it on/off according to the interviewee's wishes, can tell the interviewee the recorder allows you to listen carefully, etc.

Follow-up training (on group interviews)
Another training session on group interviews was held on March 4th for the Beirut research staff, at Shatila Children and Youth Center (Shatila camp). A group of five girls, ages 14-18, was interviewed.

◆ ABOUT THE FIELD SITES

JORDAN

Hay al-Mahasreh:

- There are no official statistics on population figures, however the local inhabitants provide estimates ranging between 8000 and 10,000 people. Around 96–98% of the inhabitants are originally from Bayt Mahsir, a village which was depopulated and destroyed during and consequent to the 1948 war. The other two to four percent are from other villages in Palestine. There is one Jordanian family only in the whole area and around ten families who are Egyptian, Iraqis and Syrians.

- The social relations are primarily between and among the families who live in the area, or, relatives who were originally from Bayt Mahsir and/or Hay al-Mahasreh and moved out. The social relations are strong and the family is the basic unit providing support to its members. The older generation had a larger family size, while the younger families are beginning to limit the number of children. Nevertheless, the family is an extended one and there are many nuclear families that live in the same household, or in extensions to the original house. Usually, the sons who marry build an extra room and stay close to the parents. Daughters move in with or close to their in-laws. Most of the population is 'young.'

- There is a high literacy rate for both men and women.

- Most of the inhabitants work in the private sector, with few working in the public sector, mainly as teachers, many of them women. The others work in the local industries and institutions, clerks, taxi-drivers, small entrepreneurs and so on. The official unemployment rate is approximately 17% but local inhabitants say it is much higher.

- The infrastructure is inefficient. First the roads/alleyways are relatively narrow, although some wider than others. The sewer networks and water pipes are also old and not properly extended.

- There are several health centers near the neighbourhood, one governmental, the other a private clinic and the third is provided by the Alms Committee and which is subsidized.

- Almost 90% of the students go to UNRWA schools that are close to the neighbourhood. When they complete grade ten, students move to governmental schools also not far from al-Hay.

- There is also a local market providing basic items for daily consumption and use.

Issues raised by the local community as the 'obvious' main problems:

- What is obviously lacking are play centers for children/adolescents; no social or cultural clubs for younger men and women. No public gardens. There is one kindergarten belonging to the Work and Development Society.

- Overcrowding with special repercussions on adolescent girls, the public areas are dominated by boys and young men.

- General poverty and unemployment that affects many families and hinders them from providing their children with basics such as proper nutrition, clothes and school materials. Some parents do not provide time and attention to their children.

- Alleyways and streets are dangerous for children.

- Unemployment among the youth and a lot of 'free time' spent in streets, which in turn hinders the mobility of young women and girls, due to social restrictions on them. In turn, youth are neglected and viewed negatively in social and economic terms and publicly and officially they are termed the 'future of the nation.'

- Lack of special programs geared towards the adolescents and youth.
- Gender discrimination and relatively high fertility rates.
- Lack of sufficient knowledge on general health issues. Patriarchal family structures, with the father still having a lot of power over children. Most fathers are not very involved in their children's lives.
- The emergence of a trend among young men, primarily to smoke, smell 'ago' (glue), take pills and alcohol. Although it is still limited.
- Lack of awareness in environmental issues.

Marka or Hitteen Camp:

Marka or Hitteen camp is located 8 kilometers northeast of Amman and was established in 1968 following the 1967 war. Upon establishment the population was estimated at 15,000 people who lived on 917 dunums. As of November 1999 the population according to UNRWA figures is 38,630 thousand people, that is, it has more than doubled in three decades, while the camp area has not increased. The people who moved into the camp in 1968 was mostly from the district of Jerusalem, Ramallah and Hebron, followed by people from Gaza, Beersheba, Jaffa and Ramleh.

There is a high rate of unemployment, according to the inhabitants it is over 50%. One reason is that many of the inhabitants hold the two-year travel documents, which are granted to refugees from Gaza, which prohibits them from accessing public services, or employment opportunities in the public sector.

Our approach to the camp began with the UNRWA schools as the point of departure; therefore a lot of the information on the camp came from the students. Indeed, although it is difficult to provide conclusive remarks at this stage, yet, it is one of the more impoverished camps in Jordan and in worse socio-economic conditions than Hay al-Mahasreh. Using Colin's method was helpful for example, in giving us a rough idea as to the percentage of children working, the living conditions of families, the

sources of income as children in focus groups would talk about their father's work. Many of those employed work in the construction sector and low-end jobs in mechanics shops, drivers, cleaners and maintenance. There are many that are enrolled in UNRWA's Special Hardship Program, which provides cash/food assistance to families with no source of income. Yet, UNRWA's regulations are extremely stringent, as soon as one of the sons turns 18, then the family is taken off the Program, hence it is not a good measure of poverty levels.

Comparative Dimension: Once again, it is not possible to provide a comprehensive or conclusive narrative on the comparative dimension between Hay al-Mahasrah and Marka camp. Nevertheless, one thing is clear and that is that refugees living in Marka camp have a clearer sense of social and economic discrimination and children are much more aware of their political identity as Palestinians, although they individually refer to themselves as belonging to a particular village. In Hay al-Mahasreh, the identity is centered on the village of origin and there is a sense of 'community' and intra-village relations are limited. This is not surprising, because refugees living in the UNRWA camp originate in many villages and over the years the 'camp' inhabitants have intermingled and intermarried, yet they also developed a sense of belonging to the 'camp' where people share the refugee experience – a Palestinian one. In Hay al-Mahasreh, over 95% of the population are from the same village; hence there is a stronger sense of belonging to the one village, enhanced by inter-marriage and social relations.

However, there are other dimensions to 'identity,' and children and adolescents in both areas share in economic hardship, gender discrimination, patriarchal systems and oppressive systems at school and home. There is a strong sense of marginalization in both areas, although in the refugee camp it is stronger and more clearly articulated. In both areas, children and adolescents feel 'neglected' and without a voice at home, school or society.

WEST BANK

The following are excerpts from the report received. A full report may be provided upon request.

1. Al Fawwar Refugee Camp

Location: Fawwar Camp is located about 8 km. south of Hebron. Reehiyya village surrounds it from the east, Hadab village from the south and Dura town from the west.

Topography and origin of name: Fawwar camp is located in a valley that is surrounded by mountains. The origin of Fawwar name goes back to a name of a spring of water that the camp is located nearby.

Garbage disposal services: There are 9 cleaners in the camp and one UNRWA car that collects the solid waste from both camps Aroub and Fawwar.

Transportation services: there is a bus company that serves the refugees of the camp to move to the city of Hebron. In addition to the buses there are service cars.

Education: There are two basic UNRWA schools in the camp. The girls' school is divided into two sessions, the morning session which consists of 600 students and the afternoon session which consists of 353 students. The boys' school consists of 930 students. There are also three kindergartens and one nursery in the camp.

Socio-cultural services: The Women's Center of the camp was established in 1993. It holds several courses for women and also runs a kindergarten and a nursery. The Youth Center was established in 1957. The Disabled Rehabilitation Center was established in 1990 and it runs a kindergarten. Al Sabbar Cultural Center, The Refugee Cultural Center, Palestinian Children's Cultural Center and the Multifunctional Community Center (MCC) operate in the camp in addition to three mosques. (source: the Multifunctional Community Center (MCC))

Health Status: The following information was collected from the PRA that was carried out in Al Fawwar camp by a group of students who attended a course with the Palestinian Family Planning and Protection Society between the period of 11th and the 25th of November, 1999.

The PRA team observed the following problems to be affecting the health status in the camp:

1. The problem of open sewage system.
2. The spread of flies and mosquitoes.
3. The overlook of general cleanliness and hygiene.
4. The mix of water for drinking with sanitation.

Counselling services: In the camp, there is no counselling service. Both students at schools and the women group raised the need for counsellors who can support and help in how to deal with certain problems. The women group also mentioned the problem of early marriage in the camp and the need to have awareness campaigns to families through counsellors.

2. Alaroub Refugee Camp

Location: Alaroub Camp is located about 17 km north of Hebron. Beet Fajjar village surrounds it from the east, Ifrat Israeli settlement from the north, Shuikh Alaroub village from the south and Beet-ommer village from the west.

Topography and origin of name: Alaroub camp is located in a valley that is surrounded by mountains. The origin of Alaroub name goes back to a name of the neighbouring village Shukh Alaroub.

Garbage disposal services: There are 9 cleaners in the camp and one UNRWA car that collects the solid waste from both camps Aroub and Fawwar.

Transportation services: As the camp lies on the main road between Hebron and Jerusalem, the inhabitants of the camp use the public transportation.

Education: There are basic UNRWA schools in the camp.

GAZA

Bureij refugee Camp

Bureij refugee Camp is located in the central area of Gaza Strip to the east of the main north–south road, which runs to the Egyptian border. Before the establishment of the camp in 1949, British army barracks took up some of 528 dunums site. A number of the original 13,000 refugees in the camp were housed in the barracks and the rest in tents. UNRWA provided cement block shelters in 1950. At present 80% of roofs of the camp shelters are covered with asbestos sheets. Shelters are served by water supply from the Israeli Mekorot Company. The camp has sewage system and sewage runs in open drains and accumulates in Wadi Gaza to the north of the camp, representing a health hazard especially because of the breeding of mosquitoes. The current number of population is 28,298, who live in crowded shelters and unsanitary conditions. Some people work in Israel, other people run their own shops and workshops. Many people work in Government and UNRWA schools, others work in the neighbouring farms and citrus groves. There is a public market held every Thursday attracting traders from all over the Strip. There are also a Women's Program Center and a Youth Activity Center in the camp. A new Community Rehabilitation Society was opened late 1997 using an annex building of Women's Program Center. It serves about 30 disabled children.

Khan Younis Refugee Camp

Khan Younis Refugee Camp is located about two kilometers from the Mediterranean coast north of Rafah. It was established in 1949 to the west of Khan Younis town, a major commercial center and stopping–off point on the ancient trade route to Egypt. The original 35,000 residents, most of them from villages in the Beersheba area, were housed in tents on a 549-dunums site. Today, the camp is home to 56,873 refugees, most of whom live in cement brick shelters with asbestos roofs. The Camp is divided into 13 blocks, some of which are in low–lying areas are flooded in winter. The western block of the camp "bock I" is very close to the municipal and private wells. People have different jobs, some work in Israel, some have shops and workshops. Many work in government and UNRWA educational institutions. Others work in agriculture and fishing and in order to reach the farms in Mawasi area and other fishing areas they have to pass through the Israeli checkpoint at the entrance to the Gush Qatif Settlement area. A public market is held every Wednesday. There is no sewage system in the camp. UNRWA operate 18 schools in the camp, 14 of them are elementary and the others preparatory schools. The number of pupils is 16,495. Only four schools are run in single shifts. UNRWA's Health Center including its maternity wards underwent comprehensive maintenance in 1994. 65 health care workers assigned to morning and afternoon shifts staff it. On average 16,663 consultations are held there each month. 2,442 families (10,307 individuals) are registered as Special Hardship Cases. The women Program Center of the camp was reconstructed in 1992 and 7,000 women have participated in programs offered at the center since the new facilities opened. The administrative committee of the center is appointed by the Agency. The youth activity center, which offers sports, culture and social programs, had recently a new extension built with donations from various sides. A community Rehabilitation Center offers services to over 30 disabled persons.

Beach Refugee Camp

Beach Refugee Camp lies on the Gaza beach in the northern part of Gaza City. It is known locally as the "Shati" refugee camp. The camp was established after the 1984 war to house some 23,000 refugees from Lydda Jaffa Beersheba and the south coastal plain. Today the camp has 72,888 residents on 747 dunums (less than one square km). The refugees first lived in tents and were assisted by relief organizations such as the International Committee of the Red Cross. UNRWA replaced the tents with mud brick shelters in the early 1950s, which in turn were replaced in 1960s, with cement block shelters with asbestos roofs. At present, some houses are concrete and two-or-three floor buildings. The main income for the people in Beach Camp comes from employment in Israel and work in small workshops and sewing factories. A sizeable number of families depend on fishing for livelihood. Some are owners of small shops at the market place and others work in several places in Gaza City itself. After the Israeli authorities demolished more than 2,000 rooms in Beach Camp in 1971 to widen the roads for security reasons, about 8,000 presents moved out of the camp into the nearby housing project in Sheikh Radwan. The environmental situation in the camp has improved with the completion of the new sewage project, pavement of roads and storm water drainage. Water is supplied by Gaza Municipality, which charges refugees the same rates as city residents. UNRWA operates 20 schools, 14 of them elementary and six others preparatory. Enrolment in the current academic year totals 17,019. Only six of the 20 schools are run in a single shift. A new school is currently under construction. A new Health Center was constructed in the Camp in 1994, on average, 9,500 consultations are held there each month. The refugees living in the camp also receive health care services at the Agency's Rimal Health Center. Located just east of the camp. 2,014 families (9,110 individuals) are eligible for relief assistance under the Agency's special hardship category. The women Program Center of the camp was reconstructed in 1994 and around 2,800 women have participated in programs offered at the center since the new facilities opened. A youth Activity Center offering athletic, social and cultural programs was reconstructed in the Camp in 1994.

A new community Rehabilitation Center for the disabled opened in April 1997. It offers rehabilitation services to about 70 disabled persons. The center was constructed UNRWA's assistance and funds from the Japanese Government. ■

4. FIELD WORK

SYRIA

Since the beginning of February our researchers started informal visits to specific Palestinian families in Damascus and the neighboring camps around Damascus. First they studied the surroundings of these families including the sub-structure, social relations, cultural and recreational and social institutions. They also contacted notables in these surroundings and got information on families and the villages of their fathers and grandfathers in Palestine. They also paid several visits to these families in order to study their family life and to examine their readiness to interview our researchers.

At the end of February our researchers began their formal visits, discussions and interviews with these families. They are now in process of interviewing the members of ten families in and around Damascus. The first two families live in a very poor hilly area on the steps of Qassiyoun. These interviews included grandfathers, mothers and their sons and daughters. The third family is a

Palestinian Christian family living in Damascus (in Bab Touma in the old city of Damascus). Manar is busy working in Yarmouk camp interviewing the members of three families. The first is living in Al Kuds Street in the camp, the second in Haifa Street and the third in Safad Street.

Mai is working with families in Jaramana camp on the way to Damascus airport and another family in Husseiniyeh camp and with another two families living in Sbeineh camp on the way to Amman. She plans to organize interviews with a family in Homs refugee camp near Homs. We hope that at the end of next month we will be able to cover the twenty families assigned for the project.

During our meetings we discuss the interviews reports' draft and try to analyze the interviews' technique and content. We noticed that our researchers tend to forget that in spite of the fact that we need the fathers and grandfather's testimonies and their memories of the 1948 forced migrations, we have to take care of children and adolescents' testimonies and their interpretation of the 1948 tragedy through their fathers, mothers and grandfathers' memories.

We also noticed that timeline technique is effective but it is not sufficient. We asked our researcher to offer the interviewed the right to express themselves freely in order to get a genuine, honest and spontaneous testimonies. We didn't face unexpected obstacles or refusal, but we believe we are still in the first steps of our fieldwork.

Reporting of the interviews still represents a qualitative and quantitative problem - they are full of unnecessary details and events. We hope that our researchers will improve their abilities of brief and useful reporting. We are planning to organize a meeting in Beirut with our colleagues in Lebanon to study and analyze together our fieldwork

and to exchange our experience in order to improve our approaches and techniques.

JORDAN
It is important to mention here briefly that we adopted two different approaches to the study of both communities.

Marka Camp:
We followed Colin's method and did the following:

- Established rapport and trusting relations with students in grades seven and ten in both the boys and girls schools. In all our interactions with the students we requested teachers and school staff to leave. They were four classes in total and over two hundred students.
- We provided them with empty sheets of paper and asked them to write down everything that occurs to them as a cause of anxiety, we provided some examples, but not too many so that we do not influence their answers. More explanation had to be done to the younger grades (ages 12-13)
- We sorted these into the various categories, such as community, family, school, etc.
- We developed a questionnaire based on the issues raised by the students and they amounted to fifty.
- We entered the information on the computer and we have almost completed that process, the results for most of them are out. However, another meeting is still needed to discuss the results first with the research team and then with the students.
- We selected girls for the focus groups and were able to get quite a lot of information which did not appear in the questionnaire, particularly issues relating to gender, such as early marriage, problems of abuse and oppression at home, etc. From this focus group we selected girls whom we will visit at home. Focus groups at the boy's school are yet to be done.

- I collected a few life histories from women I met at the Women's Program Center (UNRWA) and others at the Camp Services Office. Both life histories and focus group discussions need to be transcribed and typed.
- A general visit to the camp and the main centers providing services were conducted.

Hay al-Mahasreh

In Hay al-Mahasreh, we followed a different approach: we began with boys' gatherings in the streets and stopped to talk to them. Yousef, who is from the area, knew many of them and asked if they are interested to join and many if not most showed interest in the study. We met in a 'neutral area' i.e., away from their homes and they were very eager to express their views. With girls, who do not 'gather in streets' as this is a male-dominated space, we began with one of the families that Yousef knew and we asked around seven girls to join the focus group. Again, the focus group discussion was taped. With the girls we asked them to collect stories from their grandparents and parents. Households have been selected (differentiated and as much as possible representative of the population).

Although in al-Amir Hassan (unofficial camp) we conducted a workshop, yet we realize that the age-range is so large (8 – 18) which makes it unreasonable to include it extensively as part of the research, therefore we are focusing mainly on the two areas mentioned above.

Next Stage: We plan to have all the data ready by the end of May for analysis. During this period, we will focus mainly on girls and boys we have been working with in the context of their households. Ten in Marka camp have been identified and ten in Hay al-Mahasreh.

LEBANON

The following are excerpts from the report received. A full report may be provided upon request.

Group Interview

The first group interview in Beirut took place at the Shatila Children and Youth Center (Shatila camp), on March 8. This center is also frequented by children/youth from Gaza Center for the Displaced (one of our selected field sites).

The Lebanon team ... met with a group of eight boys, ages 16–19. Four reside in Shatila camp and the other four live in Gaza Center for the Displaced. Most are still students, four are at school and two are at a vocational training institute studying hotel management, while the remaining two are working. Ahmad, 16, is a car electrician and Mohammed Khalil, 18, is a laborer. It is to be noted that Jamal, 16, attends school and works as well (laborer).

At the start, many of them got their notebooks out thinking that there was going to be some kind of lecture, but we told them to relax, as we are interested to hear about problems faced by Palestinian youth, by them. Mohammed Hamzeh, 19, immediately volunteered his disdain of having to be home no later than 21:30 (mother's rule / father is deceased). Abdul Rahman, 16, spoke of the meager health services and lack of space in the camp (for outdoor activities). Ayman, 18, mentioned the insults of teachers. Mohammed Khalil, 18, was concerned about the negative influence of the political parties on the youth (males), such as smoking and drinking. He then added that this also happens with youth not affiliated to any party and noted that some are addicted to sniffing paint thinner. Mohammed Hamzeh agreed with him and added that others are addicted to tranquilizers.

It was at this point that Mohammed Hamzeh geared the conversation towards talking about other types of concern – "Why not talk about our emotional issues?" All faces lit up with shy grins. He started speaking of how he was in love with his neighbor and that it was impossible for them to date, due to tradition. Mohammed Khalil then mentioned how many parents (non-Palestinian) would not allow their daughters to date Palestinians. Ahmad, 16, complained that girls demand a lot from the boys. Abdul Rahman admitted to loving two or three times so far, but all from a distance – without really talking to them or knowing them well. The rest of the group all felt the need to know the girl before loving her, to know how she thinks, behaves, etc. Jamal, 16, revealed his readiness to marry as his father married at 17. Mohammed Khalil showed his disdain about the fact that all girls want to settle down but still boasted his ambition to meet as many girls as possible. Nader, 17, offered a solution to the dating problem by seeking girls in other areas. To prevent being caught, "a boy living in area Z, would seek a girl in area Y and they would meet in area Z," he added.

Ayman stressed the need for relationships. The couple can forget about the difficult living conditions and comfort each other. Mahmud, 17, is currently seeing someone, and is serious about her for he wants to get engaged as soon as he finishes school. He sees difficulties in having a relationship in a traditional society and financial constraints for settling down but he stressed the need for "positive thinking."

We then moved to another topic, gender discrimination. They all agreed that most parents favor boys, giving the girls less freedom and loads of housework. Mohammed Khalil noted the hassle girls suffer on the street, such as "sweet talking." Mahmud said that he has four brothers and a sister, who's often the scapegoat of their agitation and is overburdened with their demands...(he said it in a semi-apologetic/guilty way).

The boys later engaged in a ranking exercise. They were given a number of problems which one may face and were asked to rank them according to their personal concerns: Failure at school/inability to enroll in a university/inability to find work/illness/parent(s) falling ill/eradication of Shatila camp/parents divorcing/ domestic violence/father's unemployment/lack of pocket money/another camp siege (camp war)/religious fundamentalism/ not following religious teaching.

The most serious concerns were "failure at school" and "inability to find work," followed by "domestic violence" then "another camp siege" and "parent(s) falling ill." Both "religious fundamentalism" and "not following religious teaching" ranked lowest.

Mohammed Khalil added "rejection/dislike of Palestinians" on his list.
Others shared their view on this. Abdul Rahman, for instance, described his isolation when he was at a Lebanese elementary school. He often tried to tone down his Palestinian accent to combat his feeling of isolation.

Discussing internal displacement, all agreed that it has affected their parents more than them. Still, both Ayman and Abdul Rahman recall moving two or three times (displacement) before "settling" in Gaza Center. Mahmud said that he's been living in Shatila camp only for the past six years. Before this, they were living down south, where his family was displaced to earlier. They had to leave their place and so moved to Shatila. It was very hard for him to adapt to the overcrowded camp, little space, especially after living by the sea.

We thanked them all for sharing their thoughts, feelings, and time with us. They all invited us to come again and to have more meetings. Mohammed Khalil said "talking to you was good, it is a relief to talk and let things out."

It was a good session. All the boys were relaxed and not much probing was needed to let them speak, probably due to their age (upper teen). Taking into consideration that we were a team of four, we were fortunate that they were not intimidated by us, and we were pleasantly surprised by their candour regarding their emotional needs. Considerations for gender and age of both participants and interviewers will be more planned in the future.

EXCERPTS FROM SUMMARY REPORTS – FIELD WORK

Some initial assessments/impressions (to be further investigated):

- we are dealing with a traditional patriarchal community;
- the youth suffers from bad treatment (abuse) at school; lack of privacy; meagre health services; lack of space; internal displacement; isolation from and discrimination by the host community; types

of addiction; emotional frustrations; girls suffer from gender discrimination;

- they have common fears such as failing school, domestic violence, parent(s) falling ill and particular fears such as not finding work and another camp siege (particular as related to their status/history as refugees). ◼

A FIELDWORK TIP

From 'Listening for a Change'; Hugo Slim & Paul Thompson; Panos Publications; 1993

On interviewing...
(Thus) a good interview is semi-structured and improvisational, and a good interviewer's aim is to say as little as possible and to listen and learn as much as he or she can. Good questions are those which make sense to and animate the narrator; guide the direction of the testimony while giving him or her plenty of space for self-expression; and ensure that the necessary topics are covered and all leads, however unexpected, are followed through.

On transcription and translation...
The interview should (then) be transcribed and/or translated to make a written copy...

The basic rule of transcription is to render the original speech into written text as accurately as possible by including hesitation, repetition, exclamation, emphasis and dialect. It is important not to correct grammar or word order, or to attempt to make the account read more like a written one. It should remain the spoken word in the style of the narrator, with all the meandering inconsistencies this may imply. The interviewer or project coordinator should make sure that any references within the text which might not be clear to an outsider – for example, allusions to local dignatories, organisations, cultural events – are briefly explained in notes at the end of the transcript.

- Similarly, **translation should seek to be as accurate as possible in meaning and style**. This can be one of the most difficult aspects of oral testimony work. Some of the issues which arise in translation are related to the general area of interpretation of testimony ... Transcriptions and translations should always include figurative speech, such as proverbs and sayings, which should be translated literally, and where they are too culturally specific for others to glean the meaning, followed by an explanation in brackets. ◼

DRAFT BIBLIOGRAPHY-IN-THE-MAKING – PART II

Author	Name of Resource	Publisher	Date	Language
–	Working papers / Conference 'Refugees in the Bethlehem Area' / 4 – 14 July 1996	50 Years Under the Tent – Campaign to defend the rights of Palestinian refugees	10/97	Arabic
AbdRaba, Salah	Refugees, and the dream of returning to the land of the sad oranges	Alternative Information Centre	7/96	Arabic
Al-Zabin, Samir	Palestinian Refugees Situations in Lebanon	Palestinian Diaspora & Refugee Centre (SHAML)	2000	Arabic
BADIL Resource Ctr.	Al Majdal Newsletter, Issue #1 – Palestinian Refugees: Reclaiming the Right of Return	BADIL Resource Ctr.	3/99	English
BADIL Resource Ctr.	Al Majdal Newsletter, Issue #2 – Reversing Ethnic Cleansing in Palestine	BADIL Resource Ctr.	6/99	English
BADIL Resource Ctr.	Al Majdal Newsletter, Issue #3 – Palestinian Refugees and the Final Negotiations	BADIL Resource Ctr.	9/99	English
BADIL Resource Ctr.	Eviction from Jerusalem: Restitution and the Protection of Palestinian Rights	BADIL Resource Ctr.	4/99	English
BADIL Resource Ctr.	Right of Return Campaign Updates	BADIL Resource Ctr.		Arabic & English
BADIL Resource Ctr.	Yoom ilak, Yoom aleik: Palestinian refugees from Jerusalem – culture, dispossession and hope (video).	BADIL Resource Ctr	1998	Arabic
Gassner, Ingrid (ed.)	ARTICLE 74, Issues No. 12 – 26 (April 1995 to December 1998)	BADIL Resource Ctr.	1/99	English
Local Newspapers	Articles and Caricatures			Arabic
PCBS	Population, Housing and Establishment Census – 1997 (Statistical Brief)	PCBS	1/99	Arabic & English

PCBS	The Children of Palestine: Issues and Surveys (Annual Report, Child Survey Series No. 1)	PCBS	4/98	Arabic
Peters, Joel; Tamari, Salim et al	The Question of the Palestinian Refugees and the Multi-lateral Talks	Palestinian Diaspora & Refugee Ctr (SHAML)	1998	Arabic
Pulfer, Gerhard & Al-Mashni, Awni / BADIL team	Palestinian Refugees in Exile (Country Reports) – West Bank & Gaza Strip: Palestinian Refugees Five Years After Oslo	BADIL Resource Ctr.	1999	English
Pulfer, Gerhard & Gassner, Ingrid	UNRWA: "Between a rock and a hard place", between politics and the service of refugees	BADIL Resource Ctr.	8/97	Arabic
Samara, Adel	Palestinian Refugees between the right of return and accepted defeat	Al-Mashriq Al-A'amil Center for Cultural Development Studies	1999	Arabic
Shiblak, Abbas & Davis, Uri	Civil and Citizenship Rights of Palestinian Refugees	Palestinian Diaspora & Refugee Centre (SHAML)	1995	English
Tamari, Salim	Palestinian Refugee Negotiations: From Madrid to Oslo II	Institute for Palestine Studies	1996	English
Tamari, Salim (ed.)	Jerusalem 1948: Arab neighbourhoods and their fate in the 1948 war	Jerusalem Studies Ctr. & BADIL Resource Ctr	1999	Arabic
UNRWA	UNRWA Gaza Field Office – fact sheets	UNRWA	7/99	English

These were obtained either during the literature search here in the U.K. or during our field visits abroad. This list shall be updated as more literature is uncovered. Please send us copies of any literature you find that is relevant to the project.

＊ **A special mention and thanks to the West Bank team, who provided us with originals of all but one of the resources listed above.**

SUMMARY REPORT FRAMEWORK *PLUS*

TASK	DESCRIPTION	
15. Literature search		
(g) Search results – what is available	• It would be enriching to know of the results of the local literature searches: what type of studies have been done in the area before, with this target group, etc.	
(h) Analysis of the search	• A brief analysis of this literature as is relevant to the project.	
(i) Photocopies	• Everybody is encouraged to make photocopies of studies/ publications that they consider relevant or important, and to either mail them to Oxford, or leave them for Dawn or Gillian to carry back with them from their field visits.	
16. Contacts & meetings in the community	• Briefings on meetings with concerned local IGO's and NGO's. • A suggested emphasis on meeting with UNRWA and Save the Children Fund (if they operate in the area) as the more important foci to the research project, in addition to other organisations working in relevant domains. ⊃ *Descriptions of the meetings with / in the community (members of the community, active individuals and organisations, meetings with IGO's working in the area such as UNICEF, UNRWA, etc.)*	
17. Research staff (assistants and interviewers)	• A brief description on the how and why the research assistants and interviewers were selected.	
18. The training of the research staff.	• A summary of the type of training offered to the research staff as preparation for the fieldwork.	
19. Selecting the field sites	• A brief description of the selected field sites. • Reasons for selecting these field sites. ⊃ *Sociodemographic data of the population under study* ⊃ *Description of the socio-economic variety of the population under study (as well as ensuring some form of socio-economic variety)* ⊃ *Illustration of the gender balance in the study population (as well as ensuring some form of gender balance!)* ⊃ *Comparative information about the population in terms of those living in camps and outside of camps.*	Report 1 & 2 **January 2000**
20. Implementation of PRA/social mapping/timelines /othersocial research tools	• A summary of the process of implementing these social research tools in the fieldwork. • A summary of the results of this field work. ⊃ *Description of the social mapping and PRA (results, analysis, inherent meaning).* ⊃ *Comparative information about the population in terms of those living in camps and outside of camps.*	Initial phase of research/ report 3 **March 2000**
21. Interviewing and narrative phase of the project	• **A summary of the process of implementing these social research tools in the fieldwork.** • **A summary of the results of this fieldwork.** • **A narrative report of the research from the teams.** ⊃ *Details of the narratives being collected (parents, grandparents, caregivers and other adults or relatives).* ⊃ *Comparative information about the population in terms of those living in camps and outside of camps.*	**Next phase of research/ report 4 May 2000**

Glossary

al-Aqsa Intifada	uprising of September 2000
al-Dabka	type of dance
al-Istishehad	martyrdom
al-Hajj	pilgrimage to Mecca
al-Intifada	he Uprising of 1987-93
al-Nakba	Catastrophe; the expulsion of forced migrants of 1948
al-Naksa	Débâcle; setback of 1967
Druze	a Muslim sect
fedayeen	freedom fighters
fellaheen	peasants
dunum	measure of land equivalent to 0.1 hectares or 0.247 acres
hara	quarter in a neighbourhood
haram	poor; pathetic
hay	neighbourhood
intifada	uprising
himar	donkey
kubkab	wooden shoes
laje'een	refugees
mokhtars	local notary
mowatneen	residents
mukhayyamji	belonging to the refugee camp
mukhayyamjiyyeh	people who live in a refugee camp
qafla	group
shabab	youth
Shhour	time of the day when the fast is broken during Ramadan
Tawjihi	General Secondary Education Certificate Examination
thouar	fighters

wateneen	nationalists
yindhabbu	restrained; brought into a physical place, usually the home
zu'ran	hooligans
First-generation (G1)	Palestinians who lived in Mandatory Palestine (pre-1948) or were born there.
Second-generation (G2)	Those born in exile after 1948. Many of then also lived in the West Bank or Gaza prior to displacement in 1967.
Third-generation (G3)	The children, grandchildren, or great-grandchildren of second-generation Palestinian refugees

Index

www.ingramcontent.com/pod-product-compliance
Lightning Source LLC
Chambersburg PA
CBHW060029030426
42334CB00019B/2251